There's Always the Hills

Also by Cameron McNeish

Highland Ways, (KSA)

The Spurbook of Youth Hostelling (Spurbooks)

The Spur Master Guide to Snow Camping (Spurbooks)

Backpacker's Scotland (Robert Hale)

The Backpacker's Manual (Nordbok)

Ski the Nordic Way (Cicerone Press)

Classic Walks in Scotland, with Roger Smith (Oxford Illustrated Press)

The Munro Almanac (NWP)

The Corbett Almanac (NWP)

The Best Hillwalking in Scotland (The In Pinn)

The Wilderness World of Cameron McNeish (The In Pinn)

The Munros, Scotland's Highest Mountains (Lomond Books)

Scotland's 100 Best Walks (Lomond Books)

The Edge – One Hundred Years of Scottish Mountaineering, with Richard Else (BBC)

Wilderness Walks, with Richard Else (BBC)

More Wilderness Walks, with Richard Else (BBC)

The Sutherland Trail, with Richard Else (Mountain Media)

The Skye Trail, with Richard Else (Mountain Media)

Scotland End to End, with Richard Else (Mountain Media)

There's Always the Hills

Hills

Cameron McNeish

Foreword
by
Sam Heughan

SANDSTONEPRESS
HIGHLAND | SCOTLAND

First published in Great Britain by
Sandstone Press Ltd
Dochcarty Road
Dingwall
Ross-shire
IV15 9UG
Scotland

www.sandstonepress.com

The publisher acknowledges subsidy from Creative Scotland
towards publication of this volume.

ISBN: 978-1-910985-95-3
ISBNe: 978-1-910985-96-0

Jacket design by Raspberry Creative Type, Edinburgh
Typeset by Iolaire Typography Ltd, Newtonmore
Printed and bound by Pozkal Poland

For Charlotte and Grace

Contents

ACKNOWLEDGEMENTS

Looking back over my forty-year career I realise that a number of individuals have been responsible for introducing various strands to my life, elements that have morphed together to create this journey of mine.

My parents initially allowed me the freedom to discover horizons that were beyond the immediate boundary of family and home and my track and field coach, John Anderson, taught me the essential foundations of commitment, hard work and perseverance. Peter Lumley, Roger Smith and the late Clive Sandground presented me with early writing opportunities and Duncan Kirk, Mike Ure and Darren Bruce have been supportive and encouraging magazine publishers.

For radio and television opportunities I'm indebted to the late Murdoch McPherson, Christopher Lowell and David Harron, and Richard Else and Margaret Wicks continually encourage and inspire my television work as well as being close friends and neighbours in Badenoch.

Many thanks also to Robert Wight and Garry Fraser of the *Scots Magazine* for giving me permission to plunder and re-work some features that have appeared in their magazine and a heartfelt thanks to those wonderful colleagues who loyally assisted me on the various magazines I edited over the years, in particular Tom Prentice, John Manning and Emily Rodway.

Individuals like Tom Weir, Bill Murray, Hamish Brown, Jim Perrin, Chris Townsend, Chris Brasher, Jim Crumley, Dick Balharry, Dave Morris and Hamish Telfer here in the UK and Ray and Jenny Jardine and Annie and Dave Getchell in the US have all given freely of their knowledge and experience to make my time in the wild places so much more meaningful and I owe a real debt of thanks to Glenn

Rowley, Tim Greening and Rex Munro of KE Adventure Travel for giving me the chance to travel extensively to the Greater Ranges and beyond.

And a very special thanks to my publisher and editor Robert Davidson of Sandstone Press for his support and encouragement and giving me the benefit of his considerable experience and wisdom.

Sincere thanks also to fellow hill goer and actor Sam Heughan for taking time out from a very hectic filming schedule to read my book and write a foreword to it. I'm looking forward to many more hill days in Scotland with Sam showing him some of the wild places that his alter ego, Outlander's Jamie Fraser, may not have been familiar with.

Finally, my own family have been constantly supportive and have given me hope for the future. My two sons are frequent companions on various adventures and my wife Gina continues to be the love of my life after forty-five years of marriage. I'm delighted that in the autumn of our years we can still enjoy the hills and wild places together and more importantly, simply enjoy each other's company. We look forward, in the near future, to introducing our two grand-daughters to the joys of the outdoors. This book is dedicated to them.

LIST OF ILLUSTRATIONS

Section 1

1. With my Grandfather, Grandmother and parents

2. On an early summer holiday at Dunbar, birthplace of John Muir, although I didn't know it at the time.

3. King's Park Secondary School photo, c1963, Cameron in the back row, third from the left.

4. My first love, long jumping. I became Scottish Junior Champion in 1968.

5. Learning to shot put with John Anderson.

6. A very special day over 45 years ago. Cutting the cake with Gina.

7. Lomond Mountaineering Club, c1975. I'm at the back, fifth from the left.

8. During a wonderful Cairngorm to Ben Nevis backpacking trip in 1975.

9. Cameron the Youth Hostel warden at Aviemore SYHA.

10. Gina with Gordon and Gregor cross country skiing. They're never too young to learn.

11. Seventies climbing pal Jeff Faulkner near the summit of A'Mhaighdean.

12. Long time friend and colleague, Roger Smith, leaving Ben Macdui with Braeriach in the background.

13. On the Robert Louis Stevenson Trail in France with old pal Peter Lumley.

14. My good friend, mountain guide John Lyall, as we climbed January Jigsaw on the Buachaille Etive Mor.

15. A favourite shot of Gina at Carnmore below A'Mhaidghean.

16. On the Matterhorn summit as part of the celebrations of the 125th anniversary of the first ascent by Edward Whymper.

17. Family outing to Yosemite in 1997.

18. Gina, Gregor and me on the summit of Mount Whitney, at the end of the 221 mile John Muir Trail in California.

19. Getting all nostalgic in a favourite howff in Glen Coe, a place I often frequented in my rock climbing days.

20. Of all the great mountaineers and naturalists I have met, none was more encouraging than my old friend, Tom Weir (with thanks to D.C. Thomson Ltd).

21. The redoubtable Chris Brasher, athlete, journalist, mountaineer, and one of the greatest characters I've ever met (Richard Else with permission).

22. With Chris Townsend after we had completed the GR20 over the mountains of Corsica.

Section 2

1. Gina on the Pinchot Pass, John Muir Trail, Cailfornia.

2. With Donnie Munro, former lead singer with Runrig, on his home territory of the Isle of Skye.

3. With writer and broadcaster Lesley Riddoch on the summit of Carrauntoohill, the highest mountain in Ireland.

4. With the legendary Hamish Brown in the High Atlas mountains of Morocco.

5. My dear friend Jim Perrin and me, enjoying a televised pilgrimage in Ireland for our *Wilderness Walks* series.

6. Ray and Jenny Jardine, lightweight backpacking gurus who taught me about 'connecting' with the landscape.

7. The Ordesa Gorge in the Pyrenees with writer and broadcaster Nick Crane.

8. My good friend, film producer and Newtonmore neighbour, Richard Else.

9. With Jimmie MacGregor at the unveiling of the Tom Weir statue.

FOREWORD

Bodach nam Beann - the man of the hills.

Adorned with woolly bonnet, walking poles and rucksack, Cameron McNeish can be recognised by his silhouette alone. The most highly respected voice now speaking for and from Scotland's mountains, and their most instantly recognisable figure, his knowledge and expertise derives from his every footstep on every remote Munro and Corbett, and his crossing of each mountain burn. *Bodach nam Beann* could have given me sound advice when I first discovered the hills for myself . . .

The icy surface stretched before me, sloping down across a rock shelf to the cliff edge, a fatal ice slide for the unwary hiker. I could barely see a few metres ahead in the mist, and the snow was beginning to fall again. Behind me a white uneven landscape, covering the rocks and gaps between them, would make my eventual retreat slow and tentative. Only my footprints to this point indicated a safe way back and they were already filling with fresh snow. Sheltering behind a boulder, knowing that the summit cairn of Schiehallion was only metres away, I fingered the small pink stone in my pocket, quartz hard enough to cut glass, picked up an hour or so earlier to add to the summit cairn.

A local taxi had dropped me beside the single track road at Braes of Foss, next to a group of trees that partially hid the mountain. I had practically rolled out of the front seat, my head fuzzy with last night's birthday celebrations and a long week of filming in the outdoors. In my tweed hip flask was a drop of the smoky whisky I'd been given as a birthday present, a memento from a fellow mountain enthusiast after my first (failed) ascent of a Munro a few months earlier. There had been a few since, and it had become a tradition to take a nip or two after reaching the peak, 'easing' the journey down.

Now though, the thought of alcohol was not so appealing.

I considered whether an attempt across the icy surface was worth the risk.

In reasonable hiking boots, several base layers and a technical winter jacket, I wasn't feeling cold, although my hands would turn bright red - then white - if I took them out of my gloves for too long. I'd been in this situation before when I foolishly tried to climb Ben Lomond in the snow with no crampons. The closest Munro to Glasgow, it is a popular climb in summer but hazardous in winter. Lost somewhere on the mountain's Ptarmigan[+] ridge, its lower peak, I climbed too high before losing my balance and sliding downwards for twenty to thirty metres. Digging my raw and frozen fingers into the snow to break the descent I realised that, displaced only a few metres to the right, I could easily have slipped off the mountain. I had become one of 'those' people: foolish, dangerous. The mountains need respect and I resolved to always be not only cautious but also prepared. Then I would enjoy their great heights all the more, and adventure even further into their lesser known world.

Remembering that possible fatal experience, I accepted that this was as far as Schiehallion (and the conditions) would let me go. I took a celebration nip, fumbled for the small rock in my pocket and placed it on the snow drift next to me, a temporary cairn, for this trip.

We had been filming *Outlander* near Loch Rannoch for a few days, among the magical setting of standing stones that the main character Claire travels through, back to Scotland in 1745. I had spent my 35th birthday on the side of a mountain, filming a 'picnic' in the driving rain and fog, and even the bannock we had to eat was soggy. Dreich and damp as we were, it felt momentous, remarkable even, the ever-changing summit of Schiehallion standing like an extinct volcano, cloud continuously masking then briefly revealing her sharp peak, the magical backdrop to our scene.

I looked towards where I knew our crew would be working, at least a kilometre down, in the valley. The wind was getting stronger but the snow had eased. As if in answer, the cloud briefly parted allowing me to see down the long sweep of the valley to a silver-grey loch in the distance. I could make out the circle of trees that marked the location of the standing stones, the cherry picker cranes carrying the enormous lights that pretend to be a dim Scottish sun. I even spotted a few black figures, unrecognisable in wet weather gear, moving slowly around. The crew would be cold and wet and only halfway through their day and I felt so fortunate to have the time off. As quickly as they had parted, the clouds closed again and I was alone. It was time to get down, in case the weather got worse and I lost my way.

Schiehallion - fairy hill of the Caledonians. Castail Abhail - castle of the fork. Beinn Alligin - the jewelled mountain. Càrn Mòr Dearg - the big red cairn. These were the names that conjured the history, and mythology, that drew me first to their wild peaks, challenging me to be brave enough, daring me to uncover their secrets. Even the rivers, burns, woods, towns and meeting places have a complex history, each hidden meaning bringing new insight to the story and character of the land. The list is endless!

Returning to Scotland to shoot our TV series I fell in love again with my home country: the history and culture, the mix of language and tradition. Gaelic, as we spoke it in the show, was our main focus, but I soon realised that many names come from the Picts, the Welsh, Scots and even the Norse. The mountains to me have always felt like places to escape to, places of freedom, to discover and reach new perspectives when looking back on the journey. Climbing in rain, sun or snow (often all in one day!), one can find a new perspective on life below. It is a way to journey through time.

Walkers, film-crews and historic moments may come and go but the mountains always remain. Each of us will have a personal relationship with them, but not all go equally deep. Cameron McNeish is very much the Oracle, *an t-allaban mór* - the great wanderer, wise man of the Scottish hills. Someone who has not only knowledge of the Thieves Road* and crossed The Stream of the Boundary** but who has watched the sun rise above Kingussie from the summit of The Old Woman (*A' Chailleach*).

Knowing this and having admired him from afar, having been obsessed with any Outdoor and Adventure related subjects, it was a dream come true when Cameron asked me to appear on the

Adventure Show on TV with him. I had followed him on social media as I was becoming more active on Twitter and Instagram, great resources for information and an access to many of my idols and their achievements. Surprisingly to me, Cameron not only followed back but also sent a direct message. Hearing of my passion for the hills, he suggested that we meet for an interview to be followed by an article.

I had created My Peak Challenge the year before, now nearing 10,000 subscribers, it is a healthy lifestyle and activity charity fundraiser. The idea came from wanting to share my love of the Outdoors, challenging oneself to reach new peaks and discover new horizons. Our community, or 'Peakers' have accomplished so much, raising hundreds of thousands of dollars for charity, formed new friendships, lost weight, gained mobility, discovered new skills and increased confidence. It's a global movement, with scalable programs to suit everyone, with members from every walk of life, including: Olympic athletes, expectant mothers, those with mobility issues and some very active tenacious pensioners. I want to share what is special to me about the mountains and the solace they give.

Throughout Cameron's life the mountains have also been a constant presence, his sanctuary and retreat. They were and are a proving ground, providing an anchor, source of adventure and discovery. Yet there is much more to his life, of course: his enduring marriage to Gina, their children and grandchildren, a deep connection with earlier writers such as WH Murray and Tom Weir, a video record of the highlands - that will surely be a treasured archive to future historians. Cameron has written many books and magazine articles sharing his great knowledge, his vocal commitment to Scottish independence, athletics and leadership. This book is an insight to the driving force, the man, behind all this productivity. Yet at the heart of it and the centre of him, there is always the hills . . .

In this book, his keenly anticipated autobiography, we get a glimpse of his journey, his indelible marriage to the mountains - a distant ridge of snow covered peaks, revealed briefly through the clouds.

Sam Heughan

Foreword

+ The bird after which this ridge is named is described by the Royal Society for the Protection of Birds as a plump gamebird, slightly larger than a grey partridge, that breeds in the highest mountains of the Highlands of Scotland on the Arctic like landscape there.

* (Rathad nam Mèirleach)

** (Allt na Crìche - between Strathspey and Deeside)

INTRODUCTION

The film producer Samuel Goldwyn once said he didn't think anyone should write their autobiography until after they were dead. It's also been claimed that a definition of an autobiography is an obituary in serial form with the last instalment missing. So, given that I'm still relatively hale and hearty I might argue against this story of mine being described as a pure autobiography and, as I have done in so many aspects of my life, will happily follow in the footsteps of my old friend Tom Weir who once suggested that his own story was more of an 'autobiography of sorts'.

More importantly, if you'll excuse the religious parallels, the following chapters represent more of a book of thanksgiving, my way of saying thanks to the dozens, if not hundreds of individuals who have influenced aspects of my life, a life that has been shaped by so many into a journey that has allowed me to follow my dreams, and none more so than the late Chris Brasher.

From my own days in track and field athletics, I was well aware of Chris' achievements – a vital pace-maker when Roger Bannister became the first person to run a mile in less than four minutes; 1956 Olympic champion in the 3000 metres steeplechase; founder of the hugely successful London Marathon; and along with John Disley, the man who was largely responsible for introducing orienteering to the shores of the UK – but Chris Brasher was also an enthusiastic and entrepreneurial mountaineer and hillwalker.

He had been a member of various international climbing expeditions and, during his time as head of outside broadcasts at the BBC, produced and presented the incredibly popular Old Man of Hoy climb in Orkney with a stellar cast of climbers including Dougal Haston, Joe Brown, Chris Bonington, Tom Patey and others.

1

I first met Chris when the Ministry of Defence tried to buy the Knoydart Peninsula in the early eighties. I was in the early days of my writing career and he quickly enlisted my help in publicising the situation, a state of affairs that became the genesis of the Knoydart Foundation which, in turn, spawned the well-known wild land charity, the John Muir Trust.

In the following years, I came to know Chris very well and we enjoyed plenty of great hill days together in the Lake District and in various parts of Scotland, so he was an obvious choice when I had to choose guests for my first BBC2 television series *Wilderness Walks* in 1996. The idea was that we'd take a multi-day walk in the Cairngorms and discuss how wild landscapes had affected his life and career. Shortly after he arrived in Aviemore to begin the walk Chris asked if we minded if he disappeared for a day during the week. Further to all his other interests he and his wife Shirley owned several race horses and that week one of his horses was due to run at Punchestown near Dublin. He was keen to see it perform.

As you can imagine, this posed considerable problems for our filming schedule, but director Richard Else came up with a plan. He would hire a helicopter to take all of us, the whole five-man crew, across to Dublin for the day. We would film Chris and me going to the races and use it as part of the production. Initially all went well. The helicopter picked us up at Glenmore Lodge near Aviemore, we flew the length of the Kintyre Peninsula and across to Northern Ireland and then along the Irish coast to Dublin and Punchestown. Brasher was in his element, showing off to his horse racing friends. It's not every day you arrive at a race meeting in a helicopter with a television crew following your every move, not unless you're the Queen or a very rich Middle-Eastern Sheik.

I put a tenner on Chris' horse, the first and only horse racing bet I've ever made – I had to ask Chris how you went about it – and we wandered to the stand for a better view. All the time I was wondering why Chris hadn't put money on his own horse. We got into position midway up the stand, with my old friend Duncan McCallum operating the camera and a young Keith Partridge (long before he became a well-known adventure cameraman) recording the sound, and it wasn't long before the horses were paraded out, lithe, muscled and shining in the afternoon sun. Chris pointed out his own mount, appropriately named Mister Boots, and then they were off.

The least I expected was a decent race after all the effort it had taken to get there, but the gambling gods decided otherwise. Brasher's horse fell at the very first hurdle.

It was a disaster. With his jockey dismounted, poor old Mister Boots took off and was last seen galloping in the direction of County Kildare. I half expected Chris to be distraught but he simply shrugged his shoulders, gave a wan smile and said, 'Ah well, there's always the hills.'

It's a simple notion, pure escapism if you like, but I sense there's something deeper than mere escapism in the idea of returning to the comforting bosom of Mother Nature. For as long as I can remember, that has been my panacea for times of disappointment or grief. The hills have always been my salvation.

As a young international long-jumper, I was very disappointed not to make the team for the Commonwealth Games in Edinburgh in 1970. I took myself away from the sports stadium to the summit of Arthur's Seat, that wonderful old volcano that dominates our capital city, and gazed across the Firth of Forth to Fife and the Highland hills beyond. Up there, with the skylarks singing, life felt less dark and gloomy.

I remember climbing a hill called Beinn Fhionnlaidh a few days after my mother's funeral. As with many people when a parent passes away I was overcome by a sense of guilt – I should have done more for her, I should have visited her more often, I wasn't as good a son to her as I could have been – a guilt list that I guess was largely unjustified, created by grief, sadness and a profound sense of loss. In considerable mental turmoil, I took to the hills and chose a rather isolated Munro. Beinn Fhionnlaidh lies between the great sea lochs of Loch Creran and Loch Etive and is a long whaleback of a mountain that rises fairly gently from the wooded flatlands at the head of Loch Creran to a steep blunt nose overlooking the densely forested slopes of Glen Etive. I knew from previous experience that the hill's summit not only felt appreciably shy and retiring, as the old guidebooks would have it, but was positively misanthropic.

I made my way past some old shielings and onto the lower bracken-covered slopes of this north-north-east ridge where an argocat track gave me a line to follow, all the way up the ridge to a high corrie below the steep rocky slopes of Fhionnlaidh's north-west top. Some steep scrambling took me through a band of crags to the stony summit ridge and over a couple of rises to the summit itself, with its small cairn. My arrival at the cairn coincided with a rain shower so it was no place to linger, but as the shower abated on my descent the long views began to appear, out the length of Loch Creran to Loch Linnhe and the Sound of Mull. I could see the Paps of Jura and Ben More on Mull and, closer at hand, the Corbett of Fraochaidh and the twin tops of Beinn a' Bheithir dominating the forested pass that runs from Elleric to Ballachulish.

Moments like these are special. It's when you tend to feel most insignificant, especially when compared to the lasting reality of wide open skies, mountains and forests. It's when you realise that our human lifespans are a mere flicker in the geological sense of time. As I looked out across that dimming horizon I felt a growing sense of peace, an awareness of my own destiny and a realisation that my dear mother was now free from pain and turmoil. It was a cathartic moment.

There have been lots of these liberating moments in my life. When I was in my forties a hill-running accident (I tripped and fell down a crag) left me with a broken wrist, a broken ankle and forty stitches in my head. During my period of convalescence, I was aware that I was becoming depressed. I wasn't sleeping well, I had become short tempered and comparatively slight setbacks cast me into a slough of despond. I wasn't a very nice person to live with. While I was thankful to be alive, it wasn't until I was well enough to limp out into the forest on crutches that I began to feel a mental improvement. I recognised almost immediately the healing nature of this kind of exposure to the natural world and those short excursions into the forest quickly became a crucial element in my recuperation.

In these early years of the twenty-first century, political events sometimes move so fast, and often in the strangest ways, that it's very easy to feel alienated and ultimately stressed. We become aware that other people govern and control large portions of our lives, and some of these people (usually remote politicians) make decisions that directly affect us, whether we like it or not. Many of the daily schedules that we adhere to are not of our own making but are imposed on us by others. In our capitalist society we are urged, and sometimes compelled, to work harder and harder, not for our own personal satisfaction but to satisfy the unquenchable thirst for profitability of those faceless folk we call shareholders. We live in a technological world that appears to be moving faster and faster and, if we can't keep up with the pace, society will find a robot to do our job for us. It's scary and it's no small wonder more and more of us want to cry out, 'Stop and let me get off!'

In distant times people lived their lives in fear of invoking the wrath of the gods. Today we live in fear of upsetting shareholders, or the handful of individuals who keep a tight rein on our media outlets.

Over the years I've slowly become more and more aware that the foundation of my love for Scotland has become a blend of Scotland's glorious landscapes, our history and culture and the rich diversity of people who live here.

Nationalism and patriotism are complex issues and I don't really want to get into that argument here, but the truth of the matter is that my connection with Scotland, especially wild Scotland, will always remain beyond and above politics.

The first time I experienced this sense of connection was on a youthful three-day trip on the Isle of Skye. Having reached the jagged crest of our toughest hills, the Cuillin, I experienced such a combination of ecstasy and relief that I could exalt in the wild surroundings in a way that could only be described as euphoric. In that heightened state it became clear to me that for the first time in my life I felt at one with the mountain. I wasn't simply a visitor casually climbing some scree and rock – I felt I was part and parcel of the *fabric* of the mountain, the rock, air, water and light. For the first time I experienced a sense of kinship with that wild and inhospitable landscape. I had connected with the mountain and, in a sense, transcended my own being. It's all to do with belonging and kinship, a sense of home and familiarity, like sitting down in an old armchair by your fireside and feeling at ease with the world. It's not a bad place to escape to from time to time.

Today I rejoice in the fact that I can escape the constant barrage of negative news and ease myself into that comfortable chair, dram in hand, and enjoy those things that are wholly Scottish and mean a lot to me – listening to the haunting songs and fiddle music of friends like Julie Fowlis or Duncan Chisholm, reading or re-reading some of the old Scots classics like *Sunset Song* or George Mackay Brown's *Greenvoe*, or I can take to the hills and connect with their timelessness, immerse myself in their beauty and majesty and wonder again at the contrasting insignificance of man.

The Harvard sociobiologist E. O. Wilson once wrote, 'Wilderness settles peace on the soul because it needs no help. It is beyond human contrivance.' Beyond human contrivance. I like that, and I've discovered throughout the years that there is something fundamentally satisfying in those things that have not been manufactured or created by man: the song of a blackbird, the scoldings of a red squirrel in the pines above you, the magnificence of the Aurora Borealis. These are things that have always been, things of eternal value.

This book is essentially about a journey, a long and winding route from the backstreets of the South Side of Glasgow to the wild places and hills of Scotland and some of the mountains of the world where I've been fortunate enough to live out a dream. I've been living that dream for over forty years.

There have been many signposts along that route, often pointing in different directions, but the one element that has kept me to the true path is simply this – no matter what life throws at me, there's always the hills.

Go and enjoy them while you can, before age and infirmity rob you. Love them and respect them and they will be kind to you, offering far more than you can give. Inhale deeply and allow the purity of the mountain air to bless you: run the rivers and explore the forests. Hug a tree or two. Contemplate the longevity of these wild places and compare it with our own brief flicker. Sit still and hear the silence or strike a rhythm to the music in a mountain stream and above all consider yourself a part of it all. You are not a stranger here and you are not an outsider. You belong here. And when you are living life in that other world to which you also belong, if things should appear dark, or gloomy, or sad or when plans go awry, just remember ...there's always the hills.

1

GOVAN TO GOAT FELL

Winter arrived overnight with a flurry of mischievous wind, suddenly turning the ochres and russets of autumn into a world of pallid white. At a stroke, the fields and lanes around the village turned curiously unfamiliar and a deep hush fell over the woods. On the outskirts of the village, where ordered gardens give way to moorland scrub and grassy hollows, the white blanket had silenced the chatter of the streams and the only sound to be heard was that of a surprised blackbird, grumbling at the sudden loss of food and water. It was cold but the rising sun brought an illusion of warmth as it cast a golden glow across the delicate whorls and ripples of the snow surface, each tiny, unique snow crystal reflecting the light in a way that both twinkled and dazzled. The patterns of wind-blown snow ebbed and flowed, sometimes in great curves of drift, at other times in straight corrugated lines. Each fence post was topped by a white powder puff and drystone walls stood black and defiant against the white shroud.

In the days that followed more snow fell until I couldn't hold out any longer. I had to climb a hill. The snow was deep, up to my calves, so I grabbed my snowshoes and made my way to higher ground. A groove of sheep tracks cut their way across the flanks of the hill, single-filed and delicate-hooved impressions, betraying small feet for such cumbersome beasts. Not far away a kestrel hovered in the sky, watching its prey that had suddenly become so exposed. There were few hiding places in such a white landscape.

I climbed all morning, delighting in the vibrancy and sharpness of the air. On the high point of the hill the wind that had brought the snowstorm had scoured the tops clear and the heather and grasses looked strangely unfamiliar. I lay against the cairn, my waterproof jacket below me for protection and my flask offering something hot and comforting. Away in the distance, above the deep valley, a pall of smoke hung in the air. Beyond it, etched against the icy blue of the sky, lay white horizons, as far as the eye could see – familiar shapes in unfamiliar shades – the line of the Glen Feshie hills and, beyond, the high Cairngorms, icy challenges for another day. Closer at hand the rolling uplands of the Monadh Liath lay as a winter wonderland for the wild land connoisseur. Gloriously beautiful, the snow simply wiped out the handiwork of man and returned the high places to a state of ice-cold wilderness. It was what mountaineering dreams are made of – the peace and beauty of the season, the stern fights with the elements, the memories of freedom and challenge. A return to something our ancestors held dear, something we may have lost.

I have no idea where my love of hills and wild places comes from. It could be a random gene, or an unconscious consequence of some early childhood experience, or something deeper and more profound than that. I'm often asked what it is about hills and mountains that attracts me so much and the simplest answer is that such landscapes make me feel happy. I feel comfortable in a mountainous landscape and extremely uncomfortable in the middle of a city. A forest walk heightens my spirit, an urban walk tends to depress me. I've never felt lonely on a mountain-top but a roomful of strangers can be wholly unnerving.

To my knowledge my parents had never set foot on a mountain before I came along. I suspect neither of them had ever even seen a proper mountain, other than in the cinema. Curiously, I recently had a conversation with my 99-year-old Aunt Jenny, my late mother's sister, who told me that she would have loved to have climbed mountains as I have done, as there was always something inside her, a strange feeling, that attracted her to wild places. She simply never had the opportunity.

However, my father's younger brother, Willie, emigrated to Canada in his twenties and, according to my Canadian cousin Laurie, spent a lot of time paddling his canoe in the Algonquin Provincial Park in Ontario. Some of the guys at Algonquin Outfitters apparently still remember him.

Another of my father's brothers lived in Renfrew and regularly spent his summer holidays with Willie in Canada where they went hiking and canoeing together. I remember my Uncle John as a keen cyclist who often made long forays into the Scottish countryside. If there is such a thing as an 'outdoor loving gene' it may have come from one or all of these relatives.

It would be too easy to suggest that I was typical of those who were born in the slums of Glasgow and who grew up with a determination to flee the city streets at every opportunity. It's certainly not an unfamiliar story. Ever since the dark days of the 1930s Depression, working-class climbers and hikers fled to the hills as often as they could and plenty of my peers had found themselves on a similar route. Poverty was rife in Glasgow in the thirties and it wasn't a whole lot better in the streets of Govan where I entered the world in June 1950.

My grandparents' house in Uist Street, where I was born (my mother refused to be admitted to a maternity hospital) was at the posh end of Govan – the Drumoyne end. Their house wasn't one of the ubiquitous Glasgow tenement flats but a four-in-a-block apartment with a front and back garden. From their upper flat window you could look across the road into the playground of Greenfield Street Primary School. My father used to joke that so many of the local children had long marks running up their cheeks as a result of being breastfed through the school railings. Our kitchen window looked down onto a lawn and a bit of a garden, with trees – a small oasis that my grandfather cultivated and cared for with a passion.

In Glasgow, most schoolchildren are segregated into schools where different religions are taught. Greenfield Street Primary was the local non-denominational school. St Constantine's Roman Catholic Church was just along the road, and youngsters who often lived next door to one another were separated at the absurdly early age of five. Beyond St Constantine's was the Fairfield Working Men's Club. My grandfather, William Brown, was a caulker in Fairfield's Shipyard – a responsible trade that completed the process of making new hulls and decks watertight and leak-free. He was a quiet and dignified man who had fought at Ypres and the Somme with the King's Own Borderers.

Quiet and dignified he may have been for most of the time, but he liked to let his hair down on a Saturday night. My mother and her sisters enjoyed telling the story at family gatherings. Wull would listen to the football results on the wireless before getting himself ready for his once-a-week visit to the pub. He would put on his good suit (his only suit), a collar and tie and slick his hair back with Brylcreem. My grandmother, grumbling quietly, would brush him down and send him on his way. He would return some hours later, the worse for wear, but Gran and her daughters would be waiting for him. The front door of the flat was at the foot of a long flight of stairs and Gran and the girls would lie in wait, anxious to hear the sound of Wull's key in the lock. When he spotted Gran he would apparently greet her with a fond and slurred request, 'Give us a kiss Lill,' to which she would invariably respond, 'Kiss my arse!' The girls would help him up the stairs, then, on Gran's command, would hustle him into the bedroom where more instructions were given, 'Jaicket aff,' she would command, followed by 'troosers aff noo ...'.

No sooner had poor old Wull been de-trousered than Gran would take the large white handkerchief from the breast pocket of his suit jacket and spread it wide over the bedspread while the girls raided his trouser pockets for loose change.

Gran would then take a few handfuls of the change, tie them up in the hankie and put it in her peenie pocket with the promise, 'That's for ma weans.'

Next morning Wullie, now sobered up but suffering a hangover, would say to my grandmother, 'Lilly, have you seen my loose change? I thought I had more than that in my pockets.' Gran, without a grain of guilt, would confront him with the words, 'Are you suggesting I stole it? Eh, are you calling me a liar?' To which Wull would respond by retiring to his chair by the coal fire, his dignified demeanour unsullied by needless argument.

William and Lillian Brown were my mother's parents. There were seven in the family and my mother, Helen, was the youngest. Her sisters claim she was spoiled rotten, which my mother always denied. However, Mum, bless her, was a strong-willed woman who did like to get her own way.

My mother and father, Robert, who everyone knew as Bob, met at the dancing – the Dennistoun Palais or some other such popular Glasgow dance hall where the patter was as good as the music.

'Are ye dancing?' was the time-honoured request, to which the negative response was frequently, 'Naw, it's jist the way ah'm staundin.'

Once the couple took the floor the patter continued. 'Aw, hen, ye're wan in a million.' The maiden might then respond, 'Aye right' (that lovely Glaswegian double positive that is actually a negative), 'and so are yer chances.'

Years later, the Hamish Imlach song, 'Cod Liver Oil and the Orange Juice', celebrated the Glasgow dancehall humour, the story of Hairy Mary and her Weegie suitors and I remember, as a teen-ager, singing it to my folks. They both instantly recognised the old romantic come-ons . . .

My father was from Drumoyne. The McNeishs had historically fled south from Highland Perthshire in search of work and had settled in Lanarkshire, near Lesmahagow, where my great-grandfather worked in the coal mines. In search of better prospects he moved into Glasgow to work in the early days of the Clyde shipyards where my father's father, another William, worked all his life. We knew him as Pop, a tiny man in stature but immense in character who was convinced he was the next Robert Burns. He was certainly an avid reader, like many working-class men of his generation, and was passionate about classical music. He was, in the widest sense of the words, self-educated, and all through his life he sincerely believed that if he emigrated to Canada like his youngest son he would be heralded as a great poet and Scots musician.

He played the fiddle, and that's perhaps where my own love of traditional Scots and Irish music comes from. Pop played in a Scottish country dance band until he was into his nineties and turned up at my wedding with his fiddle case under his arm. My uncle Donald suggested he looked like an ageing Al Capone and the fiddle case perhaps hid a machine gun! My best man on the day, my old pal

13

Hamish Telfer, was gracious enough to allow Pop to play a couple of tunes at the reception and he did – 'The Old Rugged Cross' and something else that no-one recognised. I think it might have been 'Oh, Rowan Tree'. He was about to set off on his third refrain when Hamish managed to drag him from the stage, listening patiently to Pop's complaints that the rest of the band were completely out of tune.

Shortly after I was born in my grandparents' house in Uist Street, my parents managed to rent a ground floor flat around the corner in Elderpark Street and that's where I spent my toddler years. My father, a carpenter to trade, worked as a ship's joiner in Fairfields where his father and his grandfather had worked before him. Around about this time he began taking night school lessons to get some qualifications that would allow him to train as a teacher.

Unlike today, when some mothers of young children go out to work to bring in a necessary second income, my mother didn't work, but spent her days looking after me with the devoted help of her own mother. For some reason, probably because I was her youngest daughter's firstborn child, my granny spoiled me, and she would often take me to one of Govan's four cinemas for the matinee. I would sit on her knee and she would feed me sweeties: liquorice allsorts, soor plooms and chocolate toffees, bought with the proceeds of my grandfather's Saturday night trouser pockets.

Dad eventually got his qualifications and spent a year training to be a teacher at Jordanhill College in Glasgow. On graduation he began teaching ship joinery at Glasgow's Stow College of Building, from where he eventually transferred to Anniesland College of Further Education. I remember going for a walk with him when I was a young man and he proudly told me he had been promoted to the role of Senior Lecturer and that he would now have a reasonable income to spend on my mother, myself and my two younger sisters. His dreams never came to pass. He died suddenly at the age of 52 from a heart attack, the victim of forty fags a day.

Once Dad qualified as a teacher my parents decided to buy their first house, a Western Heritable bottom floor flat in a four-in-a-block house in nearby Cardonald. I remember that house with fondness – my sister Helen, five years my junior, was born there and I loved this leafy suburb where I could play with my pals, in particular Sidney Paton, who went on to become Vice-Chair of Scottish Natural Heritage, and Ian Cochrane.

The three of us began primary school at Angus Oval Primary on the same day and I have bittersweet memories of that introduction to learning. The school itself sat on top of a hill above the River Cart and the remains of Crookston Castle and I loved looking out from the playground across the fields towards the distant Gleniffer Braes, fields that were shortly to become the huge housing scheme of Pollok.

The downside of these early primary school days was my first teacher, a Mrs Ferguson, who often lashed us across the back of our legs with a twelve-inch wooden ruler if she didn't think we were trying hard enough. She didn't have a lot of patience with five-year-olds and soon I was looking for ways to avoid going to school. And there were better, more exciting things to do.

The River Cart flowed through the city from its source high in the Lanarkshire hills. By the time it reached Cardonald it was fairly mature and slow moving and absolutely ideal for rafting. My pals and I spent hours building rafts, largely inspired by two great boyhood novels, *The Adventures of Tom Sawyer* and *The Adventures of Huckleberry Finn*, by Mark Twain. It took a lot of imagination to compare the White Cart with the great Mississippi but imagination was something we had in abundance.

Those early years also developed a skill that was to hold me in good stead for the rest of my life. Risk-taking is something that many youngsters are unfamiliar with these days and that, I believe, will have serious implications in generations to come. We knew that building a raft from oil cans and planks of wood and trying to float down the River Cart was risky but wasn't life about adventure and fun? Wasn't risk-taking worthwhile?

Occasionally we fell in the water and got wet but we soon learned how to swim; now and then someone would fall out of a tree and hurt themselves; it wasn't uncommon to tear our clothing because of the old nails that were still imbedded in the planks of wood, but we never looked for someone to blame. We knew accidents happened, and most of the time we expected accidents to happen. The idea was to manage the risk in such a way that the expected accident could be avoided. Frequently we would argue and fall out and it would end in fisticuffs but more often than not we were pals again next day. We all wanted to play football in the school team but rarely felt inferior because we weren't good enough. We simply learned how to deal with failure and disappointment. We drank from streams and pools of water and public fountains, ate blackberries from the bushes, stole rhubarb and crab apples from folk's gardens and survived. Indeed, we survived with aplomb.

Our biggest fear was not being allowed out to play. This was the ultimate sanction for bad behaviour. Generally speaking, during holidays and at weekends, I left the house after a breakfast of tea and toast and turned up for a bite of lunch, usually a bowl of soup, before disappearing again until teatime. During the summer months, I would be outside again until bedtime. What did we do all the time? We had adventures, we explored, we spent very dirty hours playing in the old steam train engines at Corkerhill Junction and at one point built a den in one of the old passenger carriages, a den that was ours for the entire summer holidays. Part of the fun was evading the old watchman. We played in and on the river, cycling once we were old enough to get a bike (but never owned a helmet). We played football and roamed freely and, curiously enough, I only remember one incident that involved the police. I don't recall what it was about but I do remember getting a clip round the ear from this big Highland polisman. Once was enough . . .

Young, well-groomed American men would often approach us and offer to teach us baseball. They were evangelical Mormons and, while we loved to play this curious American version of rounders, I don't recall any of us attending any of the religious classes. We had become streetwise and I suspect that the streets of Cardonald were not a particularly fertile grooming ground for the Mormon faith.

We would build carts, called bogies, out of scraps, and ride them down the hill only to discover that we had forgotten to fit any brakes. We soon learned how to stop without brakes. We ate all

16

kinds of rubbish: crisps, chocolate and sticky sweeties and we drank fizzy, sugar-laden drinks like Tizer and Irn Bru and Dandelion and Burdock but we never got fat – we were always too busy running around. If I wasn't riding around on my bike I was just running, pretending I was Roger Bannister, or Emil Zatopek, or the great Herb Elliott. We didn't walk anywhere.

The fifties and early sixties were memorable years. The austerity of the immediate post-war years was over and with it came the end of rationing. The Cold War cast a long shadow over the world but, despite that, remarkable things were happening. Ed Hillary and Tenzing Norgay climbed Everest, the highest mountain in the world, and the following year Roger Bannister became the first man to run a mile in less than four minutes. An American actress called Grace Kelly married Prince Rainier of Monaco and became a Princess. The Soviet satellite, Sputnik, launched the Space Age and a few years later the Soviets launched the first man into space in the shape of Yuri Gagarin and of course the Beatles produced their first of many hit singles, 'Love Me Do', and in so doing changed the whole nature of popular music. In 1954 IBM announced the development of a model 'electronic brain' – it was the dawn of the computer age, and a biologist by the name of Gregory Pincus led a team of scientists who invented the pill, the symbol of the UK's most defining decade, the Swinging Sixties.

Maybe it's not surprising that this particular generation has produced some of the finest risk-takers ever. Look at the legacy of innovation the past 50–70 years has produced. Freedom went hand in hand with occasional failure, as did success and responsibility, and we learned how to deal with it. Our youngsters of today are like a protected species and I often ache at the thought of their lack of freedom. I've no doubt it will have repercussions for society in the future.

From the perspective of a doting grandfather I can sympathise with my son and daughter-in-law who worry constantly about my two granddaughters and tend to keep them close at hand. It would be very easy nowadays to suggest that my own parents were irresponsible, but the fifties were very different from today. None of my peers had an inkling of what a paedophile was. We knew a few adults who seemed to our innocent eyes a little bit odd, but we simply avoided them. We were young active lads living in a fairly pleasant suburb but we were pretty well-informed about the birds and the bees and what delineated right from wrong, and we knew what it was like to get a good thrashing from our folks if we misbehaved. My dad had big joiners' hands, like great bunches of bananas, and more than once I was at the receiving end of them, but never did I think I was being abused or assaulted. I knew my parents loved me and I also knew that if I did wrong I'd be punished. I knew how far I could push it, all part of the risk-taking learning curve.

I saw a map recently that graphically illustrated how times have changed. It was a map of the Sheffield area and it suggested that in the early part of last century it wasn't unusual for a young person to have a 'play radius' of six miles or more. It told of an 8-year-old, called George, who was allowed to walk six miles to go fishing in the river. By 1950 George's son Jack, also aged eight, was generally allowed to walk about a mile from his home to play in the woods. Jack's daughter, Vicky, was allowed to walk half a mile to the swimming pool in 1979 and her son, Ed, is currently only allowed to walk on his own to the end of his street, about 300 metres.

Such are the fears that exist in our society today that many parents simply don't allow their children out of their sight. I fully sympathise with every parent who would rather not lose sight of their children but how many of the potential nightmares have been promulgated by an obsessive media and a nanny-state that has created an over-reaction by the general public?

I don't really know, although in recent years I have learned from my own two sons of some of the things they got up to when they were young. Bear in mind they grew up in a small Highland village where everybody knew each other and the biggest risk they would take would be in criticising the efforts of the neighbouring town's shinty team! I'm truly grateful for the opportunities I had to be an adventurous youngster and can honestly say that such early adventures and explorations laid a firm foundation for my later career as a mountaineer and wilderness backpacker.

Not long ago I met some youngsters walking along the Kincardine ridge, from Meall a'Buachaille along the tops to Craiggowrie above Glenmore, near Aviemore. It was a raw and blustery day and what was unusual about meeting them was that they were unaccompanied by adults. I spoke to them briefly, assuming they were on a Duke of Edinburgh Award expedition, or something similar, but they weren't. They had simply come out for a walk in the hills, and not one of them was more than fourteen. I was delighted, largely because they reminded me of what I did at that age, borrowing a tent from school and some old pots and pans from my mother's kitchen to go off for a long weekend, exploring the Campsies and the Trossachs and on the way learning the rudimentary skills of hill-going. Even today I can look back and remember, with utter delight, that sense of untrammelled freedom and exploration.

Sadly, most youngsters today miss out on an aspect of that notion of freedom. Mountaineering, for youngsters, has become very regulated and that's a pity. In a book I wrote a few years ago to accompany a television series, *The Edge – One Hundred Years of Scottish Mountaineering*, I had the privilege of interviewing Jimmy Marshall, one of our finest climbers of the fifties and sixties. I asked him about the importance of 'exploration' in climbing, and this is what he said:

'Apart from the few people climbing at the forefront and the height of their skills, we must acknowledge that the mass of people in the mountains must be deprived of the exploration. It's not even a tick-the-guidebook mentality, it's just that everything today is exposed and people aren't allowed to do things for themselves. If you go to the hills as a youngster of 15 or 16 and you're ill clad and you end up in the wrong glen and have to be rescued, you're abused for being reckless. But that's the very mold in which we went to the hills – badly clad, no knowledge of where one glen went from the other or what it looked like, finding precious wee notes of information – but now the information about things is printed so fast that I think it deprives the whole adventurous quality of mountaineering for the masses.

'I'm not depressed by what's happened. I just feel sorry for the young folk that they've missed such an era. I still go crazy as I recall the pleasure and wildness of mountains. It's so enriching. I mean nowadays you never see kids out on the hills unless they've got anoraks and proper boots and there's somebody organising it and directing them.'

Mountaineering clubs were once the obvious conduits for introducing young people to the mountains but the risk of litigation has made most club members wary about taking on such responsibilities. The likes of the Duke of Edinburgh Award, the Scouts and other youth organisations still introduce young people to wild places but many young teenagers who might experience a natural urge to go to the hills are often not the kind who will be comfortable within the more regulated discipline of such bodies.

Occasionally, concerned parents ask me how their son or daughter can take up mountaineering. My gut reaction is to tell them to simply go and do it. Go to the Campsies or the Pentlands or the Lomond Hills of Fife if they come from the Central Belt. These areas are well served by public transport and the journey to and from the hills should be part of the exploration experience. The youngsters just need to be encouraged to go, and parents need to learn how to let them go, to release them, to shove them out of the nest.

A number of years ago the Ordnance Survey came up with a scheme to encourage young people to learn navigation, but, rather than persuade them to head into the great outdoors, they encouraged them to spend more time indoors at a computer terminal. Their interactive website was probably very educational but missed the point. Outdoor education should be about getting youngsters away from their computers, away from gymnasia and climbing walls and out to where they can smell raw earth, get their hands dirty and hear the birds sing as they learn to climb or to navigate. Spending time outdoors is vitally important for our young people; if they can't experience the natural world in childhood then it's highly probable they will never want to care for it or protect it come adulthood, but I'm getting ahead of myself.

Perhaps I'm looking back through rose-tinted specs and the nostalgia of a happy childhood, a period of family life in Lammermoor Avenue in Glasgow's Cardonald that was very settled and happy. As I mentioned earlier, one of my two sisters, Helen, who is five years my junior, was born there, and we grew up in a household that was far from wealthy but which provided everything we could want. I recall when Dad brought home our first family television set. It was in a wooden cabinet and had a tiny black and white screen but Helen and I were overjoyed. I suspect she was no more than a toddler but I remember us holding hands and dancing around the living room. I was excited at the thought of seeing children's programmes like *The Lone Ranger* and *The Adventures of Robin Hood*, while Helen, a little younger, became a big fan of *Watch with Mother*. Andy Pandy, Loopy Loo and the Flowerpot Men became a part of our everyday life.

Regular gatherings of my mother's side of the family were a notable part of our early life. We would all congregate in my grand-parent's house in Uist Street in Govan, usually about ten adults and seven or eight cousins and, after a steak pie and tattie supper, the women would retire to the kitchen, having told my grandparents to sit with the kids and have a break. The womenfolk would hastily wash the dishes, dry them and get on with the real object of the evening: sharing a few fly cigarettes, blowing the smoke out of the window under the illusion that my gran would go berserk if she caught them smoking. Fags were for men, not women.

Back in the living room my uncle Tommy would then strum a guitar (he couldn't actually play any chords) and sing a song called 'Down Mexico Way'. There would be a bit of a sing-song and at some stage there would be a lemonade advocaat for the women and a wee dram for the men. Just the one mind you!

Life at this time had a simple routine. Dad went off to catch the bus to work just after eight when Mum would attend to Helen's needs. I generally organised myself to go off to school, calling on my pal Jim Wallace who lived next-door, to walk the half-mile or so to Angus Oval Primary. Later, after Primary Three, we went from the infant school to Cardonald Primary, a dour and dark Victorian building that sat at the junction of Paisley Road West and Lammermoor Avenue, a 5-minute walk from our house.

Jim was a constant companion in those days. His dad was a butcher, a big and burly man who didn't hesitate in voicing his opinions in all manners of colourful language. Jim's mother, unusually in those days, had a job too and when the weather was bad Jim would often have to wait in our house until his parents came home from work.

One day I happened to mention to my mother that Jim had said a 'bad word'.

'What did he say?' she demanded.

'Oh, I can't repeat it,' I said, in an angelic voice.

'Oh, for God's sake,' she replied, 'spell it out.'

'Okay, F-U-C-K...'

Wallop! 'Don't you ever say such words in this house.'

I wasn't aware of it then but money was tight. My mother was an ambitious woman and had encouraged my father to take out a mortgage on the house in Lammermoor Avenue. I think we were the first in our extended family to have such a thing as a mortgage, but it soon became clear that it was stretching my father's meagre wages as a newly qualified teacher. On a Friday night he would come home and sit down with my mother at the table, make a list of all the weekly outgoings, bills to be paid, the mortgage repayments, money for food and bus fares and fags, and then tally it up. He'd then open his pay packet and take out the cash, giving some to my mother for housekeeping. The rest he'd balance up with the list of outgoings he'd made. There was joy if anything was left over - a real Mr Micawber moment.

However, my parents must have been good at economising and saving a few pennies for, a few years later, they had enough money to buy a holiday caravan. My uncle Donald and aunt Chrissie, my father's sister, had a holiday caravan in Saltcoats on the Ayrshire coast and, after visiting them a few times, my mother decided we should also have one. If my shipyard worker uncle Donald could afford a holiday caravan then we could too. The caravan was far short of luxury. It was sixteen feet in length and had a coal fire and Calor Gas lamps. The beds were made from the cushions that formed the seats during the day and there was barely room to swing a cat, never mind provide holidays for four people. We loved it with a passion.

The caravan site was for static caravans only and was owned by a chap called Tommy Hamilton who had been goalkeeper for the famous Glasgow Rangers Football Club between 1923 and 1934. It was a small site backing on to some tenement flats on one side and the local abattoir on the other, and it wasn't unusual to be wakened in the morning by mooing cows, followed by the crack of a gun as the beasts were put down. My cousin Donald and I had a morbid fascination for the place and we used to climb the wall in the hope of seeing the action. On one occasion, we spotted a pool of blood and for some reason this excited us much more than it should have done. It should have turned us into lifelong vegetarians, but didn't. We were hardy bairns from Govan.

My cousin Donald Regan and I were firm pals. He had a younger brother, David, who was keen to hang around with us but we didn't like the idea of having a 'wean' to look after. Donald also had an older brother, Michael, but we were too young to hang around with him. There was a third member of our gang. A family from the East End of Glasgow called Flanagan had the caravan next to ours and the son, Peter, was a few years older than us and had learning difficulties. He also had a bad stammer, wore thick specs and was as clumsy as an elephant in a ballet class, but we enjoyed having him along, largely because we used him as a bit of a fall guy. We would send him into the local bakery to ask if they had any broken biscuits they were going to throw out and he would regularly pop into Veronicas, the Saltcoats newsagent, to nick a few bread rolls for us all.

Because he was a few years our senior, and looked considerably older with his thick Pyrex-plate specs, he could lift us over the turnstiles when we went to watch Ardrossan Winton Rovers play, a team my uncle Tommy had once played for. It wasn't uncommon for young boys to be lifted over the turnstiles by a responsible adult without having to pay, but Peter was far from being a responsible adult. He was a mild-mannered lad, but that changed when he watched the football. He could curse and swear with the best of them, and with absolutely no hint of a stutter. Donald and I learned a fine vocabulary from big Peter. He also had the habit of throwing his half-time pie at the referee, often, I'm ashamed to say, after our encouragement.

Holiday weekends, Easter and summer holidays were all spent 'at the van' in Saltcoats and Donald and I were like two sun-bronzed waifs, fishing from the harbour walls or from the rocky coastline; swimming in the sea from the sandy beaches; climbing on the crumbling walls of Ardrossan Castle or eyeing up the girls at the summer fairground. These were the years just before the big pop music explosion of the Swinging Sixties when Elvis Presley, Buddy Holly and the Everly Brothers were the kings of popular music and their songs blared out from the fairground loudspeakers every summer evening. That was soon to be replaced in the early sixties by the chart-topping hits of the Beatles, the Rolling Stones, Cilla Black, the Kinks, the Searchers, Brian Poole and the Tremeloes and all the rest. It was an incredible and wonderful time to be a teenager.

Donald and I shared a radio that we tuned every night to Radio Luxembourg. We inevitably managed to hear a few bars of a popular song before it faded into crackles and high-pitched whines, despite the fact that Radio Luxembourg boasted the most powerful privately owned transmitter in the world. It was a very frustrating experience but Radio Luxemburg was the forerunner of pirate radio stations like Radio Caroline, which was launched by Irish music entrepreneur Ronan O'Rahilly, who started broadcasting from a ship off the Essex coast in 1964. By 1967 ten pirate radio stations were broadcasting to an estimated daily audience of ten to fifteen million. Astonishing figures at a time when British pop ruled the world. Other than the music, these Saltcoats holidays were notable for something else: my first emotional stirrings towards mountains and wild places – the foundations of what was to become a lifetime's passion and career.

We normally travelled to Saltcoats from Glasgow on one of the red Western buses on the Friday evening, making the long, slow and tortuously winding journey through Renfrewshire and into Ayrshire via Paisley, Johnstone, Kilwinning and Stevenston. The bus journey gave me the chance to think through plans for the weekend, usually with my cousin Donald, but as soon as we arrived at the caravan site, just off Raise Street, we would dump our bags and go on a walk, usually to the seafront and along the esplanade with a bag of chips to share. It was on one of these gloaming strolls that I first noticed the hills of Arran. I remember it as though it was yesterday, so clear and vivid was the impression it made. The waters of the Firth of Clyde were calm and there was still enough daylight to make out the small print of the impressive scene that lay across the water – the black crags, the shades of the grass and heather and the white tumbling burns on the hillside. I didn't know the names of any of the peaks but my father told me to look at the shape: a head and a body lying prone, the shape of the legendary Sleeping Warrior. The mountain was Goat Fell.

2

RUNNING AND LEAPING

It was probably the romance and mystery of seeing those first views of Arran's Sleeping Warrior across the Firth of Clyde that initially inspired me to climb hills and mountains and take to the quieter byways of Scotland. I recall childhood visits to the Kelvingrove Art Gallery and Museum in Glasgow – cavernous halls stuffed full of fascinating artefacts: models of steam trains and ocean-going ships; suits of armour and ancient weapons from all over the world; stuffed animals and birds and the skeletons of dinosaurs, but it was the voluminous art galleries that drew most of my attention. Here I would spend hours gazing at the Victorian landscapes of Highland Scotland, the paintings resonant with the mystery and enigma of that period known as the Celtic Twilight, great canvasses full of exaggerated splendour, misty with promise of another world, a world far removed from the city in which I was growing up.

James Docharty's 1868 masterpiece, *The Heart of the Trossachs* was achingly beautiful, portraying the 'majestic mountains' of Walter Scott's poetry. Gustave Doré's *Glen Massan* was filled with stormy clouds and kinks of light while the grandest painting of them all was Horatio McCulloch's 1864 masterpiece, his hugely romantic view of Glen Coe. This is generally regarded as McCulloch's finest work, making an enormous impact through the artist's ability to interpret the sheer majesty of the forbidding scenery. The dramatic lighting and fleeting weather effects highlight the rocky cliffs in an awe-inspiring scene, a scene that I was to become intimate with as the years went by.

Now, suddenly, on the Ayrshire coast, I found myself looking at that same promise of things untold, a land of rock and heather and ragged streams that flowed down the mountainsides into the sea. It was only a dozen miles away, but it could have been another world. I've never been able to fully articulate the powerful emotions those Kelvingrove paintings aroused in me, or the sense, the premonition, that such passions were to be a driving force in my life, shaping and forming the years ahead. I always had a deep-felt intuition though, that there was something curiously familiar about the atmospheres, colours and shades of those wild landscapes. Something strangely instinctive, a longing perhaps for some desire buried deep in my soul. It was to be some years before I actually climbed those hills of Arran and that, oddly enough, was also a formative and important experience. I remember it well.

My first visit to the Isle of Arran was on a sun-kissed day. I was 21 and a bunch of us had wandered over the tight and exposed crags and ridges, over Beinn Tarsuinn and the A'Chir Ridge, over Cir Mhor and on to Goat Fell. So beguiled were we by sun-scorched granite we almost missed our ferry and eventually had to jog down the hill and all the way back to Brodick pier. We made the ferry with minutes to spare, sunburnt, sweaty and breathless. I remember leaning against the boat's railings gazing at the outline of the Arran hills against a cobalt sky, and it was then I decided that, somehow, I was going to spend the rest of my life amongst mountains. It was a decision I would never regret, but it was a few years before it became reality.

As a youngster it was sport that was my first love. During my teenage years sport was the discipline that shaped my formative years and created the characteristics that would hold me in good stead for the rest of my life.

Although I flirted with hills and mountains during my teenage years, my real love at that time was remarkably different. On my very last day at primary school, aged 12, somethng happened that amazed and surprised me. On Sports Day I won every race and it was with some astonishment that I realised I could run faster than anyone else in the school. This was an important revelation because I was mad keen on sport, but not all that good at it. I was never good enough to get into the school football team and although I was quite keen to play cricket and rugby, no one else wanted to play those games. They were regarded as 'English' or 'public school' games. It tended to be football or nothing; not too surprising in West Central Scotland where football is more important than life or death. But I could run, boy could I run, and in my first couple of years at King's Park Secondary School I made it very clear to the PE staff that I wanted to be a top athlete.

While my early primary school days were close to idyllic, things changed when we moved across the city to Croftfoot. My youngest sister Heather was born there and while we still appeared to be a happy suburban family my mother never settled in that part of Glasgow. I think she missed the close embrace of her brothers and sisters and her own parents in Govan and Cardonald. Although I didn't know it at the time she went through a nervous breakdown and suffered from bouts of depression, which made the atmosphere at home strained and awkward. I usually managed to make my escape and learned quickly to appreciate my own company, taking long walks through the park just to keep out of the way.

This period more or less coincided with me going to secondary school and I didn't like it. I didn't like it at all.

School felt like a form of imprisonment. I was held indoors against my will and made to sit through lessons that didn't interest me and appeared to be pointless. To this day I'm not sure what purpose algebra and trigonometry plays in the great scheme of things, although I'm certain there must be a point, but as a 15-year-old rebel I was looking for any excuse to dodge classes and re-assert my freedom. My school, King's Park Secondary, was built on top of a hill from where I could gaze across the city to the blue outline of the Campsie Fells. The Highland hills lay beyond. In maths I would gaze at that view and daydream, much to the annoyance of my teachers.

In Third Year I had to choose between various subjects: history or geography, woodwork or metalwork and French or German and, by chance, I avoided languages completely. I went through a year of school when the German language teacher thought I was taking French and the French teacher thought I was in the German class. The ruse earned me a few 40-minute periods off in the course of the week – time that I put to good use by wandering through the park or locking myself in one of the toilets to read a book, usually the autobiography of some great athlete like Emil Zatopek, Herb Elliott or Peter Snell.

My family moved to Glencroft Road in the Glasgow suburb of Croftfoot in 1962 and the back garden of the house overlooked King's Park, whose green wooded acres became my playground and sanctuary. I would wander here when dodging school lessons, learning what a blackbird's warning cry sounded like or discerning the difference between a sparrow and a chaffinch, or a thrush and a fieldfare. I took delight in recognising the footprints of various mammals and even made plaster casts of them.

In time, my class-dodging schemes were discovered by my father. Being a teacher himself he had a pretty good idea of what I was up to and, after several warnings to which I paid little heed, I was dragged to the school and the headmaster's office. Willie Barge was the heidie, a Captain Mainwaring of *Dad's Army* lookalike. Indeed, he looked more like a bank manager than a school head teacher. After a quiet tête-à-tête with my dad, while I was left sitting outside in the corridor, the head gave me a strict lecture on the importance of attending all school lessons and a palm-warming with six of the best. The fabled leather tawse was still being used with enthusiasm by most schoolteachers at the time. I was also given a 'dogger's card', a clocking-in type document that my various teachers had to sign before every lesson to make sure I was in attendance. School became even more of a purgatory.

The only thing I enjoyed about school was sport. Despite my misdemeanours I was eventually appointed school Athletics Captain, and I was an enthusiastic member of the basketball team. On Saturday mornings my cousin Alan Elliott and I played football for a junior football team that went under the name of Rampant Dynamo, a feeder team for Sunderland FC. I started as a full-back and after a few unspectacular games was pushed forward to inside left. I'm not sure what that position is in modern terms, probably a cross between a striker and a midfield player, but it was a role in which I excelled. However, football wasn't to be my game. As in other aspects of my life, I was fast reaching the conclusion that I wasn't a team player. Later, on the long-jump runway and in the mountains, I depended on no one but myself, and that was the way I liked it: an independence, a maverick attitude, that has shaped my entire life.

Although I depended on no one else, it is fair to say that I couldn't have achieved the minor successes I did in athletics had it not been for my school's PE teacher, Hector McIntosh. He was also our basketball coach and was an excellent player himself. During my school years Hector encouraged me in a way no other teacher did, taking me to school athletic meetings in his own time and in his own car, usually at weekends, and sending me off during regular PE periods to do my own athletics training. He also convinced the school janitor, on my behalf, that I should be allowed to come to the PE department after school and use the weight training facilities. I couldn't have had a more encouraging and inspirational teacher.

The only other lesson I enjoyed was English, and that enjoyment was down to the enthusiasm of one particular teacher, a Glaswegian by the name of Rab Dickson. Mr Dickson had a great sense of humour and instinctively knew that we'd prefer the robust language of *The Miller's Tale* in Chaucer's Canterbury Tales to the stifling, stuffy language of William Shakespeare. He knew all the best Robert Burns lines, although Burns wasn't on the official school syllabus. In those days Scottish poets were ignored, and Scottish history was deemed less important than purely English events like the Battle of Hastings or the Magna Carta. I have Rab Dickson and not the Scottish education system to thank for introducing me to the likes of Burns, Norman MacCaig and Hugh MacDiarmid.

Although I wasn't aware of the term at the time I guess I was introduced to my very first backpacking trip when some schoolmates and I borrowed gear from school and set off on our Duke of Edinburgh Award Bronze Medal expedition across the Campsie Fells from Blanefield to Fintry. The Campsies frequently beckoned through the urban haze with promises of escape and fresh air. The fells make up a surprisingly large area, from the prominent top of Dumgoyne in the west to the Carronbridge to Kilsyth road in the east, and are bisected by the B822 Crow Road from Lennoxtown to Fintry. The eastern fells tend to be dominated by forestry plantations but further west, particularly above Strathblane, access to the tops is far easier. I would often gaze from my classroom window across the city to the promise of those high hills, desperate for the weekend when I could pack my 'Bergen' and set off from Blanefield, exploring the crags and high moorlands to the accompaniment of whaups, oystercatchers and lapwings.

The Campsie Fells are made up of layers of lava flow and Dumgoyne, the 'fort of the arrows', the thumb-like addendum that sticks up at the western end of the fells, is an ancient volcanic plug whose name suggests that it was once a defensive site. Curiously, neighbouring Dumfoyn could be the 'hill fort of the wart', which probably best describes its appearance. The area's highest point, Earl's Seat (578 metres/1,896 feet), on the Fintry side of the fells, is probably named after the Earl of Lennox whose lands once extended on the south side of the Campsies. A good hill walk, with much rough walking over trackless hill country takes in Earl's Seat and Dumgoyne, a fairly straightforward route with the promise of wide-ranging views to the urban skyline in the south and in complete contrast, Ben Lomond and the jumble of hills that mark the beginnings of the Highlands in the north.

My first expeditions to the Campsies were not all cherries and cream. Almost inevitably we burned our hands trying to cook on an open fire; we didn't sleep because of the cold and the rock-hard ground and we ate all our grub within the first few hours of the expedition. We managed to get ourselves lost in the mist on Earl's Seat, dropped down a steep gully on the north side of the Campsies and became lost again looking for Fintry. We found Balfron instead. We were only a few miles out and our teacher, Fred Connor, didn't seem to mind too much. We were all eventually given our Bronze Award but I don't recall any of us going forward for the Silver. We had grown bored with the Duke of Edinburgh's scheme by that time. However, in spite of the hardships we had experienced, the expedition itself, and the training with Fred Connor that led to it, had given me a taste for camping in wild places that soon became a habit.

It wasn't unusual for two or three of us to borrow a tent from school and pinch pots and pans from home and head off to the Campsies or the Trossachs. Tartan blankets, wrapped around our bodies and held in place with safety pins were our sleeping bags, and we learned that old newspapers, placed below us, would ward off the chill from the cool breast of Mother Earth. Naturally, we cooked on open fires. It didn't take me long to learn that our activity embraced simplicity. What could be simpler than walking all day, then sleeping all night to get up in the morning and walk all day again?

At the ripe old age of fourteen I made my debut as a track and field athlete representing my school. Mr McIntosh drove me to the Scottish Schools Athletics Championships at Pitreavie in Fife where I was entered into the Under–15 220 yards and the long jump. I finished second in both events but it was the long jump that I wanted to make my own, largely because that same year I watched a 22-year-old Welsh long jumper called Lynn Davies win the gold medal at the 1964 Tokyo Olympics.

Lynn was competing against the two finest long jumpers in the world, the joint world record-holders: the American, Ralph Boston, and the Russian, Igor Ter-Ovanesyan, and on a wet and cool day, reminiscent of his native South Wales valleys, Lynn Davies pulled it off with a personal best leap of 8.07 metres/26 feet, 8.5 inches. With that leap I found a new hero.

'Lynn the Leap' came from a small coal mining village called Nantymoel, near Bridgend in Glamorgan. I wrote him a long letter, congratulating him on his Olympic success and, rather naively, asked him for some tips. Much to my surprise Lynn replied to my letter; the beginning of a correspondence that was to last for several years. Lynn Davies was a role model in every way, a man hugely committed to sport and to helping others achieve their potential.

In my second year at secondary school I was asked if I'd like to attend the Scottish Schoolboys Athletics Training Course at Inverclyde Sports Centre at Largs. This was a week-long residential course run by the Scottish Amateur Athletics Association and directed by their new national coach, a charismatic and hugely inspiring individual by the name of John Anderson. John was a short, ginger-haired Glaswegian who simply vibrated with enthusiasm for sport. He had played football to a fairly high standard and his best pal had been Ally MacLeod, later to become the Scottish football team manager, but it was track and field athletics that he loved. He had never been a successful athlete himself but had trained as a PE teacher at Jordanhill College in Glasgow and subsequently studied for a degree at the Open University. He eventually became a national coach in England before being offered the post of Scottish National Coach.

At one point during the week's training at Inverclyde John took me aside and in a conspiratorial tone suggested that if I worked hard enough I could become the first Scot to jump more than 25 feet. If I really committed myself I could become the first to jump over 26 feet and perhaps even 27 feet. The world record at that time was 27 feet, 5 inches. I was stunned, and hugely excited. I responded by politely asking him (I actually called him Mr Anderson. I never called him John until I was about 18) if he would consider coaching me, and he agreed. My young life was about to change in a dramatic way.

John Anderson was a very influential and successful coach who went on to work with five world record holders and 170 Great Britain internationalists including distance runners Dave Moorcroft, David Bedford, Liz McColgan, Sheila Carey and Lynne MacDougall. He also coached successful sprinters like David Jenkins and sprint hurdlers David Wilson and William Sharman. In later years, he even achieved television personality stardom as the referee in the popular programme, *Gladiators*. His 'Gladiators ready?' and countdown, 'Three, two, one,' in his thick Glaswegian accent, were so successful that they were copied by the original American Gladiator show.

John's influence on my life at that time was massive. He taught me the importance of having a vision, and working hard to fulfil that vision. His confidence in my potential gave me self-belief, not a thing that comes easily to those of us born in Govan (perhaps with the exception of Sir Alex Ferguson and Rab C. Nesbitt), but most of all he taught me the value of commitment – something that he demanded from all his athletes. One of those, Hamish Telfer, was my best friend, training companion and occasional hill-going buddy, and we were affectionately known to the others as Hammie and Cammie. I first met Hamish when we joined the West of Scotland Harriers in 1964, a well-respected running club whose coach, a lovely old gent by the name of Johnny Todd (Mr Todd to us), took Hamish and me under his wing. In those days the West of Scotland Harriers was predominantly a cross country running club and, although Hamish and I considered ourselves sprinters, we were encouraged to become involved in everything that was going on – no bad thing for youngsters. That included winter Saturdays at the Stannalane running track, near Rouken Glen in the south-side of Glasgow, where we went cross country running with some fine old timers including the legendary John Emmet Farrell, Gordon Porteous and Andy Forbes. Together with Shettleston Harriers's Davie Morrison the foursome were to become known to everyone in the Scottish athletics scene as the 'geriatric rat-pack'.

For Emmet Farrell, there had been national records for the one-hour run in 1945 and 1950; Scottish track titles at six miles in 1938 and 1946; and 10 miles in 1938, 1939 and 1946. He represented Scotland ten times in what is now the world crosscountry championships, the last of these aged 43. With his international days behind him he simply kept on running. When veteran athletics came into vogue, Emmet embraced it. In reality he had never stopped running so at seventy years of age he swept the world 1500, 5000 and 10,000 metres titles, setting world records at the shorter two. He won gold at the world 10,000 metres road race, successfully defended the track crowns at 1500 and 10,000 metres in New Zealand and also won the world veteran cross-country title.

At the time Hamish and I were pretty ignorant of Emmet's pedigree. We just knew him as one of the old guys who went running at Stannalane, but he always kept us amused with his stories, particularly this one.

'I often run in Rouken Glen Park because it's quiet and provides a nice scenic atmosphere of path, grass and trees. On one occasion as I passed by, the local park ranger, who knew me well, commented to a worker nearby "That chap's been running for over forty years." The worker replied, "Can he no stop?" He was right. Out of the mouths of babes and sucklings cometh truth.'

Included in our Stannalane running group was another young athlete by the name of Ian Walker, who went on to become a Scottish international 400 metre runner before swapping his spiked shoes for a banjo. Ian is now an established folk singer and I often bump into him at festivals.

I have some very fond memories of dank, wintry Saturday afternoons at Stannalane. We probably ran between 5 and 10 miles, mostly around the Barrhead waterworks, and on our return to the 'pavilion', a basic wooden shack, we all had to share one shower to scrape off the cow shit! That was followed by a cup of tea and a biscuit for which we all donated, if I remember correctly, tuppence. It was all very Alf Tupper'ish and I absolutely adored it. I clearly remember one particular Saturday afternoon when it had snowed all morning. By lunchtime the clouds had rolled away and the sun came out. Everything sparkled and shone and it was so bright we ran with sunglasses on. The familiar fields and lanes where we ran week after week took on a different aspect: they were pristine and clean and vibrant and for the first time in my life I saw how fresh snow can change and refresh a familiar landscape. It was a phenomenon I was to become very aware of in years to come.

At that time Hamish showed some promise as a cross country runner and he and I used to finish reasonably highly in Under-15 and Under-17 cross country events, although the lads of Shettleston and Springburn Harriers usually dominated such races. We used to go for long runs together. Although I was specifically training as a long jumper, Hamish was always happy to do some sprint training with me and I was always willing to go for some long runs with him. On one occasion we had the idea of running down to visit my aunt Nancy and uncle Tom in Bishopton in Renfrewshire. We got there in reasonably good shape, had a cup of tea and then ran home again. Or at least I did – I had to get my father to go out in the car and search for Hamish. I think we ran about eighteen miles that night and Hamish later claimed that rigor mortis had set in at about sixteen. On another occasion, some years later, I rang him out of the blue and asked him to partner me in the Saunders Lakeland Mountain Marathon. We did manage to win a minor category but Hamish reckoned 'he died the death of a thousand dogs'.

The truth of it was this: we both simply loved athletics and we both loved training. Since Hamish and I were virtually inseparable, John Anderson took him under his coaching wing and the pair of us would often travel to Hamilton, where John lived with his first wife Christine, to help him collate training films, do some filing or wash his car. On one later occasion, when Hamish and I were both 17, I bought a Honda motorbike while Hamish splashed out on a wee scooter-type thing which barely went above 15–20mph. We decided to go out to Hamilton to visit the Andersons on a particularly cold winter day. I got to Earnock about an hour before Hamish and when he appeared Christine had to take him into the house, place him in front of the fire and thaw him out.

Our teenage weekends were entirely taken up with training sessions – usually meeting John Anderson somewhere and going to the all-weather running track at Grangemouth Stadium. Later, that changed to Meadowbank Stadium in Edinburgh. We were in an excellent group of athletes that John coached; today it would be called an 'elite' squad. It included Scottish shot put champion Moira Kerr, marathon runner Leslie Watson, hurdler Lindy Carruthers, 400 metres runner David Jenkins (who later became infamous as a drug cheat), the decathlete Stewart McCallum, middle distance runners Dunky Middleton, Graeme Grant, Hugh Barrow and the sisters Alex and Jinty Jamieson.

Hamish and I were working hard and training in exalted company. Because of our commitment to athletics our teenage years may have innocently bypassed many of the things other teenagers enjoyed: discos and clubs, boozy weekends and parties, but we loved the social scene that went hand in hand with our training group. As young red-blooded males we had a succession of girlfriends, particularly from the ranks of the Maryhill Ladies Athletics Club, and John Anderson became something of a confidante in matters relating to the opposite sex. These were issues that we found difficult to discuss with our own parents and John had an amazing ability to sense when one of us was going through a love-torn period. When either of us was dumped by a girlfriend – a fairly regular occurrence – he would prescribe a session of twenty-second runs, so we could run the heartbreak out of our system. This was a form of athletics torture consisting of a flat-out run for twenty seconds. The distance you achieved in that time was then marked on the track and you then subtracted ten yards from it. The idea was to then run that distance as many times as possible with a 90-second recovery between each run. When you failed to reach the distance more than twice, the session was over. I was never sure if this was the most appropriate type of training for a budding long jumper, but for a heartbroken teenager it was perfect. Running your frustrations out on the track is hugely cathartic and if the ex-girlfriend was around to see you retching your breakfast up after a hard session, as she invariably was, she witnessed at first hand how much you were suffering for her. It was all very gallant and romantic . . . or so we thought.

In comparison with some of my training companions I never made it big in track and field. In 1968 I won the Scottish Schools AAA long jump championship and in the same year became the Scottish Amateur Athletics Association (SAAA) Junior Long Jump Champion with a leap of just over 23 feet. A few weeks after that success a letter arrived from the SAAA inviting me to represent Scotland in a Home Countries International athletics match in Leicester, an event in which I would compete against my boyhood hero, Lynn Davies. In international terms it was a baptism of fire. Lynn, the reigning Olympic Champion represented Wales; Fred Allsop, another Olympian and at that time the UK triple jump champion, represented England and this 18-year-old youngster represented Scotland. Not surprisingly I was last, but I obviously made enough of an impression for the Scottish selectors to invite me to compete for Scotland again at an international indoor meeting at RAF Cosford near Wolverhampton the following winter. I competed in the long jump and the triple jump and once again finished bottom of the pile in both events.

The major target for most of us in the John Anderson coaching squad was the Commonwealth Games in Edinburgh in 1970, but John moved on from his role as Scottish National Athletics Coach in early 1970 and was replaced by Frank Dick, a former 400 metres runner who became one of the UK's most respected and influential coaches. I badly missed the close, almost fatherly relationship I had enjoyed with John Anderson. I suffered a long series of injuries, my performances suffered and I became rather disillusioned with track and field athletics. After particularly hard training sessions at Meadowbank Stadium, where the Commonwealth Games would be held in 1970, I got into the habit of taking myself off to Arthur's Seat, high above the city of Edinburgh, to gaze out across the stadium, across the Firth of Forth to the outline of the Lomond hills of Fife and the dim horizon of the Highland hills beyond. Up there, away from all my training companions and training schedules I could think and I knew, deep in my heart, that very soon I would have to make some tough decisions about the direction my life was going to take. The hills were gently calling me.

Needless to say, when I left school I had absolutely no desire to endure another three or four years' education at university or college. I wanted out of the system as soon as possible but what was I to do? It was to be another seven years before I settled into a job that gave me the time and space to plan a proper career and in that time I tried my hand at being a policeman, a part-time barman, selling weighing machines, selling insurance and had a year-long spell in the financial sector.

I was also disappointed not to have been selected for the Scottish team for the 1970 Commonwealth Games, especially since many of my friends had made the team and were having a wonderful time in anticipation of the grand event. Since becoming Scottish Junior Long Jump Champion in 1968 I had gone through a series of injuries that had really affected my confidence. First of all I suffered some hamstring tears, then I developed a heel problem and that's bad news for a long jumper. No sooner had I recovered from the heel problem than I developed a sore Achilles heel but, despite the injuries, I was beginning to realise, somewhere deep in my knower, that I simply wasn't good enough to reach the higher echelons of this sport that I loved. My enthusiasm for athletics, and the hard training it involved, was steadily diminishing.

I was also becoming aware of another issue, one that in years to come would rock the world of sport to the core, and in particular, cycling and athletics. One of our training squad, David Jenkins, was destined to become the European 400 metres champion in 1971 and went on to represent Great Britain in three Olympic Games. We were all thrilled for him until the thunderbolt arrived. Jenkins was convicted for distributing anabolic steroids. Whether he took them while he was competing and training with our squad we'll never know, but others certainly were. Our training squad knew all about steroids. I don't believe anyone in the John Anderson camp took drugs but I do recall a young and gangly long jumper turning up the next year having put on about two stones of muscle. That wasn't normal. We knew who the drug-takers were and we also knew that the authorities were turning a blind eye to them. I often wonder if things are different today. I'm not involved in track and field athletics any more so I really can't say for sure, but I do know that in 1970 athletics was changing as a sport, and I was changing too.

Despite these issues, Hamish and I went through to Edinburgh as often as we could and enjoyed the 1970 Games as spectators. They were a huge success and Scotland finished fourth in the medals table behind Australia, England and Canada; an achievement that's fairly hard to believe nowadays. Rosemary Stirling won the women's 800 metres; Lachie Stewart beat the great Ron Clarke, the Australian world record holder in the 10,000 metres; Ian Stewart and Ian McCafferty took gold and silver in the men's 5000 metres while Rosemary Payne took the women's discus. But the event that really stood out for us was the closing ceremony – an afternoon of joy and fun that proved beyond all doubt that these were the 'Friendly Games'.

As the international teams paraded into the Meadowbank Sports Stadium for the ceremony there was a shout from somewhere in the crowd and suddenly hundreds of spectators jumped down from the stands to join in the parade. Hamish and I didn't need any encouragement – we joined them, found our friends in the Scottish athletics team and danced around the track with them to the strains of 'Scotland the Brave'. It was complete and utter turmoil. The officials, who had initially tried to prevent the crowd coming onto the track gave up and joined in themselves. Black African athletes wore the kilt and one athlete pedaled around the track on a child's bicycle, his knees hitting the handlebars. All official formality was lost until the Queen's horse-drawn carriage entered the stadium, the words of 'Auld Lang Syne' flashed up on the scoreboard and everyone joined in, arm in arm, competitor and spectator alike. Compared with the formal, carefully orchestrated theatre of modern sports events, the 1970 Commonwealth Games were truly the Friendly Games, and one of the very last true amateur Games. Despite the disappointment of not competing myself, I'll never forget that wonderful afternoon in Edinburgh. It would have been the highlight of my year had it not been for a significant meeting in December that same year.

3

May the Fire Be Always Lit

Gina Devine was a nurse in the Southern General Infirmary in Glasgow – a place known to Glaswegians as the Suffrin' General. And she just happened to be on duty one night when I, as a young policeman, had to accompany a very drunk Danish sailor to the casualty department, nowadays known as the accident & emergency unit. He had fallen down the ship's gangplank and broken a leg, but threatened violence to anyone who attempted to touch it. Not a nice situation for a young nurse to be faced with but I was impressed with Nurse Devine's firmness. She plastered up the leg while I held the sailor down, to a tirade of what I assumed to be the finest of Danish abuse.

It all sounds very romantic, a young police officer stands by to protect a pretty young nurse from possible assault, and it would have been nice to consider myself in the Sir Galahad role but, in truth, Gina had it sorted. These A&E nurses had their own ways of dealing with awkward patients and I was impressed. So impressed that I used some internal hospital and police contacts to find her phone number. I rang her up, asked rather naively if she remembered me, and asked her out. Much to my surprise she did remember me and accepted my invitation for a date.

It was very much a whirlwind romance. We met in December 1970 when I was 20 years of age and we were married in April 1972. By all accounts we were very different: I was a sports fanatic, Gina wasn't. I liked to go for wanders in the mountains, Gina didn't. I was impetuous and took risks, Gina didn't. I came from a Protestant background, Gina from a Roman Catholic one, but it worked and, after 45 years, two sons and two granddaughters, it's still working. Gina is not only my best friend and my favourite hiking buddy, she's my soul mate. I know that sounds a wee bit cringeworthy but I would describe a soul mate as a stable and secure individual who you can lean on, trust and depend on to help you through life. There is a mutual feeling of love and respect and you are each in sync with each other's needs and wants. It would be lovely to write that we have never had an argument or said a harsh word but that would be silly. Like most couples we have our disagreements but the secret, if it is a secret, of a long and successful marriage is not to allow those disagreements to fester. Agree to differ if you must, then move on.

We didn't see the religious issue as a problem, and neither did Gina's parents or my own, but plenty of others did. There were several quiet, well-intended words of warning, and some folk who were invited to the wedding didn't come because it was a 'mixed marriage'. We didn't care, we treated the whole issue very lightly and I even had some valuable and friendly assistance from the official Roman Catholic Church. We decided to marry in Gina's church in Stirling so off we went to see her local priest, Father O'Hanlon, a lovely amiable man who nevertheless insisted we do things by the book, the RC book. Since I wasn't of 'the Faith' I'd have to receive some instruction in the ways and workings of the Catholic Church. That meant six weeks travelling to Stirling to see Father O'Hanlon. We realised this might be difficult so the good Father asked if I knew any Catholic priests in Glasgow where I lived. As it happened I did – my parent's next-door neighbour was Father James McShane, a Canon in the church (my father used to describe him as a 'big shot'), and it was arranged that every Wednesday evening, at seven thirty, I would pop next door and have an hour's instruction from James.

On the first Wednesday I nervously went next door, rang the doorbell and waited. Eventually he opened the door, looked a little perplexed to see me, and hustled me in.

'Look,' he said in a conspiratorial tone, 'I completely forgot. Celtic are playing in a European Cup tie tonight and it starts in a few minutes on the telly. If you're happy enough I can give you some books to look through and as far as everyone's concerned you'll have had your instruction. Okay? Now, do you fancy a can of beer?'

That was it, although as he showed me the door later in the

evening he did ask me why on earth I wanted to marry a Catholic?

The wedding, in April 1972, was a huge success and Father O'Hanlon and my parents' Church of Scotland minister, the Reverend James Barr, jointly officiated. The reception was held in the church hall in Stirling's Raploch area and we danced to a terrific local band that soon had everyone up on the floor, including the priest. We reckoned we were the only married couple who enjoyed their wedding reception so much we didn't want to leave, but we did, and soon were off to the Isle of Skye on a short honeymoon. I had thirty quid in my pocket to last us a week.

Those early days of our marriage could have been incredibly difficult. Money was scarce and we had a mortgage to pay. Interest rates were soon to reach an all-time high, there was industrial turmoil in the country and I had no idea what I wanted to do for a living. I left the police force convinced I had what it took to earn a fortune in the life insurance business but, after selling a policy to my pal Hamish, and another to a friend of his, sales more or less dried up and I had neither the skills nor the enthusiasm to sell any more.

On a hot summer's day in June 1974 our first son, Gordon, was born in the maternity unit of the Southern General, the hospital where we first met, and for the first time in my life I experienced a real sense of responsibility. As I cradled that little bundle of life in my arms I was overcome by a profound sense of determination. I was going to do everything I could to give my young son the best possible start in life in an environment that was neither threatening nor deprived. A short time later Gina and I decided the best way to achieve that was for us to move away from the city, to the Scottish Highlands if possible, where I would start a career of some kind, preferably in the outdoors.

At the time I was working for the Ford Motor Credit Company but not enjoying it. I had to wear a suit and a collar and tie and my boss constantly complained because I'd grown a beard. I was becoming increasingly frustrated by city and corporate life and I needed a break. When I eventually handed in my resignation the boss asked what I really wanted to do with my life. When I told him I wanted to earn a living climbing mountains he just laughed and shook his head. It soon became the office joke. I couldn't really blame him since I wasn't all that sure myself how I was going to achieve my goal.

By this time I had more or less given up athletics and went off to the hills whenever possible, either with Hamish or with the Lomond Mountaineering Club. Even when I was training as a long jumper I had enjoyed the occasional sortie, although some of my earliest expeditions were rather questionable in terms of safety. I remember Hamish and I eyeing up Stob Ghabhar as we travelled to Glen Coe, and on a whim decided to climb it. I still shudder involuntarily every time I drive north from Bridge of Orchy and see Stob Ghabhar, for this was the first mountain we ever climbed in winter conditions. Looking back on that adventure with the benefit of hindsight I guess we were lucky to escape with our lives. We were so excited by the idea of a winter climb that we kicked and lunged our way up thigh-deep snow in the middle of the mountain's south-east corrie, plunging our new hickory-shafted ice axes deep into the soft, unconsolidated white stuff. By rights we should have been swept to our death in an avalanche, and if avalanche warnings had been given in those days this would have been high-risk: category 4 or 5. Few Scots mountaineers knew much about avalanche forecasting in the sixties, never mind two spotty-faced youths, and there was still a general consensus that avalanches were something that occurred in the Alps or the Himalaya, not in Scotland. Consequently, we were completely oblivious to the risk and had a wonderful time.

Thrilled with getting to the summit, we decided to have a go at a real classic winter climb, the Upper Couloir of Stob Ghabhar. I think we became a little infatuated by the mix of French and Gaelic and 'couloir' sounded so much more Alpine than 'gully', which is what it is. Hidden away above the mountain's glacier-scarred eastern corrie, the extravagantly named Upper Couloir was a target for many strong climbing parties in the latter years of the nineteenth century. It was eventually climbed by the united efforts of AE Maylard, Professor and Mrs Adamson and a Miss Weiss in 1897. Nowadays it's a fairly straightforward winter route when conditions are good, but conditions were not particularly good when we tried it. More to the point, we didn't have a rope, belaying gear or crampons. Our sole winter equipment was one hickory-shafted ice axe each. One look at the climb's bulging ice pitch had us hurrying downhill to think again.

We were more interested in rock climbing than hillwalking in those days and Glen Coe was the usual haunt of the Lomond Mountaineering Club. I have fond memories of brewing up tea on an old Primus stove in the little stone howff opposite the east face of Aonach Dubh. I was new to climbing, a little nervous and unsure of the techniques, but was literally shown the ropes by cockily confident gangrels who were hardly any older than I. There was little difference in age, but light years in experience and attitude. I learned a lot on these early climbs but, more importantly, in climb after climb, I learned to love this place, its crag and its burn, and its little stone howff. Even today I often divert from the footpath to clamber up there and enjoy a few moments of pure nostalgia. The east face of Aonach Dubh had long offered exciting, if modest climbing routes. Among the best of these are the Long Crack, Spider and Archer Ridge. Even on a lousy weather day the combination of Bowstring on the Barn Wall and Quiver Rib, two straightforward, easy routes, can offer immensely fulfilling outings.

In much the same way as Muriel Gray's 1991 television series on Munro-bagging inspired a generation of hillwalkers, so it was a 1967 television show that opened the eyes of youngsters like me to the adrenaline flow excitement of rock climbing. A year earlier, Rusty Baillie, Tom Patey and Chris Bonington had made the first ascent of the 450-foot, crumbling, sandstone pillar that had been severed, by the wind and the erosive power of the sea, from the cliffs of St John's Head on the Orkney island of Hoy. Their ascent of the Old Man of Hoy encouraged Chris Brasher, at that time head of outside broadcasts with the BBC, to film a climbing extravaganza on the sea stack, with fifteen million viewers getting a gull's eye view of the technicalities, the interaction between the climbers themselves and the sheer gut-wrenchingly vertical rock hundreds of feet above the churning sea. Many of those viewers must have been convinced that rock climbers were quite simply mad. Even today, a considerable part of the electorate, and sometimes their elected representatives, are quick to criticise the irresponsible and foolhardy selfishness of climbers who require to be rescued from crag or mountain, but for every one of those unfortunates there are thousands of rock climbers who go about their chosen sport in complete safety. Rock climbing, thanks to modern equipment, is a relatively safe activity that can be pursued in a variety of environments from indoor climbing walls to some of the most breathtaking landscapes in the world.

It was the late Mo Anthoine who coined the phrase 'feeding the rat', not only describing the overwhelming desire to climb, but also something deeper and more fundamental. Anthoine's addiction, like that of so many climbers, was an obsession with risk and adventure, and with the wonderful sensation of wellbeing that follows a climb, as the endorphins surge through the system in a natural high. That's not to say that rock climbing is all roses. Sometimes, just sometimes, we remember that the rose grows from a prickly stem. Climbing is often wet, cold and uncomfortable and can involve hanging around, literally, in damp and exposed situations for hours on end. Sometimes it can be scary, even life threatening. The element of risk is always there, the prospect of serious injury, even death, could be the outcome of a simple mistake but, as Chris Bonington suggests, it isn't so much a matter of doing something dangerous as being master of that danger. In essence, that's what climbing is all about. It's about eliminating as much risk as possible, of reducing the odds between you, the climber, and the rock you are attempting to climb, to an acceptable level.

In one of his books, Sir Chris, probably the most boyishly enthusiastic climber I've ever met, wrote: 'Mastering danger ... is perhaps at its most elemental in rock climbing, either climbing solo or at the end of a long run out with very little protection. You reach a difficult section, pause, work out the moves, evaluate the risk, feel a tinge of fear. Maybe, there is no retreat. You can't get back down so you've no choice but to go on. You make a tentative move, back off, try to rest, and then commit yourself, putting the planned moves into action, staying relaxed, in control, every sense sharpened, as you move upwards over the rippled rock. You've made it. There is a great sense of elation, euphoria and, at the same time, release, followed by a vast satisfaction as you bring up your second.

Your awareness of the mountains around you, of a pattern of lichen on the rock just below, the heat of the sun on your skin is all intensified. The sensation is even stronger if it was a new route, if you have touched rock that has never felt a human hand, if you were unable to predict the outcome. This is what makes climbing so addictive.'

Unlike Chris Bonington, most of us will never experience the euphoria of climbing a new route, or become the first person to set foot on the summit of a remote Himalayan peak, but we can all have our own Everests, our own Old Man of Hoy. In a society that is becoming increasingly nanny-state-like, when risk is being reduced for the safety of all, many of us want to escape the clutches of the health and safety regulators and return to an environment where we can, for a while, be totally responsible for our own actions, and can, if only for a few hours, be in control of our own destiny.

I recall a turning point in my own climbing career when I was leading a route and suddenly reached a point where I wasn't sure if I could go on. I certainly knew I couldn't go back. As I considered my options I became vaguely aware that the physical flow that had brought me to this point would carry me through. The complete involvement with the rock, the very totality of the experience, amounted to a heightened sense of control. I waited and allowed the thought to take root. Once that happened I felt confident and reached above my head into a small crack. Something seemed to click. My fingers curled round a wonderfully reassuring rugosity within the crack and I pulled up on it, my feet finding holds of their own. Within two or three moves I was moving calmly, confidently and climbing away from the sheer drop that a few minutes earlier had threatened to swallow me up. As I pulled over the lip and found a belay to bring up my mate, exhilaration washed over me and I dropped to the ground consumed by a sense of wellbeing and intense satisfaction. It was as though my consciousness had been isolated during the previous few minutes, allowing only a limited selection of information to penetrate my awareness. Now, my mind was awash with awareness of the views around me, the smell of green grass, awareness of a sense of achievement, the overcoming of fears and doubts, and the sense that I had been capable of exercising control in a situation that had been potentially hazardous. It's only when the outcome of such a situation is in doubt and you're in a position to actually influence the outcome that you begin to appreciate whether you had been in control or not.

The pioneers of rock climbing were most certainly exploratory adventurers and as the sport, and particularly equipment, developed, new sets of ethics were formulated that set precedents for the next generation. The term 'climbing' essentially incorporates a number of games that climbers play. It was an American climber and mountaineer, Lito Tejada-Flores, who said that climbing is not a homogeneous sport, but rather 'a collection of differing (though related) activities, each with its own adepts, distinctive terrain, problems and satisfactions and perhaps most important, its own rules'.

For example, the rules, or ethics, of Scottish winter climbing may allow a climber to hammer a piton into a crack to tie on to, but the ethics of modern rock climbing would frown on such an action. You might use an aluminium ladder to cross a yawning crevasse on a Himalayan glacier but you wouldn't use that same ladder to climb the crags of the mountain. Environmental questions arise when climbers use expansion bolts that are drilled into the rock, or when modern winter climbers use ice axes and crampons to climb routes that have very little snow or ice on them. The fundamental problem of climbers damaging the rock they climb on is now a very real one and in the self-policing world of climbing I've no doubt new sets of ethics will be formulated to deal with such problems.

Tejada-Flores' differing activities nowadays range from bouldering and scaling indoor climbing walls, to taking part in full-scale mountaineering expeditions, to far-flung corners of the globe. Twenty years ago, climbers generally made a progression from hillwalking to rock climbing, then Alpine climbing to tackling the Greater Ranges – a natural development that produced climbers with a great range of skills. Today, such progression is less prevalent and it's not uncommon to find indoor climbing-wall enthusiasts who have never climbed on a mountain crag. Likewise, there are those who wouldn't be seen dead on a climbing wall in a gymnasium. Rock climbing truly is for all.

With the inclusion of sports climbing in the 2020 Olympic Games it will be interesting to see how the sport develops. While climbing will probably benefit from an influx of grant-aid and sponsorship, I have particular fears about climbing becoming an Olympic sport. I recall how athletics changed when it became professional: how top athletes would choose which event to compete in depending on the fee; how coaches demanded larger and larger sums for their time; how the love of the sport in many cases was exchanged for the love of money. Most important of all, how winning became synonymous with earnings and a win-at-all-cost mentality, even if it meant taking drugs.

For me climbing is all about the outdoors: being in the fresh air, challenging yourself on a natural crag or rock wall, hearing the call of birds, respecting the environment. Climbing an artificial wall in a gymnasium seems so alien to me. You may as well do a few press-ups and learn a few gymnastic tricks. I took up climbing because I wanted to be outside in the fresh air, and usually in a beautiful setting, not a sweaty gym. I had enough of that when I trained for athletics. Here in Scotland we are fortunate to have an enormous range of natural rock climbing venues, from the crags of Craig-y-Barns at Dunkeld to Dumbarton Rock; the magnificent vertical sea of granite that makes up the Etive Slabs to the multitude of crags at Polldubh in Glen Nevis; the mountain routes of the Buachaille Etive Mor, Ben Nevis, the Cairngorms and the mountains of the far north and a host of others, too numerous to mention, in all areas of the land. And the Old Man of Hoy is still there, still being climbed, an iconic monument to all the traditions and past glories of Scottish rock climbing.

The lads (I'm afraid I can't recall any lassies coming to the club) of the Lomond Mountaineering Club used to meet every Wednesday evening in the Wintersgill's Bar in Great Western Road. The first night I went along I asked the barman where I'd find the Lomond guys. He nodded to a corner of the room, 'That lot there,' he said, 'wi' the big jaickets oan.' It's an odd thing about climbers but they like to look the part. This lot certainly did – most of them were sitting in front of a blazing pub fire wearing down-filled duvet jackets, the mountaineering identity badge of the time. Those were good nights, blethering about the hills and climbing routes and planning the weekend's outing. I seem to recall we mostly went to Ben A'an in the Trossachs or Glen Coe and I still have a great photograph of the guys posing Victorian-style in the Coire Ghabhail or the Lost Valley: Willie Johnstone, Dougie Benn, Alan Paterson, Hamish Teale, George Christie, Ray Stokes, Eddie McWilliams, Eric Duncan, Phil Schrieber, Dave MacDonald and Brian Johnstone. Some of the stalwarts of the club are missing from the photo, guys like club secretary Bill Lindsay, Tommy Hardy and Ken Johnstone, who was probably the best climber in the club.

Along with Pete Ogden, Ken made the first ascent of Spacewalk on Aonach Dubh and a couple of years later climbed three new E5 routes on the Cobbler with Cubby Cuthbertson, one of the finest climbers Scotland has ever produced.

Throughout this climbing period Gina was incredibly supportive and encouraging, but had no desire to climb mountains herself. I had taken her to the Luss hills by Loch Lomond before we were married and stomped off uphill leaving her in my wake. I was probably showing off, but when I turned around she was sitting on the grass. I went back down to her and she looked up at me, burst into tears and said, 'I'm sorry, I hate this!' She probably didn't appreciate the pair of climbing boots I bought her for a wedding present.

She may not have enjoyed climbing herself but Gina quickly recognised the mental and physical release the hills offered me, a release from the frustrations of jobs I didn't like and from the continual worries about providing for a young family. It was some years before she eventually joined me on the hills, and I'm proud of what she achieved in a relatively short time. Together we have enjoyed some big multi-week walks in the Alps and North America, long treks in the Himalaya, Morocco, Jordan and Guatemala and regular outings in the Scottish hills, a way of life that has helped cement our marriage over a long number of years.

From an early age I'd had drummed into me, by my parents, the importance of having a good career with a good pension at the end of it, my own home, and the importance of not spending beyond my means. It was all sensible advice but increasingly the idea of a long career and the entrapment of a nine-to-five, five days a week routine depressed me. Gina and I had bought a nice mid-terrace house in Barrhead in Renfrewshire and moved in immediately after we had married. It was in the Crosstobs area, just below the Gleniffer Braes, but we wanted to be more 'in the country' so a couple of years later, after Gordon came along, we bought a slightly bigger house in Neilston, at that time a small dormitory village with a history that went back to the twelfth century. During the Industrial Revolution textile processing was introduced to the village and by the beginning of the twentieth century there were about four hundred mill-workers' houses.

It was undoubtedly a pleasant place to live, with lochs to swim in during the summer and the crags of Neilston Quarry to climb on but we were finding things tough financially, as was much of the country. The governing Conservative and Unionist Party had instituted a three-day working week to conserve electricity; the shortages blamed on a succession of miners' strikes. The UK economy was being affected by record rates of inflation, up to 17 per cent, and the government was recommending pay caps for the private as well as the public sector. Continual industrial action was eventually to bring down Ted Heath's government and, despite assurances of a New Jerusalem from Harold Wilson, the incoming prime minister, the immediate future looked bleak.

At that time Gina occasionally flicked through the pages of her hometown newspaper, the *Stirling Observer*, and an advert caught her eye. The Scottish Youth Hostels Association was looking for a married couple to warden their Trossachs Youth Hostel. Suitable applicants were invited to apply. We decided to try for it. I had been a member of the SYHA for some years and had used the network of hostels on various weekend sorties. I had even spent a couple of night at the Trossachs hostel some years before and vaguely remembered it as an old rambling building set in its own grounds near

Brig o'Turk. Could this be what we were looking for? Could this be my portal into the professional world of the great outdoors? We decided to cast our fate to the wind and go for it.

In 1931, a party of Scottish Youth Hostel Association officials crossed the remote Minch Moor between Traquair and Yarrow in the Borders. They were heading to Broadmeadows to officially open Scotland's first youth hostel. The principal aim of this new charity was to enable everyone, but particularly young people, to know, use and appreciate the Scottish countryside and places of historic and cultural interest. Within seven years the SYHA was able to boast 70 hostels and a membership of 20,000 and the charity was well on its way to achieving its aim of providing cheap accommodation throughout Scotland for young people and those of limited means.

The international youth hostel movement was conceived in 1912, in Altena Castle in Germany, where a schoolteacher named Richard Schirrmann created the first permanent *Jugendherberge*. These early hostels were inspired by the vision of the German Youth Movement to give city youngsters an opportunity to breathe the fresh air of the countryside. The youths were supposed to manage the hostel themselves as much as possible, doing 'hostel duties' to keep costs down and build character. The growth of this new international youth organisation didn't please everyone. A report in the *Glasgow Herald* in June 1938 quoted cynics who decried the hostels movement, 'A waste of money and effort alike. In pandering to a craze (to die in a year or two) among irresponsible youth for dressing-up in ridiculous garb at the week-ends and disturbing the peace of the countryside in 'hiking' – odious word – or cycling 'gangs'. However, the craze didn't die off. In his wonderful book, *Always a Little Further*, first published in 1939, author and climber Alastair Borthwick reflected that eight years previously, 'fresh air was still the property of moneyed men, a luxury open to few.'

The thirties saw huge changes. The years of the Depression encouraged many to leave the squalor of the cities and take to the road, searching out adventure and new experiences in the Highlands.

One man who was caught up in this new spate of exploration was the climber, naturalist, author and television presenter, Tom

Weir, from Springburn in the north of Glasgow. Tom suggested that, although Glasgow was a poor place in the thirties, it was rich in green places, but so many of those semi-rural areas were soon to be swallowed up by the vast housing schemes of the forties and fifties. 'In those days,' he recalled, 'there was plenty to explore on your own doorstep, and when motor cars were scarce, cycling was a pleasure.'

Many of those working-class outdoor pioneers would congregate around the now legendary Craigallian fire, near Milngavie, in a secluded pine-fringed hollow near Craigallian Loch. Here, most Friday and Saturday nights would see a gathering of like-minded souls, swapping yarns, making plans, re-telling adventures, a fellowship of outdoor enthusiasts, socialists, adventurers, working-class lads and lassies. While the more affluent climbers of the day travelled north to Glen Coe and Ben Nevis by motor car, giving the Scottish Mountaineering Club the nickname of the SMT, or the Scottish Mountaineering Transport, this new, working-class group travelled less widely and, when they did go beyond their immediate vicinity, their favoured modes of travel were Shank's Pony and hitch-hiking.

In 2012 a new memorial stone was erected to mark the exact location of the Craigallian Fire but before that a large stone block exhibited an explanatory sign:

'Here Burned The Craigallian Fire. The Eternal Fire was a beacon which attracted those industrial working-class Wanderers who wanted to escape from the stone jungle of Glasgow into the countryside during the Depression of the 1930s – and during which, it was said, the Fire never went out. From here, the Highland of Freedom and all Scotland beckoned them: the Fire was the cradle for all the other fires which warmed Wanderers in howffs, dosses, bothies and caves as they explored further north.

'Some remained in the hills or at the Fire most of the week and only returned to the city to claim their dole money from 'the buroo'. Within its glow, philosophy, socialism and hill-lore were discussed at length and the fire-flickered woods echoed to songs which were sung well into the night. The Ptarmigan, Lomond and Creagh Dhu Climbing Clubs were all born here and many who sat round the fire fought in the Spanish Civil War (1936–39). Several Wanderers who used the Fire would be notably instrumental in fighting for the freedom of all people to enjoy the Scottish countryside through the development of such things as our Rights of Way and National Parks.

'Long may old Craigallian woods
Send forth abundance of their goods;
May the fire be always lit
So that we may come and sit.'

By the end of the thirties things had changed. The growing popularity of 'hiking' had an incredible effect. A chain of youth hostels grew across the Highlands and lightweight tents became available. Many of those hillwalkers and climbers who didn't like the simple rules of the youth hostel movement developed their own chain of caves, howffs and barns, generically known as 'dosses' and, in some quarters, the hills were regarded as being unpleasantly overcrowded. Environmental problems, too often associated with modern times, were experienced too. The Craigallian Fire was banned because of litter, possibly one of the first negative effects of the hiking boom, and mirrored in recent times by the ban on wild camping on lochsides in the Loch Lomond and Trossachs National Park. Some said the hills were being loved to death and Alastair Borthwick, amongst others, voiced the concern that 'cheapness and popularity have their dangers, particularly for those who climb. The sport is growing too quickly.'

I had always been impressed by the idealism of the youth hostel movement and particularly the notion of inexpensive, simple accommodation in remote areas. Not so many of these remote hostels exist today but Loch Ossian (where I was thrilled to officially open the refurbished 'green' hostel in 2003) and Glen Affric are still there as a reminder of the early ethos of SYHA. Gina and I had swotted up on that SYHA ethos. In response to our application to become wardens of the Trossachs Youth Hostel we were asked to attend the SYHA offices in Glebe Crescent, Stirling, for an interview. We were ready to give a good account of ourselves but were a little concerned that having a 1-year-old child might go against us.

The Hostels Manager, an amiable and mild-mannered man called Jim Martin, met us at the Stirling office. He ushered us into a dark wood-panelled room where a table had been placed directly in the middle of the floor. On one side were two chairs, presumably for us, and on the other side sat three elderly gentlemen, one of them puffing on a pipe. My first thought was that it was unlikely that any of them had ever spent a night in a hostel, or strode up a mountainside. Jim Martin introduced us before taking his own seat at the back of the room. The interview panel was made up of members of the local Stirling Area Committee who asked us all the expected questions. Confident in our answers we began to relax. I felt it was going very well indeed and quietly chastised myself for my earlier, uncharitable, thoughts. One of the gents even expressed his delight that we had a young child, 'He will give the hostel a nice family feel,' he said.

We had moved on from formal questioning to general small talk when one of the men looked as though he had just remembered something. 'Oh, before you go,' he said, 'what religion are you?' We were taken aback but, encouraged by the way things had gone so far, I answered immediately. 'I'm Church of Scotland,' I said, 'and my wife is Roman Catholic.' There was a palpable silence. The man sat back in his chair, glanced briefly at his two compatriots before glaring at Gina. 'You know you won't be able to go to the chapel?' he said. 'You'll be far too busy on a Sunday morning.'

Gina tried to explain that she wasn't a practising Catholic and neither of us were actually church-goers but the tenor, the feel, of the interview had dramatically changed. The three men began gathering up their notes as though to signal the end of the interview. The pipe smoker dismissed us with the words, 'Thank you, we'll be in touch.' It felt like the kiss of death.

Jim Martin ushered us from the room and firmly closed the door behind him. 'I can't apologise enough,' he said, looking very embarrassed and uncomfortable. 'That was completely unacceptable, but I heard enough in there to convince me you are both the kind of folk we'd like to have running one of our hostels. Let me make you a proposition. I think it's fair to say you won't get the Trossachs job and I know you want to run a countryside hostel but we need wardens for our Aberdeen Youth Hostel. You'll need to go through another interview with a different Area Committee but I can guarantee it'll be a very different experience to the one you've just gone though. If you accept that position then as soon as a hostel that you fancy becomes vacant you can have first refusal. How about it?'

We were still a little shell-shocked from the interview but told Jim we'd think about it. Neither of us had even been to Aberdeen before and moving to a city certainly didn't fit our plans of being close to the hills. As soon as we could, we drove north to have a look at the place and although the hostel, a huge Victorian mansion, was in Queen's Cross, a very pleasant and quiet residential area on the west side of the Granite City, the wardens' accommodation couldn't have been worse. The living room and kitchen were on the ground floor, immediately behind the warden's office, but the two bedrooms and bathroom were on the fourth floor. To get to bed at night we had to climb the stairs through the entire building.

Gina wasn't keen. Neither was she particularly enthusiastic about the idea of cooking meals for 128 people. Aberdeen Youth Hostel was a 'catering for groups' hostel. While most hostellers cooked their own food in the hostel kitchen we would have to prepare and serve meals for any large groups that booked in, like school groups. Poor Gina, who had never cooked a meal for more than two or three people, was mortified at the thought.

I mentioned earlier that I'm considerably more prone to risk-taking than Gina, and after a lot of discussion she reluctantly agreed to give it a try. We would put our Neilston house on the market and bank any profit, saving it for a rainy day. If we were working for SYHA we would have our accommodation supplied so we wouldn't need a mortgage, and we wouldn't have to pay for heating or lighting. When we were catering we'd get our meals on the house. The wage wasn't great and when I say wage in the singular that's what it was. Although the contract was for a married couple only the husband got paid. There was no such thing as equal rights in those days.

Philip Lawson, a head teacher from Edinburgh, who was also chair of the SYHA East Area Committee, interviewed us for the Aberdeen post. He was friendly and approachable and, I suspect, well primed by Jim Martin. The interview was a positive and friendly affair and, after thirty or so minutes, Philip formally offered us the job. We accepted, and our life was about to be completely turned around.

4

ABERDEEN ANGUS YEARS

We moved to Aberdeen in the January of 1975, at a time when the city was undergoing dramatic change. The economic boom triggered by a massive oil find in the North Sea had transformed the place and the city was quick to adapt to the benefits and challenges of being the oil capital of Europe.

Thousands of Americans descended on the area to show us how to drill for the black gold, sparking a huge demand for housing, hotels, construction sites, shipping and labour. Hundreds of jobs were created as oil production grew faster than in any other major petroleum province in the world and Aberdeen Youth Hostel, being in the lower bracket of cheap accommodation, became the target for every roughneck and roustabout on the lookout for well-paid offshore jobs.

According to the youth hostel rules you weren't strictly allowed to use hostels as a means of cheap accommodation while you were working, but I soon reached mutually acceptable agreements with a few regular roustabouting hostellers from overseas, mostly Australians and Kiwis.

Much of the offshore work was on a two-week-on, two-week-off basis, so when the lads came back I allowed them to stay for a couple of nights before they went travelling around Scotland for the rest of their onshore period. I also allowed them to stay for a night or two before they went back offshore. This arrangement had several advantages. We got to know the regulars fairly well and there were always some of them around when we had problems with unruly hostellers.

Aberdeen was gaining a reputation for being a 'good-time' city and Union Street, the city's main thoroughfare, was thought by many to be paved with gold. There was plenty of money on the go and most of the oil rig workers were earning big bucks and freely splashing it around. The thought of all that dosh inevitably attracted some less salubrious types to the city: neds, drug pushers and prostitutes, and these people wanted cheap accommodation too. If, for any reason, I experienced grief for refusing someone a bed for the night I would invariably find a couple of the regular roustabouts standing immediately behind me ready to pile in if things got rough. They tended to be big, brawny guys, the type you wouldn't want to argue with. Having them around also made me feel more confortable about leaving Gina and Gordon behind if I nipped off to the hills for a couple of days. Many of them became firm friends who were always keen to lend a hand in the hostel, doing a bit of painting here, a spot of joinery work there, in return for a few free bed nights. Despite her earlier concerns about cooking for groups, Gina handled it all magnificently and we soon worked out menus and systems for providing good sustaining meals without tying ourselves in knots in the kitchen.

As it happened we didn't have too many groups wanting meals and life took on a new rhythm and routine: opening the hostel at 7a.m. and closing between 11a.m. and 2p.m., and shutting down for the night at 11p.m. Because Aberdeen was a big and busy hostel, we were able to employ an assistant warden on a full-time basis so Gina, young Gordon and I could escape every so often for a weekend away. Working hours were long though and, despite the fact that hostellers had to do a 'hostel duty' before they left for the day, there was always a lot of cleaning and maintenance work to get on with. It was rare to find time to relax during the three hours the hostel was closed. Occasionally we grabbed a couple of days off and went off with a tent somewhere. This was an unknown part of Scotland to us and we always enjoyed a real sense of exploration and anticipation on these little family forays. We were peeping over new horizons all the time, and we loved it.

On one occasion we drove to Braemar and Gordon, aged two and a bit, walked most of the three miles between Linn of Dee and Derry Lodge, where we camped for the night. It was our first experience of family camping, the first of many we would enjoy over the years with Gordon, and then Gregor, who was born in Aberdeen a year later. The Derry Lodge outing was a short, but memorable trip, made after I bought a cheap tent with enough space for all of us. We had added two dogs to our small family: Jasper, a labrador and Flora, a golden retriever. It wasn't unusual to see the McNeish clan wandering along a track to the hills, Gina pushing Gregor in an old pram, the wee soul firmly wedged between a couple of rucksacks, and me more often than not with Gordon sitting comfortably on top of the pack that I was carrying. We must have looked like a bunch of tinkers. We also spent a lot of time on the beaches of Balvenie and Menie Estate, just north of Aberdeen, a magnificent area of natural beach and sand dunes that were later to be destroyed by the multi-millionaire businessman and future president, Donald Trump, for a luxury golf course.

These family away-days and weekend trips to the hills of the eastern Highlands were totally exhilarating and memorable and, as often as the hostel demands would allow, and with Gina's blessing, I would head off on my own to climb the hills of Deeside, the Cairngorms and the Angus Glens. During my time as a member of the Lomond Mountaineering Club I considered myself to be a climber and the lads in the club tended to refer to anyone who walked in the hills as 'padders' or even 'dirty Munro-baggers'. There was a strong sense amongst climbers in those days that walkers were lesser beings and you really only went hillwalking when the weather was too violent for climbing. In Aberdeen I didn't have anyone to climb with and the unsocial hours I worked would have made it very difficult to go out and climb with a club, although I did become a member of the Aberdeen Mountaineering Club for a time. So, I had to swallow my pride and become a padder. Becoming a dirty Munro-bagger would have pushed my credibility too far.

The secretary of the Aberdeen Mountaineering Club at the time was a nice guy called Erland Flett and he invited me along to one of the club outings to the Crianlarich area. The Club had booked a private hostel and we took it over for the weekend. On arrival on the Friday night I settled into a cosy bunk with my labrador,

Jasper, curled at my feet. Saturday dawned cloudy and gloomy and we decided to climb Ben Challum, just north of the village. It was a day of peering at maps and compass directions and we plodded up the hill from the ruins of St Fillan's Priory, just beside the Kirkton farmhouse. Faolan, or little wolf, was apparently the son of Kentigerna, a princess from Ulster, and for centuries after his death it was believed the bones of his left arm held miraculous properties. Indeed, according to the writings of Seton Gordon, the silver reliquary that contained St Fillan's bones was presented by the Abbot of Inchaffray to the kneeling Scottish army on the morning of the Battle of Bannockburn.

There wasn't a lot left to see of the Priory, and my companions appeared to be completely disinterested in such historical things. They were more intent on 'bagging' the Munro so no sooner had we put on our boots than we were off, up past a couple of ancient graveyards, across the railway line on a long serpentine route, wriggling our way over bracken-covered hillocks towards the rocky outcrops of Creag Loisgte. From there, old fenceposts marched uphill offering a secure navigational aid to what we thought was the summit cairn. We reached the cairn but it was so cold and windy we immediately retraced our steps back down. Several years later I realised that we hadn't reached the summit at all. Ben Challum has two tops, and we had only climbed the lower one. This south top can be confusing in the mist for you have to descend slightly west to gain a short, rocky ridge which, in turn, descends to a high bealach. From there it's an easy climb to the real summit from where, as one of the highest hills in the old hunting forest of Mamlorn, the views can be spectacular, with Ben More and Stob Binnein dominant in the south and the Bridge of Orchy hills close by to the north.

That was my one and only outing with the Aberdeen Mountaineering Club. Despite everyone being friendly and encouraging I decided that club outings weren't really my cup of tea. I discovered that I like to do things my own way and since that day I've climbed hills more or less on my own or with one or two good pals or, in later years, with Gina.

One of the great benefits of living in Aberdeen was the

comparatively easy access I had to the big hills of the Cairngorms and the Angus Glens. These East Highland landscapes were new to me. Virtually all my climbing and hillwalking had been on the hills of the Trossachs and the west Central Highlands. I had heard much about the Cairngorms and read a lot about these big, rounded Arctic hills but I was completely unprepared for their size, spaciousness and remoteness.

Adam Watson's guide to the Cairngorms became a very well-thumbed guidebook, and I loved VA Firsoff's excellent *Cairngorms – on Foot and Ski*. Thanks to these books I almost convinced myself that I was already on intimate terms with this vast mountain range. In reality, my very first experience of the Cairngorms was cloaked in fear and apprehension, the first time I had felt such emotions on a mountain, a sensation that was new and unwelcome. I had served my hill apprenticeship on the peaks of the west, moving from the low hills of the Campsie Fells to the Lomond and Trossachs hills, before tackling the steeper flanks and crags of the Glen Coe peaks. It was a logical progression, taking on harder expeditions as my experience and knowledge grew. I learned the rudiments of navigation and ropework on these hills, but the summits were rarely more than two or three miles from a road. I had no experience of remoteness or isolation, no real awareness that if I sprained an ankle or pulled a muscle it might involve a night in the open. In the years to come the Cairngorms were to teach me much about self-reliance.

Within a few months of arriving in Aberdeen I packed a rucksack with overnight camping gear, drove to Linn of Dee near Braemar, and tackled the hills of the Cairngorms for the very first time, trekking up Glen Lui to Derry Lodge before climbing the long Sron Riach ridge of Ben Macdui, which, at 4,300 feet, is the second highest mountain in the land. My plan was to cross the high plateau to Cairn Gorm but no sooner had I passed the old Curran Bothy, crouched close to Lochan Buidhe (it was demolished in 1975) than I became aware of the sheer enormity, the massive scale of this landscape. Cloud was coming and going in regular drifts and each time the landscape around me was newly revealed it seemed bigger and wider than the time before. Never before had I seen such massive, domed skies;

never before had I felt as insignificant as I did that day and never before had I felt so incapable of dealing with it. I was tired after my long walk-in and my confidence oozed away like the stream running out of Lochan Buidhe. I became convinced I couldn't reach Cairn Gorm that day. Instead, I turned tail and scurried down beside the March burn to the comparative haven of the Lairig Ghru.

I've often pondered those negative feelings that I have never experienced before or since. I knew little, if anything, of the legend of Am Fearlas Mor, the Grey Man of Ben Macdui, an apparition that had apparently struck fear and alarm in the likes of such experienced individuals as mountaineer Professor Norman Collie and the Scots patriot Wendy Wood. I was aware that in 1971 five Edinburgh schoolchildren and their teacher had perished close to the spot where I turned tail. Was there something lingering on the bare shores of Lochan Buidhe, some spirit of place that had filtered into my psyche, dimming the sense of exploration and discovery that had accompanied me all the way to Macdui's summit and beyond? Or were the mountains and their reputation too much, just too demanding, for this tyro Cairngorm hiker? I suspect it was the latter because that initial fear and alarm was quickly and effectively submerged by a deep and passionate love affair with the Cairngorms that has lasted almost as long as my marriage. At the time of writing I'm celebrating the forty-second anniversary of my introduction to what I now like to refer to as my 'hills of home'.

The night of that first memorable day was spent in a tiny pup tent on a tundra-like swathe just below the summit of Devil's Point or, more correctly, Bod an Deamhain (try saying 'pot-in-john'). I woke in the morning in a high and magnificent landscape that was flooded with early morning sunlight. Incredibly, about fifty metres away from my camp, stood three rather threadbare and quite ugly reindeer. At that early stage in my outdoors career I was barely on nodding terms with red deer, never mind reindeer, and the sight of them was both exotic and bewildering. It was only later that I learned that Mr Utsi from Lapland and his colleague Dr Lindgren were trying to reintroduce the species into the Arctic-type landscape of the Cairngorms from their base in Glenmore. The rest of that day passed like a dream. I climbed Cairn Toul before returning to the head of Coire Odhar where I followed the footpath back towards the little Corrour bothy that lay below the steep black slopes of Bod an Deamhain. Another track followed the River Dee all the way back to Linn of Dee.

It was some years before I climbed Cairn Toul again, but this time from the comforting perspective of experience and familiarity. Some of our finest hills lie well beyond the convenience of roads or tracks and require considerable effort to reach their foot, never mind their summit. Cairn Toul is a good example. Rising in the middle of the Lairig Ghru, a geological slash that cuts through the heart of the central Cairngorms, its ascent requires a long walk-in from any direction, but, as with most isolated hills, the extra effort is worth it for that special dimension of inaccessibility.

Cairn Toul, the 'hill of the barn', is certainly one of the more shapely and elegant Cairngorms, despite its name. With its double-topped summit ridge thrown up by the apex of three well-sculpted corries, its ascent is usually tacked on to the high-level traverse of Braeriach and Sgor an Lochain Uaine from the north, or from Coire Odhar in the south. I refuse to call Sgor an Lochain Uaine Angel's Peak as the Ordnance Survey suggests. Try *skoor an lochan oo-anya,* which means peak of the green lochan and has nothing whatsoever to do with angels.

There is a story that suggests Queen Victoria was out walking with her ghillie John Brown and, when she saw the black, glistening crags of Bod an Deamhain in the Lairig Ghru, asked him the name of the hill. He told her and she then asked him to translate from the Gaelic into English. This apparently embarrassed the loyal servant as he wasn't too keen on telling the queen the name translated as the penis of the devil. 'It means, err, devil's point Ma'am,' and the name has stuck. Some years later some interfering hillwalking cleric decided that if there had to be a mountain name relating to the devil then he would create a celestial balance by renaming nearby Sgor an Lochain Uaine as Angel's Peak.

On the morning of that first wonderful camp below Devil's Point I had been greeted by a joyous outpouring of song from a little bird that I couldn't identify. Some years later I learned it had been the spring song of the cock snow bunting, as wonderful a sound as you'll hear anywhere. After the passage of still more years, my son Gregor and I made our way into Coire an t-Sneachda, the snowy corrie where three large pools reflected the cyclopean masonry of the headwall. From the largest of the pools, a slanting pathway climbs the rocky slopes to a notch in the headwall. This is the Goat Track and it's a rough, steep, loose, scree-girt trail, with some very mild scrambling thrown in for good measure. Near the top of the headwall our little Arctic visitor again made himself known. A comparatively rare breeder in Scotland, the snow bunting is a true lover of the high and lonely places, a black and white fleck of beauty against the wind-scoured landscape. Rising from the screes the bird rapidly beats his white wings until, twenty feet or so above the ground, fluttering his outstretched wings like a skylark, he glides earthwards with an explosive and intense song. The music continues as he lands, wings upstretched, and as he closes his wings the outpouring of song becomes a cry, a moving and powerful anthem for his Arctic surroundings.

The triumphant chord the snow bunting strikes is both moving and encouraging and has the capacity to refocus the jaded eye. I've no idea how many times I've climbed through Coire an t-Sneachda and made my way across the plateau towards Ben Macdui. I've now lost count how often I've wandered in a desultory way over these high and lonely mountain tops, but something as naturally simple as the song of a snow bunting can re-stimulate a sense of wonder and awe at this, the highest tableland in the British Isles.

Gregor was keen to make the most of a visit home from university to photograph some of the classic views of the Cairngorms, so we tracked across the upper slopes of Coire Domhain to cross the chortling Feith Buidhe burn before it crashed down over the red granite slabs that form the headwalls of Glen Avon. Photographed at a low angle, through the crashing waters, the view of Loch Avon in its mountain setting is, for me, one of the finest scenes in Scotland. Further round the headwall we dropped down into the bergschrund between the remains of the winter snowpack and the granite walls of the upper corrie. It was fun tracing a route along the line of the berg-schrund, a wonderful form of ice caving where the deep, glistening blues of the ice contrast with the gnarly rough red of the granite slabs – a photographer's delight. A long but easy climb took us to Ben Macdui's north summit where it was only a few minutes to the elevated trig point of Britain's second highest mountain. I love this place: its spaciousness, its vast, open skies, how it drops abruptly into the deep chasm of the Lairig Ghru, its views that can be as wide-spread as Morven in Caithness to the Lammermuirs in Lothian.

We made our return by Creag an Leth-choin, to photograph the deep cleft of the Lairig Ghru, and wonder at the miscroscopic beauty of moss campion and dwarf cudweed, the wee brother of the edelweiss. In that wonder was an instinctive recognition of the determined pattern behind the behaviour of things, a celebration of order and harmony. For those few hours we felt part of it and, in many ways, I guess that's the fundamental issue in my personal relationship with these marvellous hills. It's a sense of belonging, mixed with a more tangible sense of familiarity and appreciation. In some years I may only tramp these high hills three or four times, in others three or four times a month, yet I never feel like a stranger. It's a comforting thought . . .

During the quieter parts of the year the hours of duty in the hostel occasionally felt long and boring. We developed the hostel's garden and grew our own vegetables and I spent a lot of time reading about the hills. Sometimes people left magazines in the hostel lounge and, flicking through a couple of these one day, I read a couple of articles about what appeared to be a new kind of outdoor activity. I quickly realised it wasn't new at all, but by borrowing an American term the outdoor industry had cleverly developed a fine marketing ploy.

Backpacking: putting camping gear into a pack, hoisting it on your back and heading off to some wild land, or a long-distance trail for a few days or a few weeks. Although I wasn't aware of the term at the time I guess my very first backpacking trip was that Duke of Edinburgh Award Bronze Medal expedition across the Campsie Fells from Blanefield to Fintry. Two outdoor writers in particular caught my attention: Peter Lumley who was editor of *Practical*

Camper magazine and was a founder member of the nationwide Backpackers Club and Robin Adshead who was the lightweight camping columnist in the rival *Camping* magazine. Both writers were based in the south of England and wrote about backpacking mainly in the Home Counties, the West Country, the Peak District and occasionally in North Wales, but there was something in their descriptions of Backpackers Club outings that caught my imagination, something that prompted me to fill in the application form, pay my two or three quid subscription fee and join the Club.

There was something primal about the notion of carrying everything you required for survival in a pack on your back, stopping for the night in some beautiful location, preparing a meal and settling down as day eased itself into night. It was like stripping life down to the essentials: a minimal amount of possessions, a desire to wander at will through inspiring, wild landscapes and a basic shelter for the night. The simplicity of it all, its minimalism, really caught my imagination.

The Backpackers Club had organised a gathering at a big outdoors show just outside Birmingham. I drove down and met Peter Lumley there. We spent much of the weekend chatting about the hills, new outdoor equipment and writing. Recording my outdoor experiences on paper was something new to me. Peter suggested that I keep notes from my various walking and climbing trips and think about an article he might publish in his magazine. It was a Road to Damascus moment. The idea of writing about the hills, just like Tom Weir or the great WH Murray, had never really entered my mind and suddenly, as though a veil had been lifted from my eyes, I could clearly see my future path.

I found an old typewriter in the Aberdeen Youth Hostel basement and bought new ribbons for it, a wad of typing paper, and began to teach myself to type. Unlike Tom Weir, who learned to touch-type from his sister Molly, at the cost of two and sixpence a lesson, I had no one to teach me but managed reasonably well, although to this day I still only type with the forefinger of each hand. It was enough. I managed to tap out an article about camping on Aberdeenshire's Bennachie and sent it to Peter at *Practical Camper* magazine.

You can imagine my delight when he replied and told me he liked the feature, and could I write some more pieces. I was over the moon and from then every spare moment would find me in our youth hostel basement, tip-tapping away at my old sit-up-and-beg typewriter. Almost everything I wrote was about my new-found love of backpacking. Shortly after I joined the Backpackers Club I got notice from the club's national organiser Eric Gurney that the annual Scottish Club week would be a long walk from Blair Atholl to Aviemore. I also knew, from his comments in his monthly column in *Camping* magazine, that Robin Adshead would be in attendance.

Robin was a retired Army officer, a captain in the Regiment of Gurkhas. He was also a qualified light aircraft and helicopter pilot and an excellent photographer. He had spent a lot of time in the Himalaya and on his retirement from the army at the age of 38 he had offered to manage one of a new chain of outdoor shops owned by a charismatic American by the name of Bill Wilkins. Bill already owned a manufacturing company called Ultimate Equipment and his team had designed some superb lightweight tents. He had fully bought into this new concept of lightweight backpacking and his new chain of shops was appropriately called Backpacker Systems.

I really only knew of Robin Adshead through his column in *Camping* magazine and an excellent book he had co-authored called *Backpacking in Britain*. His writings were styled on another backpacking writer whose work I was to become very familiar with in years to come, an Anglo-American by the name of Colin Fletcher, but for the moment my backpacking literary inspirations came from Peter Lumley and Robin Adshead. I knew Robin intended walking north through Glen Tilt after leaving the train at Blair Atholl so I drove to Linn of Dee, just beyond Braemar, walked to White Bridge near Glen Geldie and started walking south to where I hoped to meet up with him. It was then that I realised what made the Backpackers Club so different from the other hillwalking and mountaineering clubs I had experienced. It's a club that likes to be known as a 'club for mavericks' or a 'club of unclubbables', for no one walks in big groups. Members, even on club meets, are encouraged to break up into very small groups to minimise impact on the landscape.

As I made my way down Glen Tilt I met some pairs of walkers and one or two individuals who told me that Robin Adshead was somewhere just behind. Eventually I wandered round a bend and there, on a flat riverbank, was a small Ultimate Equipment tent with a thickset, dark haired individual sitting outside putting on a brew. I called out, 'Hello, are you Robin Adshead?' He looked up, waved me over and said, 'Hi, you must be Hamish.'

Robin was very posh. Educated at Eton and Sandhurst, his experience with the Gurkhas of Nepal had rubbed away the more-excessive elements of his privileged upbringing. Now that he had left the army he just wanted to spend as much time in the great outdoors as possible. Considering our polar-opposite backgrounds, me from Red Clydeside Govan and Robin from the heart of Tory Cotswolds, we got on like a house on fire and became firm friends until his death in November 2005 at the age of 71. Robin often reminded me that the most important thing he learned in the services was diplomacy, which he defined as, 'the art of telling someone to fuck off in such a way that they actually look forward to the journey'.

Our evening together beside the infant River Tilt was the genesis of that long friendship, one that resulted in many happy backpacking trips with Robin over the years, at home and abroad. On one occasion we were bivvying high on the Brevent above Chamonix. It was snowing and very, very cold. We had cooked a meal and eaten it and I asked him to open the bottle of wine we had carried up the hill with us. He looked at me aghast and exclaimed, 'My dear chap, one couldn't possibly drink red wine in these temperatures.' We did without.

Our last backpacking trip together was in the Cairngorms when Robin and his son Corrin came to stay in Aviemore. We set out for the high tops but the weather was dreadful. The three of us shared a tent, to save weight, but three adult men sharing a tent for several nights has its downfalls. After a couple of nights it seemed that we couldn't pick up any item of clothing or equipment without finding body hair attached to it. It became known as the Camp of the Pubes.

Once we descended, Robin and Corrin had a meal with us before the long drive back to the south of England. Several hours later the telephone rang. It was Robin.

'Just to let you know,' he said in his crisp Etonian tone, 'Corrin and I stopped at a motorway services in the Borders and Corrin saw a book of yours in the shop. He took it from the shelf, opened it up and what do you think he discovered between the pages? A bloody pubic hair.'

As a young man passionately in love with hills and mountains there were a number of place names that thrummed my heartstrings. Torridon, Glen Coe, Kintail, Affric and the Cairngorms gripped my imagination with thoughts of jagged peaks, tight ridges and wide, open skies, but lurking in the recesses of my emotions was an area that owed its appeal as much to its cultural identity as the quality of its hills. This area was close enough to Aberdeen for me to become reasonably well acquainted with it.

Few of my gnarly climbing companions from the Lomond Mountaineering Club had ever mentioned the Angus Glens. Their route to the hill was invariably north by west and it wasn't until I moved to Aberdeen that I began to appreciate the link between two interests that I was becoming passionate about: hills and folk music. I had become a folkie after attending a series of concerts by the Corries, the wonderful duo of Ronnie Browne and Roy Williamson. I learned a few simple chords on the guitar, had a penny whistle and an Aran sweater, and turned my back on the pop music and glam rock of the seventies. The link between traditional music and the hills was a series of glens that lay north of the fertile vale of Strathmore: Glen Doll and Glen Clova, Glen Prosen and Glen Isla and lovely Glen Esk and it didn't take me long to realise that the Angus Glens, were culturally very different from the hills of the west. Gaelic place names were far fewer here and there was more of a lived-in feel to the area, the land of 40-verse bothy ballads.

It was while exploring these glens that I came to know Danny Smith, the warden of the Glen Doll Youth Hostel and his wife Nancy. Nancy was a keen hill-goer and folk music enthusiast and she introduced me to Davie Glen, an inveterate hill gangrel, musician and Scottish 'diddling' champion. This is the mouth-music familiar to most folkies, the familiar 'tiddly di, tiddly dum, tiddly doo', and Davie Glen turned it into an art form. He was also an extraordinary story teller who regaled me with his tales in dark bothies and howffs in various parts of the eastern Grampians. Nancy and her daughter later moved west to Fersit, near Tulloch, where she ran a walker's hostel and they were regular visitors to the Badenoch Folk Club which I later helped run in Newtonmore, but I'll always associate Nancy with the music and the hills of the Angus Glens.

Very different from the hills of the west, there's something about the spaciousness and the rolling heights of the eastern Grampians that I find deeply satisfying, especially when those high plateaux plunge dramatically into high-glaciated corries. A series of well-defined corries above Glen Clova are a good example. As you approach Clova from Kirriemuir, the hills of the Mounth, the vast plateau that runs south and east of Lochnagar, suddenly appear on the horizon, big frowning hills that drop steeply into Glen Clova. A trio of massive corries catches your attention. A tour of these corries, with the bonus of an ascent of Ben Tirran, a Corbett, makes a good day out.

It was Davie Glen who introduced me to another Angus glen, Glen Isla. North of Kirkton of Glenisla, the broad, open glen is protected by high hills on either side – Mount Blair, Duchray Hill, Craigenloch Hill and Monamenach, the highest at 2,648 feet on the western side and the sprawling Badandun Hill, the curiously named Bawhelps and Finalty Hill to the east. To the north, beyond Glen Brighty, Glen Isla becomes hemmed in by the steep-sided slopes of the Mounth hills at Caenlochan, a National Nature Reserve so designated because of its lime-rich rocks and plethora of rare Arctic–Alpine plants.

To this day I can recall what seemed like a great barrier of mountains to the north of Monamenach. The grey screes of Creag Leacach, the enormous snow-covered mound of Glas Maol and the steep icy cliffs of Caenlochan, the southern ramparts of that vast raised plateau that lies south of Lochnagar, all looked impenetrable. Monamenach itself was fairly forgettable – the views to the north much less so. Davie and I climbed the hill from the road end at Auchavan; a young, slim and athletic hill-goer and Davie, a manky-looking bearded old gangrel. We must have appeared as a really odd couple. There was a heavy haze that softened the views of the high hills and made them shimmer in the early light. Mountain hares, vivid white against the snowless terrain, infested the high slopes, and skylarks filled the air with bubbling music. We elected to add rocky Craigenloch Hill to our day's walk, sunbathed and had an early lunch on the slopes of Loch Beanie before reluctantly heading back down the footpath in Glen Beanie. All the way down this lovely little glen I had been aware of a curious droning sound in the air and, as we made our way up the single-track road in Glen Isla, I heard it again. At first I thought it was from the electric lines that were slung above the road but it wasn't, it was the croaking of hundreds of warty toads that infested the pools and ditches at the side of the road. One pool in particular had become a great writhing mass of spawning toads, a mad and passionate frenzy of spring.

Glen Doll can be the starting point for some great high-level sorties into the eastern Cairngorms, including the Mounth roads that run from Glen Clova to Ballater (the Capel Mounth) and from Glen Doll to Braemar (the Tolmount) as well as the two Munros of Mayar and Driesh. On one wet and wild day I took the path that climbs up the length of Glen Doll north of the White Water, a footpath that has become known as Jock's Road although, traditionally, the route is called the Tolmount. Jock's Road, named after a climber by the name of John Winters, is the steep section that climbs out of Glen Doll opposite the dark crags of Craig Maud. By the time I reached this steeper ground the rain had become sleety and the wind was blowing a gale. Best thing to do under the circumstances was to find shelter, I thought, get the flask out and consider the desperate events that occurred here just over half a century ago. It was New Year's Day in 1959 when five hillwalkers set off from Braemar Youth Hostel intent on walking up Glen Callater and over the Tolmount to Glen Doll. All the men were committee members of the Universal Hiking Club in Glasgow, an active Roman Catholic club with about 80 members. After attending Mass, the men left Braemar just after eleven and not long after midday they were spotted by Charles Smith, a local shepherd, near his house at Auchallater in Glen Callater. According to Smith it was cold and breezy with rain and sleet falling. He was the last person to see any of the men alive.

Friends and family members were due to meet them at Glen Doll Youth Hostel at about 6p.m., but by that time the weather was so severe the road out of Glen Clova became blocked with snow and the single telephone line to the hotel at Clova was cut. The storm continued for two days and it was some time before the police could be informed of the missing climbers. It was 4th January before an 'official' rescue team could set out and they were hampered by horrific blizzard conditions and deep snow. They found the body of young James Boyle above the head of Glen Doll near Craig Maud. That night a temperature of -19.5°C was officially recorded in Strathdon in Aberdeenshire. The search continued on the Monday and Tuesday but was abandoned when frozen ground conditions made the hills difficult and dangerous. There was little chance of finding anyone alive, indeed the other victims weren't found until a thaw set in at the end of February. Most of the bodies were found by Davie Glen, who knew the area intimately, but it wasn't until April that the final body was discovered – that of Frank Daly, in a metre of snow near the upper reaches of White Water.

This Jock's Road disaster was a sobering reminder of how quickly conditions can change. Below me the White Water tumbled through a wild and rugged landscape before vanishing into the green choke of conifers that covers much of lower Glen Doll. On the other side of the glen Corrie Kilbo and Corrie Fee opened beyond the steep and glistening crags of the Dounalt and Craig Rennet. I silently gave thanks to Jock for his path as I climbed over the lip of Glen Doll onto the grassy plateau beyond. The traditional Tolmount route took a wet and scrambling trail up the ravine that contains the nascent White Water. Once beyond the confines of the glen the path passes the rough howff known as Davy's Bourach (built by the irrepressible Davie Glen) and follows the ridge that runs to Crow Craigies before dropping into Glen Callater bound for Glen Clunie and Braemar. I huddled below the cairn of Crow Craigies, ate some lunch and decided that enough was enough. I retraced my steps back down the glen as the wind grew stronger and the rain lashed even harder, looking forward to a hot drink in Glen Clova, but the dark cloud of the disaster hung over me all the way home.

For most hill-goers the big attraction of the Angus Glens is the pair of Munros that rise to the south of Glen Doll: Mayar and Driesh. These are the most popular hills in the area and the quickest route to the high bealach that offers easy access to both of them is via the old Kilbo hill path that climbs through the forest, runs over the wide bealach between the two hills and down into Glen Prosen. The first time I climbed these hills I must have missed it, because I found myself fighting through dense forestry as though it was an Amazonian jungle. In recent years signs have appeared pointing out the exact route.

More recently, the trees in the area have been clear-felled and Forest Enterprise has created a diversion, a long and steep haul up through the forest on what has become a very boggy and unpleasant path. The diversion climbs through the forest to meet up with the Kilbo path as it breaks free of the trees at the foot of the Shank of Drumfollow where the path hugs the steep contours to climb up to the wide bealach between the two Munros. The Shank is a long and narrow shoulder that separates the corrie below, Corrie Kilbo, with its neighbouring Corrie Fee. As you climb higher the views behind open across Glen Doll to the wide, bare tableland of the Mounth, patched with snow and sparkling under the winter sun. Once you reach the high bealach, Driesh, 3,107feet/947 metres, is a mere stroll away, easily reached in about a mile of easy walking. Continue to Mayar, 3,045 feet/928 metres, by returning to the col and following an old fence west over grassy slopes. From the summit, steepening grassy slopes drop away north to the head of Corrie Fee where a steep section to the south east of the burn leads you down past waterfalls to a footpath which continues to follow the Fee burn into the forest. The footpath becomes a forestry road leading all the way back to Glen Doll.

We stayed in Aberdeen for just over two years, a happy interlude that gave me some much-needed space to consider those things that were really important to me. Gina and I worked as a good team in the youth hostel and she earned extra money by doing part-time work as a midwife in Aberdeen Royal Infirmary. Gordon spent his toddler years in a loving family environment where both his parents were on hand all day and in January 1977 our second son Gregor was born. The timing of his arrival was perfect.

The previous December I had walked from Cairn Gorm to Ben Nevis, hoping to take in all of Scotland's 4,000-foot mountains en route. I was joined by Peter Lumley and another Backpackers Club member, Matt McKinley from Cumnock in Ayrshire, but the weather was atrocious. Deep, fresh snow thwarted our plans and we eventually decided on a lower-level walk. From the summit of Cairn Gorm we descended through the narrow and boulder-strewn Chalamain Gap into the lower reaches of the Lairig Ghru before dropping through the streets of gnarled Caledonian pines of Rothiemurchus Forest to Inshriach and Glen Tromie. From there we crossed the hills to Dalwhinnie and made our way between the Ben Alder hills to Loch Ossian and Corrour. It was a long and snowy hike from the head of Loch Treig over Tom an Eite and into upper Glen Nevis, but we soon found ourselves descending the wonderfully Himalayan gorge at Steall, down past the crags of Polldubh and down the narrow Glen Nevis road to Fort William.

This was all new country to me, and day after day I was overwhelmed by the beauty of it, particularly the ancient pinewoods of Rothiemurchus and Glen Feshie. As we wandered through the shadowed streets of the forest the rich orange-red hues of the bark of the pines were highlighted against the blinding snow, stately trees anchored deep and solid, the trunks like the foremasts of sailing ships. Some of these Caledonian Pines would have been saplings when Scotland's last independent Parliament met in 1707. Today they are granny pines, old age pensioners of the woods that provide a direct link to the first pines that grew here 8,000 years ago. It wasn't difficult to imagine a time when wolves and bears wandered freely through these forests, with wild boar scuffling in the undergrowth carpet that nature has woven, juniper bushes growing to a height of six or eight feet from a deep pile rug of bilberry and cowberry. I had never seen anything like it and suddenly realised that the high places of the Cairngorms are surrounded, skirted if you will, by forests that are every bit as impressive and magnificent as the mountains themselves. I can't recall whether I was aware at the time but something profound touched me on that trip. By the time we reached Fort William, tired, cold and footsore, I had a feeling that life was about to change again.

I had left my old car with Tom Wilson, the warden at the youth hostel in Aviemore, and after seeing Matt and Pete onto the south-bound train from Fort William caught the bus back to Aviemore via Spean Bridge, Roy Bridge, Tulloch, Loch Laggan, Newtonmore and Kingussie. It was a day in a million, the sun beating from a clear blue sky and illuminating a white, wintry landscape of snow-covered mountains and deep cobalt-blue lochs. I spent the entire journey with my nose pressed against the window, greedily devouring the magnificent scenes. At one point the thought crossed my mind that it would be wonderful to live in this beautiful part of Scotland.

At Aviemore Youth Hostel, Tom invited me in for a cup of tea before my long drive back to Aberdeen. As I supped the hot brew and munched my way through a plate of biscuits he gave me some exciting news. He had decided to retire the following spring and the warden's job at Aviemore would become vacant. I drove home with my mind in a whirl, but remembering Jim Martin's promise: when a hostel that I wanted became vacant I would get it. Should we move to Aviemore?

Immediately on my return I shared the news with Gina and she was as excited as me and then another bombshell exploded. Out of the blue Jim Martin telephoned me and told me that SYHA was building a brand new hostel in Torridon and he wanted us to be its first wardens. Wow! I had never visited Torridon but I knew all about its mountains and glens. I knew that the rocks of the Torridonian mountains were amongst the oldest in the world, and all about the challenges of the Torridon hills like Beinn Alligin, Beinn Eighe and the mighty Liathach. The new hostel was being built on the very slopes of Liathach itself, one of Scotland's most iconic mountains with the shores of Loch Torridon only a few feet away. All thoughts of Aviemore were washed from my mind until Gina, ever the pragmatist, brought me back to earth.

Is there a primary school? Where do children go to secondary school? Where is the nearest doctor? With one child of three and another only a couple of months old we had to consider such issues. We desperately wanted to live near our beloved mountains, but we also had to think of the wellbeing of our young family. After a few days of soul-searching I phoned Stirling HQ and spoke to Jim Martin, thanking him profusely for thinking of us and offering such a fantastic opportunity. I also told him I heard that Tom Wilson was retiring and that, if possible, we'd prefer to move to Aviemore. Jim, always understanding and accommodating, understood completely and told me that as soon as he received Tom Wilson's resignation letter he would contact me. A couple of weeks later Jim phoned to ask if we could move at the beginning of May. The next exciting chapter in our lives was about to begin.

5

CAIRNGORM CHARACTERS

Small but perfectly formed, Scotland can boast some of the finest and most diverse wild landscapes in Europe. Add to that the best access legislation, and what you get is a paradise for hillwalkers and mountaineers. The weather isn't perfect, I'll give you that, and we often curse the Highland climate that can feel like five months of winter and seven months' bad weather but that's rarely the whole truth. The weather can be fickle but those very complexities often create the moods and impressions, the atmospheres, that make hillwalking in Scotland a unique experience.

In world terms, Scottish mountains are not high. Only 282 summits actually rise beyond 914 metres/3,000 feet above sea level and the highest, Ben Nevis, is only 1,344 metres/4,409 feet but, because of Scotland's latitude and the cold and windy weather that this northerly position attracts, our comparatively bite-sized hills offer a very real challenge to hillwalkers. While the vast majority of the summits can be climbed comfortably in a day, mist and rain often reduces visibility and can make navigation extremely complex. In winter conditions, any time between November and April, there is a real threat of avalanches, whiteout conditions and full-scale Arctic blizzards. Only the foolhardy would treat the Scottish hills with anything less than complete respect.

Then there are the days that remain longest in the memory, when the rock is warm to the touch, the hills are purple and languid and the lazy call of the cuckoo is symbolic of the heavy, slumbering atmosphere. In conditions like this it's easy to understand what motivates those who want to escape to the hills.

The question of why people want to climb mountains is fraught with philosophical irrelevancy that has flirted around society ever since man first went to the mountains for recreation. We ask anyway, most usually in the aftermath of a mountain accident. I believe the best answer was given by the Scottish mountain-going poet Nan Shepherd. She said the most important thing about mountains was in the 'being there'. Most hillwalkers simply enjoy being amongst mountains, and are stimulated by them. The early Scottish mountaineering pioneers had a deep appreciation for this simple concept. Norman Collie, writing in the *Cairngorm Club Journal* about a hundred years ago, summed it up:

'Many are the memories one can bring back from the mountains, some of the peace and some of the stern fights with the elements, but they are all memories of freedom. The restraints of ordinary life no longer hold us down, we are in touch with nature – the sky, the winds, the waters, and the earth, surely these ancient elements of life can teach us secrets that a more protected existence hides from us. In the old Gaelic lore that deals with a people whose daily world lay close to the earth, one sees how their passion for freedom is told in their poetry. It came from their intimate relation with nature. May we not also find contentment and a larger interest in life from friendly communion with the hills and the wide open spaces of our highland land?'

I couldn't agree more, but modern society has given us additional excuses to climb hills for fun. Hillwalking is a healthy activity, a form of exercise that strengthens our cardiovascular efficiency, makes our muscles work and clears our head of the detritus of modern life. A radio interviewer even suggested to me that hillwalking was trendy, a fact that wasn't completely lost on me since she was resplendent in a fleece sweater and a pair of vibram-soled walking boots. Somehow, I suspected she had never climbed higher than the third floor of the BBC building and I doubt if it's the activity that's become trendy, more likely the gear. Smart young things, who five years ago wouldn't have been seen dead in a woolly bobblecap and hiking boots, nowadays sport brand names like The North Face, Berghaus and Lowe Alpine alongside their Tommy Hilfigers but, nevertheless, unprecedented numbers of Gore-Tex-clad walkers head for the Scottish hills every weekend, intent on the phenomenon that is Munro-bagging.

So, where are the best Munros? Well, if best means remote and inaccessible, Lurg Mhor and its near neighbour Bidein a' Choire Sheasgaich lie beyond the head of lonely Loch Monar in the northern Highlands and are girdled by trackless miles. Seana Braigh in Wester Ross, and A'Mhaighdean and Ruadh Stac Mor in the Fisherfield Forest are also extremely remote. The tough hills of Knoydart are no less inaccessible. Easier to reach but harder to climb are the jagged peaks of the Cuillin of Skye, Britain's most Alpine-like mountains. Buachaille Etive Mor near Glen Coe, An Teallach near Dundonnell and Liathach in Torridon would always be top ten favourites but, in direct contrast, on the opposite side of the country, the Cairngorms, although higher, offer more rounded slopes, thrusting massive plateaux above wind- and frost-scoured cirques, an area of genuine Arctic tundra. And my young family and I were about to set up home at the feet of these marvellous mountains.

It took me a long time to get over the novelty of living in the shadow of what I still consider to be our finest mountain range. Aviemore Youth Hostel is situated at the edge of the village, almost opposite the road that runs east across the River Spey before rising gently through Inverdruie and Coylumbridge to forested Glenmore and the sandy shores of lovely Loch Morlich. Every night, when I walked our two dogs, I would stop below a sign that pointed to the mountains – Cairn Gorm 11 miles – and every night a tingle would run up and down my spine at the thought. I had to pinch myself at the very thought of living and working in such a glorious place.

We moved into Aviemore Youth Hostel when the village was at the very height of its prosperity. This boom was largely due to the creation of the Aviemore Centre in 1966, the dream-project of Lord Fraser of Allander. 'The Centre', as it became known, was a rather ugly Stalinesque complex of concrete, sixties-style hotels, a cinema, shopping complex, ice rink and swimming pool, and a rather curious all-year-round holiday attraction called Santa Claus Land. Despite the rather dubious quality of the architecture (the architect, John Poulson, ended up in jail for bribery during a political scandal that saw the forced resignation of the Home Secretary Reginald Maudling), the Aviemore Centre quickly became a major Scottish tourist destination. In its heyday, royalty were regular visitors, including Prince Charles and Princess Anne who attended Royal Hunt Balls hosted in the Aviemore Centre's Osprey Rooms. The Christmas edition of the very popular BBC TV show, *It's A Knockout*, was held in the complex twice in the 1970s; Shirley Bassey and Billy Connolly were star attractions and the Hollywood actor Omar Sharif came and performed demonstrations of bridge. There was no lacking in ambition.

The creation of the Centre coincided with the growth of the ski development on Cairn Gorm, and Aviemore was continually marketed as Scotland's only all-year-round holiday resort, but the hard sell didn't do Aviemore any real favours. In no time the village held the dubious, though apocryphal, statistic of being the STD capital of Europe, the focus of riotous parties and stag piss-ups. A series of poor snow winters in the late seventies and early eighties coincided with the introduction of cheap flights to Europe and access to the ski resorts of France, Italy and Switzerland. This virtually put the Aviemore Centre out of business and the village of Aviemore, almost a separate entity, could have suffered drastically had it not been for the committed efforts of many local individuals and groups. Thanks to people like Willie McKenna, Ian Malcolm and others, there was a powerful and ambitious desire to turn Aviemore around, a steely determination to make a success of this strange village that was fast becoming a blot on the Highland landscape.

The focus of Aviemore's more recent development is still the concept of year-round holidays, but those snowless winters of the late seventies and early eighties pointed to a vital truth: tourism shouldn't depend on just one activity. With mountaineering, walking, canoeing, sailing on Loch Morlich, pony trekking, fishing and a host of other activities available, Aviemore didn't have to depend entirely on skiing. The concept of multi-activity holidays caught on, even during the winter months, and today Aviemore is busy all year round.

Our little youth hostel was thriving. With over 20,000 bed nights a year we were rarely quiet, other than in the month of November when we closed for essential maintenance. Despite its busyness, Aviemore Youth Hostel was a rather idyllic place to live. During the autumn we heard the roar of stags every night, and in the spring we became familiar with the piercing calls of young peregrine chicks, high in their eyrie on the craggy slopes of Craigellachie.

Before the modern slash and roar of the A9 separated it from the youth hostel grounds, the Craigellachie National Nature Reserve was easily accessed from our back door. A gate in the fence led us into this wonderful birchwood reserve where we spent hours with the boys searching for frogspawn, trying to catch the small fish in the loch, watching red squirrels, peregrines and all kinds of dragon-flies. Footpaths climbed high above reedy Loch Pulladern to natural viewpoints and glimpses of the Cairngorms across the green canopy of Rothiemurchus.

'Seas buan, Craig Eileachaidh!' 'Standfast, Craigellachie' was the ancient war cry of Clan Grant, the rousing to battle in times of the Fiery Cross. The great wooded crag is probably little changed since those days, although its foreground has changed beyond recognition. Read these words of the poet John Ruskin:

> 'In one of the loneliest districts of Scotland, where the peat cottages are darkest, just at the western foot of that great mass of the Grampians which encircle the sources of the Spey and the Dee, the main road which traverses the chain winds round the foot of a broken rock called the Crag, or Craig Ellachie.'

The dark peat cottages have long gone. Instead, the A9 runs uncompromisingly close to the base of the great rock. For all that, the Nature Reserve has remained largely unspoilt, I qualify slightly, for it is difficult to get away from the roar and rumble of the A9, the dominating concrete blocks of the Aviemore Centre, and the pulsing blare of a holiday disco disturbs the quiet evening.

Go there on a still spring morning and you'll experience something of the Craigellachie of old.

I loved wandering there on still, misty mornings when damp fingers of morning mist delicately wove through the skeletal branches of the birch trees. The rasping cough of a roe deer doe would break the stillness before the dawn chorus of chaffinch, great tit and blackbird. As I climbed higher through the trees I often broke clear of the mist into a world of vivid blue sky, to look down on a vast ocean of mist. The tip of Carn Elrig would pierce the cloud like a skerry of the sea, and the Cairngorms rose beyond, the hills framed solidly against a red and amber dawn. The beauty of Craigellachie was breathtaking, with the great black crag gleaming in the early light.

This was home and I could never quite believe it. I knew then what it was in the words, 'Standfast, Craigellachie', that made the warriors of old go and fight for their country. When Highlanders fought foreign wars, in Europe and the Commonwealth, the ancient clan war cries could not be recited without dredging deep wells of pride and emotions of birthplace and birthright. I may have been an incomer, but I could perfectly understand the emotions that resonated from a deep-rooted belonging to place and time.

While we lived in Aviemore I was Craigellachie's Voluntary Warden with the Nature Conservancy Council (Scotland). The duties weren't onerous, essentially keeping an eye on things and occasionally helping the warden of the reserve, Brian Lightfoot, whose boss, Dick Balharry, one of Scotland's most eminent naturalists, was to become a close friend in later years. I learned a lot about wildlife from Dick and even more about wildlife and conservation politics, an area I was to be reluctantly dragged into in years to come.

One of the highlights of that time was meeting the television presenter and naturalist David Attenborough (now Sir David), who was a good friend of Dick Balharry. When we took a stroll around the nature reserve I was impressed by his knowledge of the local wildlife and particularly the invertebrates. Back at the hostel Gordon, now five or six years old, asked him to sign a book but seemed to confuse him with another television naturalist of the time, David Bellamy. As the great David Attenborough signed his name Gordon asked him when he had shaved his beard off.

Most of those who stayed with us at Aviemore were outdoor enthusiasts who enjoyed skiing, walking or climbing in the Cairngorms but, occasionally, less wholesome types would disrupt the easy-going relaxed pace of hostel life. One instance sticks in my mind, not so much because of the disruption itself but how we dealt with it. During very busy spells, like holiday weekends, it wasn't unusual for the hostel to be fully booked. We always tried to keep a percentage of beds free for those who hadn't booked in advance, particularly cyclists or hikers, but sometimes we simply ran out of space.

In those days, Grade 1 hostels like Aviemore were closed between 11a.m. and 2p.m. I had a sign on the door saying 'Sorry. Hostel full for tonight.' If people turned up before we reopened at 2p.m. they would have time to find alternative accommodation, but that wasn't good enough for one guy. He approached me just as I was closing the door.

'What do you mean the hostel is full?' he said. 'You have to let me stay, even if it means I have to sleep on the floor.'

I explained that I couldn't do that. We were only allowed to sleep 80 people, any more than that would contravene health and safety legislation.

'And what if I just force my way in, you and whit army are gonny throw me out again?' he said, drawing himself up to his full height. I didn't really want to argue so I suggested if he tried to force his way in I'd phone the police. Mention of the 'P' word set him off and he became threatening.

'It's just because I come frae Glasgow,' he said. 'You Highland basturts hate us weegies.' With that he dropped his rucksack, opened it and took out an ice axe. 'So, if you don't let me stay ah'm gonnae break every windae in the place.'

It was on the tip of my tongue to explain to him that I also came from Glasgow and there was nothing personal in it, but sight of the axe convinced me I should perhaps take things to another level. I slammed the door in his face, ran through to our kitchen and asked Gina to phone the police while I kept an eye on my fellow Glaswegian. Our relationship with the local police was excellent and within minutes a white van trundled up our drive. It was Jimmy Simpson, the local police dog handler and a member of the Cairngorm Mountain Rescue Team who was also one of the most laid-back and easy-going individuals you could hope to meet. He sauntered round to the front door as though he had all the time in the world. The Glaswegian was still there, still brandishing his axe, and Jimmy gently coaxed him into handing it over. 'Stay here a minute Cameron,' he said, 'I'll take this guy round to the van and then come back and get a statement from you. Oh, and you could maybe ask Gina to put the kettle on?'

A few minutes later Jimmy turned up at our kitchen door. 'I'm gasping for a brew, Gina, and while you're making the tea I'll take a few notes from Cameron.'

'What have you done with the ned?' I asked. 'Where is he?'

'Oh him? Come and have a look. He's no' going anywhere.'

Jimmy took me out to the car park where he had parked his van. The ned was sitting in the passenger seat looking terrified. Immediately behind him, with his great slobbering jaw resting on the ned's right shoulder, was the biggest, hairiest Alsatian dog you've ever seen.

'I told Rocky to keep an eye on him,' said Jimmy with a grin. 'Now, where's ma tea?'

Another great mountain man I had come to know before actually moving to Aviemore was the author Ben Humble. I remember Ben as a rather crotchety, ill-tempered old fellow, and very deaf. He kept an Alpine garden at the National Mountaineering Centre at Glenmore Lodge and was a fairly frequent visitor there. I was usually more interested in things other than flowers and seeds but was saddened when Ben died in Aviemore in 1977, just as we moved there. I had been looking forward to getting to know him a bit better. One of the grand old characters of the Scottish mountain scene, I was truly sorry to have missed him.

He was, I had discovered, an early advocate for Scottish youth hostels, had served as a voluntary instructor in the embryonic days of Glenmore Lodge, and played an important role in the setting up of the independent Mountain Rescue Committee for Scotland. His life spanned the era from the early explorations of the Scottish hills to modern times and, in its latter stages, he was well known as the recorder of mountain accidents in Scotland. In addition, he had climbed with some of the greats of Scottish mountaineering. In his writings he tells of meeting John Mackenzie of Sconser, Britain's first mountain guide and companion to Professor Norman Collie, one of the great pioneers of Alpinism and cartographer of the Cuillin of Skye, ' . . .the most famous mountain guide in Britain, a man among men, white-bearded, ruddy complexioned and clear of eye, and though over seventy he was, up till a few years ago, leading the way to the mountain tops.'

Ben Humble also wrote of climbing with WH Murray, author of the classic books *Mountaineering in Scotland* and *Undiscovered Scotland*, two of the titles that inspired me to climb mountains. One of the chapters describes a phenomenal expedition when the two men traversed the main Cuillin Ridge, then the ridge of the neighbouring Red Cuillin, in under 24 hours – a tremendous feat which few would attempt today. The author of six books, including a now classic history of mountaineering in Skye, Ben Humble lived a life that was a simple response to the challenge of the hills, and a direct challenge to his own personal difficulties. At a comparatively early age Ben became stone deaf, and for a number of different reasons never learned to lip read. Despite this disability he became an effective and persistent communicator, scribbling in note books that he carried with him. It was the discovery of many of these notebooks that allowed his nephew, Roy Humble, to write a fascinating biography, ably illustrating the fact that Ben Humble was much, much more than a curmudgeonly old gardener. With access to all of Ben's old writings and scribblings, Roy wove the story of this brilliant dentist who made early significant contributions to dental radiology and forensic odontology before giving it all up to answer the call of the hills.

Two other men who gave their lives to the hills and settled in the Cairngorms were Iain Hudson and Jim Crompton. When I first moved to Aviemore, I was drawn like a magnet to a little wooden shack in Rothiemurchus where these two hill-going and wildlife enthusiasts had set up a company called Highland Guides. Iain and Jim may have been business partners, but they were like chalk and cheese in many respects. Jim was happy to allow Iain to get on with the day-to-day running of the business: setting up a number of guided walks to various parts of the Cairngorms in the summer and organising cross-country skiing courses and trips in the winter months, while he was more than happy to chat with the customers and occasionally lead some bird-watching groups. Indeed, Jim was an enthusiastic and well-informed ornithologist, and I enjoyed some very memorable days watching snow bunting and dotterel with him on the Cairngorm plateau. Iain continued running Highland Guides in his own inimitable way after, sadly, Jim died prematurely.

It was probably about then that he encouraged me to lead groups into the Cairngorms and, with a host of other local 'guides', including people like Pat Wells, Anne Wakeling, Jeff Faulkner and Brian Revill, groups of visitors were taken to Ben Macdui a couple of times a week, with wildlife walks to the Cairngorm Plateau in between. When the weather was bad on the high tops there would be excursions through the pinewoods of Rothiemurchus. At first, I was a little reticent about taking groups of people into these places but gradually, as my confidence grew, I came to enjoy these outings and the opportunity to meet people who were eager to learn more about the hills and their associated wildlife, lore and folk tales.

There was something deliciously old-fashioned about Highland Guides. The wooden floor creaked and there was always the smell of ski wax and pipe smoke in the air. Time after time I would wander in and knock on the counter only for a face to appear and grunt, 'Oh, it's you.' Within minutes, there would be a mug of coffee on the counter for me, and Iain would appear for a blether. What was more important was that the Highland Guides hut became a gathering place for people passing through the area, the kind of place you could drop into for a chat and a bit of gossip. Folk like Joe and Molly Porter when Molly was leader of the Cairngorm Mountain Rescue Team (the only female team leader in the country) and the great ecologist and mountaineer Adam Watson. Iain had been trained as a meteorologist in the RAF and kept all kinds of weather records. He also completed an annual survey of snow levels, an interest shared with Dr Watson. It wasn't unusual to get a phone call from him late in the evening, demanding that I jump in my car and meet him at Tullochgrue to view a particularly good showing of the Aurora Borealis. He had an almost instinctive knowledge of when the Northern Lights would appear and I shared many a happy late hour with him, viewing this fabulous natural phenomenon.

Iain Hudson's main contribution to the development of outdoor activities in the Aviemore area was his enthusiasm for cross-country, or Nordic, skiing. With his box of waxes, old leather boots and wooden skis he inspired a generation to take to the forest tracks and slopes of the Cairngorms on touring skis. Some of those he encouraged became top-class skiers and coaches themselves. It didn't take me long to be caught up. I had tried the regular Alpine skiing on Cairn Gorm but was put off by the high-octane promotion, the gaudy fashion and the crowds. Nordic skiing appealed to me more as a mountaineer and hillwalker, using the skis to take me deep into the winter woods or to the less-populated high tops. For a short spell I became the Nordic Development Officer of the Scottish Ski Council, but the politics and schism that existed between Nordic racers and cross-country tourers saw me constantly fighting battles I neither needed nor wanted. I resigned after a few months, another indication that I wasn't a particularly good team player and would, in years to come, prefer to fight conservation battles from outside the stockade rather than from within the ranks of the Ramblers, Mountaineering Scotland or the John Muir Trust. I do understand though, that those non-government organisations play important roles in protecting our landscapes and ensuring access to them.

Another legendary mountaineer I was delighted to meet was Hamish Brown. He came to our hostel door one day and introduced himself. He had read some of my work in various magazines and wanted to say hello, a social nicety that was common at that time when very few people were writing about the hills and indeed, relatively few people walked or climbed on them. Hamish was a hugely experienced mountaineer and climber and had explored wild places throughout the world. The wonderful thing about him is that he is hugely knowledgeable about a whole host of topics, from ornithology to history to poetry and books, and even ancient graveyards. He is never short of something to blether about, so it's perhaps a little bit unfortunate that he is often remembered mainly as the guru of Munro-bagging. There is much more to Hamish Brown than Munros, the Scottish mountains over 3,000 feet in height. However, having said that, I would blame him almost exclusively for my own baptism into the habit.

In April 1974 Hamish set off to climb all the Munros in one continuous journey, using only public transport to reach the islands of Mull and Skye. His journey took him 112 days during which he climbed 289 Munros, covering a total distance of 1,639 miles and wearing out three pairs of boots in the process. That mammoth expedition spawned a wonderful book called *Hamish's Mountain Walk*, a rich and fulsome compendium about the Scottish hills, landscapes, wildlife, history and hill characters. It was a book that encapsulated the very spirit of the Scottish hills at that time. More than that, it cured me of my earlier perception of 'dirty Munro-baggers' and made me take a quick count of the Munros that I had already climbed. Much to my surprise it was well over a hundred and, while promising myself I would never become addicted or obsessed, I began my own personal tick-list.

It took me over ten years to complete my first round. My final Munro was Ben More on Mull in 1990 when Gina and I celebrated in the mist and rain with a bottle of bubbly by the summit cairn. Two more rounds were to come, plus a round of the Corbetts but, in more recent years, I must admit to taking a delight in climbing hills but not necessarily going to the summit. Munro-bagging has its critics but I would defend it to the death. Provided you don't become completely obsessed it is a wonderful excuse for climbing hills, a rather curious and pointless exercise in itself, but I don't know anyone who has climbed all the Munros and not become a well-rounded and experienced mountaineer in the process. In the years since *Hamish's Mountain Walk* was published, Munro-bagging has become a popular strand of the whole Scottish mountaineering experience and I think it deserves its popularity. It's not an entirely unusual thing to do. Some people collect stamps. Others collect antiques. Some collect books. A huge number of folk nowadays collect mountain tops.

Climbers have bagged Munros ever since Sir Hugh Munro of Lindertis came up with his eponymous list in 1891. Most climbers bagged them in secret, lest their peers ridiculed them. 'Dirty Munro-baggers' were derided as lesser mortals by the hairy-arsed mountaineers but, in the years since the centenary of Munro's Tables, the number of those who have climbed them all has risen by two-thirds. As at 2017 over 5,500 hillwalkers currently have their names recorded in the Scottish Mountaineering Club's Munro records as having climbed all the 3,000-foot summits.

Munro-bagging is now not only respectable but also fashionable, and people of all ages and backgrounds have risen to the challenge. While some hillwalkers might take a lifetime to climb all 282 summits, others have done it in one long, complete journey. Some have climbed them in their retirement years, others have climbed them during the winter equinox and others have run round them. Paul Tattershall, a climbing instructor from Melvaig and a good pal of mine, even completed all 282 summits with a mountain bike (carried rather than ridden on the majority of the peaks) and it's now not uncommon for hillwalkers to enjoy several rounds during their lifetime. The 'record' for want of a better word, is currently held by fell-runner Steve Fallon and stands at 15 rounds. Add to the Munros, the Corbetts, named after their compiler John Rooke Corbett, another 220 separate hills over 764 metres/2,500 feet, scattered throughout the Highlands and Islands, and you have enough good hillwalking to last several lifetimes. Then there are the Grahams (summits of between 2,000 and 2,499 feet) and a host of others.

Until the last fifty years, the world's highest peaks were largely unexplored. Mountaineering was all about exploration, with new achievements and new adventures to be had, but, today, the number of difficult first ascents have become depleted, and exploration is not such an integral part of mountaineering any more.

Mountaineers are therefore constantly having to invent new 'firsts' and new challenges: more difficult routes, climbing without oxygen and climbing hard routes in winter. Another challenge is 'mountain bagging'.

The completion of all fourteen 8,000-metre peaks, the highest in the world, almost pales Munro-bagging into insignificance. The height is entirely arbitrary, but roughly corresponds to the 'death zone': the height at which the human body, even if kept warm and well fed, will not survive for more than a few days. The limited oxygen means that the body just cannot function properly and gradually closes down. Combined with the cold, the terrain and the sheer physical and mental effort required, climbing any 8,000-metre peak presents a near-ultimate challenge. The first 8,000-metre peak to be climbed was Annapurna in 1950. Within a decade, all fourteen had been climbed. Although thousands of mountaineers have stood on at least one 8,000-metre peak, the challenge they pose is still immense. The world's 8,000-metre mountains remain the ultimate 'mountain collection'.

The immensity of the task means that it is no coincidence that two of the greatest mountaineers of modern times were the first to pull it off. Reinhold Messner made the first solo ascents of Nanga Parbat and Everest, and in 1986 became the first to climb all fourteen 8,000-metre peaks. He took sixteen years to complete his goal. According to him, the idea grew over time and was not his objective from an early stage. 'I did not *collect* 8000ers as has often been suggested,' he once wrote. Instead, his early climbs seemed intent on pushing the boundaries, finding new routes for example, on the great peaks rather than the notion of 'peak bagging'. 'I didn't feel especially heroic to have climbed all fourteen of the 8000ers. I had seen something through, that was all,' he later said.

The second to complete all fourteen was Polish mountaineer Jerzy Kukuczka who took eight years. He completed either a new route or the first winter ascent on twelve of the fourteen.

Alan Hinkes is the first and, so far, only Briton to complete all fourteen peaks. Courtesy of BBC Scotland I interviewed him when he had just descended from his final 8,000-metre summit and asked him what he was going to do next. 'Climb the Scottish Munros,' he said. Peak bagging must be in his blood.

In the eighties, the idea arose to collect the highest peaks within all the seven continents. In 1985 Dick Bass of the US, an inexperienced mountaineer and a multi-millionaire, became the first to complete: Denali in North America, Aconcagua in South America, Everest in Asia, Elbrus in Europe, Kilimanjaro in Africa, Mount Vinson in Antarctica and Mount Kosciusko in Australia. The list, however, has been subject to many disputes, the main one being about Australia. Australia can be considered to be in the continent of Oceania, which is why Pat Morrow rejected Kosciusko for the Carstensz Pyramid (the latter being over 2,000 metres higher than the former) in Indonesia in 1986. Reinhold Messner – who again argued that he was not 'collecting' mountains, and many others, followed Morrow. Although a powerful symbol, the circuit requires comparatively little skill and experience. Everest, of course, is the great leveller but many 'seven summiteers' nowadays hire guides to take them up. The real challenges, some argue, are time – and money.

The Munros is perhaps the world's oldest 'collection'. In 1891 Sir Hugh Munro published a list of the 3,000-feet mountains of Scotland, which were then collectively named the Munros. He could have little imagined that he was instigating a challenge and a tradition that over a century later has achieved cult status. The Reverend A. E. Robertson first completed the collection in 1901. Another twenty years went by before the achievement was repeated, by another cleric, the Reverend A. R. G. Burn in 1923. Only eight people completed the Munros before World War II. The first lady was a Mrs Hirst in 1947.

Munro-bagging should have died with the maps going metric, rendering obsolete the historic height of 3,000 feet, but quite the opposite. The list of Munroists is now a long line of statistics and records and 'firsts': father and son records, people going solo, or in different seasons. Phillip Tranter did them a second time and led to a row of multiple tallies. Hamish Brown did the Munros as a continuous walk in 1974 in 112 days and held the 'fastest ever' title for many years. This record was broken by Martin Moran who completed the summits in 83 days, and managed to do so during the winter season. The ages of the oldest and youngest have changed steadily; even dogs have topped all the magic summits, and Munro-bagging shows that collecting is not just about 'firsts'.

Doing the Munros has become an immensely popular activity, made so much easier with the improvements in road networks within the Highlands, the common use of the car, along with the leisure time everyone now enjoys. It used to be a lifetime ambition to accomplish the Munros, now its is commonplace and often done much earlier in life. Nonetheless, it remains a real challenge, 282 mountains, many of which pose real difficulty. The celebrity Munro-bagger Muriel Gray wrote, 'You remember your first mountain in much the same way you remember having your first sexual experience. Unfortunately, unlike losing your virginity, Munro-bagging stays just as sore every time you do it.'

I guess the big question most non-climbers ask is: why climb mountains at all? Reading accounts of climbers' experiences, the pain and despair makes one wonder why they are constantly drawn to the mountains. Messner wrote, 'I have experienced perfect peace on a summit but also total despair.' His writing, as well as the writing of other mountaineers, is full of accounts of near-death situations, of despair and pain, and of feelings of missing loved ones at home. Alan Hinkes, for example, recounted his feelings on the summit of K2, 'My head ached and my body felt like it was being crushed by a vice. Climbing at extreme altitude is agony. Torture.' Sometimes, the challenge of the style in which the collection is being achieved seems to detract from the pleasure of the process. Martin Moran wrote in his *The Munros in Winter*, 'My appetite for the "delicious freedom" of the venture had somehow vanished, and the "euphoric release" which I was applauding but a few hours previously now hung round my neck like a Derbyshire millstone!'

So, does the process of 'collecting' detract from the enjoyment one would normally feel at the summit, or add to it? Does the process of collecting itself become an obsession? Muriel Gray has written of the obsessive 'ticking off' of every Munro peak that she came across in Scotland. She was even asked once why she had 'wasted all that time' climbing up lesser peaks? The conversation of such people is not about beauty, wildlife and experience. Rather, it revolves around the burning question of 'How many have you done?'

Serious mountaineering in the Himalayas is not just about overcoming physical objects. It means weeks and months away from family and home, and the call of the mountain seems constantly too much. Alan Hinkes does not photograph himself with a flag on top of his 8,000-metre summits, but with a photo of his daughter but, if he misses her so much, what drives him to the mountains time and time again? Uschi, Messner's wife, once asked him, 'If you had to choose between the mountains or me – which would it be?'

Without doubt, the promise of media attention is an inspiration for some. The media has changed mountaineering. Prior to World War II the greatest exploits were known only in climbing circles. That changed after the War when mountaineers achieving great 'firsts' were assured considerable attention. Although they rarely become A-list celebrities, completing new challenges will secure media coverage and book deals – and subsequent sponsorship – bringing a certain amount of notoriety, fame and money.

For the majority of us, the thought of 'collecting mountains' of any size or shape, induces mixed feelings: admiration, envy, bafflement, amongst others, but we are still left with the question 'why?' The mountaineers themselves seem equally baffled in a way. Messner wrote, 'If I have not given enough answers, don't come looking for more, go to the mountains ... the mountains have an answer for everyone.' Jerzy Kukuczka stated, 'There is no answer to the endless question about the point of expeditions to the Himalayan giants. I never found a need to explain this. I went to the mountains and climbed them. That is all.' I like that answer.

Why do we have to scrutinise our reasons for climbing hills? I'm often asked what I get from it and my answer is a very simple one: mountains make me happy. The very sight of them raises my spirits. Being amongst them is wonderful. They excite me, they thrill me, they soothe me and they refresh me. I guess others get the same feeling from being on the sea or on a raging river in a tiny kayak.

From the first sight of the mountains of Arran from the Ayrshire coast as a youngster, hills and mountains have played on my psyche in the most profound way. No more so than during our spell living and working in Aviemore.

6

DARKNESS AND LIGHT

I often look back on those Aviemore years and appreciate how time, opportunity and good fortune came together for me to grow into the role of an outdoor writer. I took the opportunity of taking a mountain leadership course at nearby Glenmore Lodge, a centre of excellence that I had come to know very well. Instructors at the Lodge at the time were like a 'who's who' of star mountaineers: Fred Harper was the principle and Roger O'Donovan was his depute. Peter Boardman, later to go missing on the north-east ridge of Everest with Joe Tasker, was an instructor along with John Cunningham, Aido Liddell, Sammy Crymble, Keith Geddes, Alan Fyffe and Tim Walker. These guys became friends and each and every one was an inspiration.

On my days off I would work as an instructor for Highland Guides, climbing hills in summer and cross-country skiing in winter, and during the day when the hostel was quiet I would write, my enthusiasm often running away with me into manuscripts of extravagant purple prose. Indeed, in an attempt to write better I took a course in creative writing and joined the Bureau of Freelance Photographers, an organisation that was founded in 1965 to help freelance and aspiring photographers sell their pictures to editorial markets. Already I had a vague notion that I might like to eventually earn a living as a photo-journalist, inspired by the failures, rather than the successes, of the UK's most accomplished and respected mountaineer, Chris Bonington. At that time I had never met Chris but I had read his books, particularly his first, *I Chose To Climb*. Not many mountaineers had made a living from their passion; very few had turned their backs on a 'normal' career to earn a crust from climbing crags or mountains. I knew it was something I wanted to do, but I wasn't confident about how my first faltering steps would develop, but Chris Bonington's experiences showed me that if you have a dream you have to reach for it.

Chris was child of a broken marriage and was brought up by his grandmother. He was sent to various private schools where he did not distinguish himself in any way. He lacked the qualifications to go to university so joined the RAF to do his national service but, 'was ham-handed in the cockpit of the aircraft'. He failed to become a flyer so joined the army, again without much success. He worked as a management trainee with Unilever but, no, that didn't work out either. By his own admission, Chris Bonington didn't really start to achieve anything until he was almost thirty and I could really relate to that. I had enjoyed some minor success in track and field but, having given up athletics for the hills, was at a bit of a loss. I had no formal qualifications, hadn't been to university and, although I enjoyed running the youth hostel, knew I couldn't do it for the rest of my working life. However, if this guy Bonington didn't begin his outdoor career until he was in his late twenties then perhaps I could too. Newly married to Wendy, his partner for the next 52 years, Chris made the tough decision to go it alone. Given the stark choice of taking part in a mountaineering expedition to South America or continuing his corporate management training with Unilever he plumped for a life of adventure, and the rest is history. Chris Bonington became the most accomplished and respected mountaineer in the world.

I had no ambitions like that, nor Chris Bonington's climbing abilities, I simply wanted to make a career out of writing about hills and mountains. Chris's first book was an inspiration to me and motivated me to forgo normal working routines and forge a life from the outdoors. I did that, but what Chris went on to achieve is incomparable.

Like many others at the time, his career followed the classic progression from the home hills of the Lake District, Snowdonia and Scotland to the Alps before his first visit to the Greater Ranges. Nepal in the sixties was a different place to that of today, long before the trekking phenomenon produced the tea-houses, hotels and infrastructure that exist now. Think of being weeks away from home, in the remote area of north-west Pakistan called Hunza, when news reaches you that your youngest son has been drowned in an accident at home. How do you cope with something so personally tragic, so far away from home and from those you love and care for? Chris and Wendy did cope, and Chris went on to lose a string of close friends in the mountains, friends that he never fails to mention in his many talks and lectures throughout the world. It's as though these personal losses have been a stimulus for him to continue and to strive ever higher, as though his successes are as much for them as for himself.

Literally, Chris couldn't have climbed any higher. After leading the successful south face of Annapurna and south-west face of Everest expeditions (in which Dougal Haston and Doug Scott became the first Brits to climb Everest), he reached the highest point on earth at the grand old age of 51. In many ways that was the beginning. Freed from the constraints of big, unwieldy expeditions, he organised a string of small lightweight expeditions with close friends and relatives to a series of smaller, more technical mountains: Menlungste, Panch Chuli, Rangrik Rang, Drangnag-Ri, Sepu Kangri and a host of others.

By the millennium, aged 66, he was feeling the first effects of growing older, but he still didn't ease up, with more expeditions to Asia and annual rock climbing trips to Morocco and Greenland. Finally, at the impressive age of 80 and only months after his wife Wendy had passed away, he climbed the Old Man of Hoy in Orkney with his great friend and protégé Leo Houlding. He had come full circle, having made the first ascent of the famous sea stack in 1966 with Tom Patey and Rusty Baillie.

What a career, and what a fine ambassador for British mountaineering Chris Bonington has been. I was under no illusions that I could carve out a career like that, but realised that I wasn't too old to take a new direction. Perhaps, just perhaps, I could make a living from climbing hills and exploring wild places. It would be great to be able to inspire others to get out there and discover more about this great country of ours, just as I had been inspired by folk like Bill

Murray, Tommy Weir and Hamish Brown. Maybe I could combine outdoor instruction with writing? Perhaps I could add more qualifications to my Mountain Leadership award and British Association of Ski Instructor certificate and get a job in an outdoor centre? I was excited by the possibilities and woke each morning with a new drive and determination to succeed, but it was an event of a more personal nature that really pushed me into doing something purposeful with my life.

I had been asked to instruct on a weekend cross-country ski course at the Lecht ski grounds near Tomintoul. The event was organised by a good friend called Andy Main who had an outdoor gear shop in Elgin and was the Scottish National Nordic Ski Coach, and often brought in keen but inexperienced instructors like me to help on his courses. On this particular day, I was busy teaching a small group of skiers how to do a snow plough when he skied over the hill and approached me, a grim look on his face. He called me aside, said he would take over my group and that Gina was looking for me. She was in the cafe.

I had no idea how and why Gina had arrived there but it was obvious from Andy's serious demeanour that something was amiss. I skied over to the cafe, took off my skis and found her waiting inside with a friend from Kingussie, Elizabeth Harkai, who had driven her the fifty miles or so to the ski centre. The news was devastating. My father had died that morning, apparently from a heart attack. My mother had been at work and my youngest sister, Heather, who has learning difficulties, found him lying across his bed. She thought he was sleeping but couldn't waken him. He was only 52. I knew he wasn't a fit man and in recent years had suffered from acute athritis in his hands and feet, which was especially bad for someone who taught carpentry. He was also a heavy smoker and the fags, or the results of smoking, had contributed to his death. A post-mortem showed his arteries were clogged with tar and his death certificate put the cause of death as ischaemic heart disease.

Dad's premature death had a powerful effect on me. Since my teenage years I had been something of a fitness fanatic. As well as climbing hills and skiing, I enjoyed running and I would easily run ten miles inside an hour. Overnight that determination to live a fit and healthy life became something of an obsession, as was the resolve to live every day as though it was my last. Years before I had latched on to some lines by the poet Robert Browning:

> 'Speak as they please, what does the mountain care?
> Ah, but a man's reach should exceed his grasp,
> Or what's a heaven for?'

I think the poet was suggesting that our dreams consistently exceed our achievements and our imagination consistently exceeds our understanding. There is also a sense that desire is more meaningful than possession and without that desire in our life, without aims and ambitions that exceed our expectations, life might become a disappointment. Following Dad's sudden death those lines took on a new meaning. My father had been robbed of years of family life; he barely knew his grandsons and my mother had her lifelong companion stolen from her. Heather, Helen and I had lost our dad. While I was aware that life itself is something of a lottery I would do all I could to live a life worth living. I wanted to see Gordon and Gregor grow up and perhaps have children of their own. I wanted to have a long, happy and fulfilling marriage with Gina. I became determined to control my own life, and not allow society, or circumstances, or a tobacco addiction, to run it for me. On the day of my father's funeral I promised him I would make him proud.

In the months that followed the death of my father I resolved to try and be a pal, as well as a father, to my own two sons. I went through a long phase of feeling guilty because I had never really enjoyed a close relationship with my own dad; in many ways I had been closer to my athletics coach, and I didn't want to pass away with my own lads thinking they hadn't really known me. It was a very difficult time, but out of adversity there is often a slow flowering, and my own aims and ambitions now appeared to take form and shape. Out of the blue I received a telephone call from a man by the name of Clive Sandground. Clive was features editor of a Scottish newspaper called the *Sunday Standard* and he had a problem. The newspaper ran a wildlife column written by the naturalist Mike Tomkies, author of the most riveting accounts of living in the natural world. He was a man who more or less shunned society so that he could live as close to his wild subjects as possible: golden eagles, wildcats and pine martens.

Every Wednesday he would write his 650 words in his cottage on an island in Loch Shiel, row across the loch to a remote telephone box near Acharacle and read his column to a copy taker in Glasgow. Sometimes the weather was so bad he couldn't get his boat into the water and would miss the deadline. In an attempt to keep some continuity with the column, Clive Sandground asked if I could fill in for Mike when he failed to get his copy to Glasgow. I was delighted to contribute and soon was filing copy most weeks.

Eventually, Mike got in touch and asked if I could just take it on permanently. He was finding the logistics of getting copy to Glasgow too problematic. That was my first contact with Mike Tomkies who, by this time, had influenced my own appreciation of wildlife in a deep and profound way through his books, *A Last Wild Place* and *Between Earth and Paradise*. These two books made me realise that to really observe wildlife in the raw you had to spend huge amounts of time immersing yourself in wild land, connecting with it, and treating the native wild population as equals.

I was keen to interview Mike and we agreed to meet. I happened to mention this to a good friend of mine, the wildlife writer Jim Crumley, and discovered that Jim had also been hugely influenced by Tomkies' work. We thought perhaps we could travel to Loch Shiel and visit Tomkies together but Mike wasn't keen on the idea. He lived a completely solitary life and apparently couldn't cope with two people at the same time. Something cropped up and I couldn't travel as planned so Jim went in my place. That was the beginning of a long and warm friendship between these two wonderful wildlife writers, two men who eventually influenced each other's work and lifted the genre to a new literary level. I never did meet Mike Tomkies face to face, but Jim frequently told me of his wildlife forays with him – expeditions where he learned much about wild animal behaviour, especially that of golden eagles, and how to observe birds and beasts at close quarters.

Mike eventually left Scotland to live in Spain where his father had a house – a crumbling mansion with no glass in the windows and no running water. He made wildlife films and wrote a book about brown bear, lynx, wolf, wild boar and vultures called *In Spain's Secret Wilderness*. Mike published his last book, *Running Wild*, at the age of 83 and died, aged 88, at his Elizabethan farmstead home in Henfield, England.

I was now getting so much writing work that it was becoming apparent that I could leave the SYHA and develop a freelance writing and outdoor instructing career. Walt Unsworth, the editor of *Climber and Rambler* magazine, asked me to contribute a regular column and I was still writing pieces for Pete Lumley's *Practical Camper* magazine. Our local newspaper asked me to write a weekly outdoor column and in 1978, the publisher Holmes McDougall, who produced *Climber and Rambler*, decided to start a magazine for hillwalkers. They called it the *Great Outdoors* and a London-based journalist by the name of Roger Smith was brought in to edit it.

Roger moved north to Peebles and got in touch, asking me to write for his new magazine. I was delighted. Things were really taking off. A writer and publisher by the name of Rob Neillands came to see me. He had a small imprint by the name of Spurbooks and he asked me to write the *Spur Book of Youth Hostelling*, followed by the *Spur Master Guide to Snow Camping*. I had already written a small book of Scottish backpacking routes for Peter Lumley called *Highland Ways* and I had just received a commission from a London-based publisher called Robert Hale to write a book called *Backpacker's Scotland*. How I managed to cram in all this writing work with my youth hostel duties I have no idea but a chance conversation with Peter Lumley in France finally produced the nugget that enabled me to leave the hostels.

Rob Neillands had been asked by the French Government Tourist Office to organise a small group of outdoor writers to take part in the inaugural Robert Louis Stevenson trail in southern France.

In 1879 Stevenson had written a wonderful account of a 120 mile journey between Le Monastier in the Massif Central and St Jean du Gard in the Cevennes, a journey on which he was accompanied by a donkey called Modestine. He called his account *Travels with a Donkey in the Cevennes*. The French tourism authority had created a walking route based on the book and thought it would be a good idea to ask some British writers to walk the route the week before it was officially opened. The idea, of course, was that we would then publicise the route. The route is now the GR70 trail.

Rob had also invited Pete Lumley, Robin Adshead, who was now writing for the new the *Great Outdoors*, John Traynor from *Camping* magazine and Don Philpott, a journalist with the Press Association in London. We flew from Heathrow to Clermont Ferrand; this was only the second time I had been on an aeroplane, the first being when I flew from Glasgow to Manchester as part of the Scottish athletics team. Our arrival at the dusty little village of Le Monastier coincided with a period of high pressure – it was very, very hot!

Whether it was the heat, or whether my companions were just unfit, I'll never be really sure but it was not a very happy trip. The two Robins were in constant competition as to who could catch the eye of the prettiest barmaids and Robin Adshead and Peter Lumley almost came to blows on a couple of occasions. I didn't add to the general camaraderie by insisting that we walk every inch of the hundred-mile route, even in the heat of the day. I was probably a real pain, but I didn't think it was fair on the French Government Tourist Office, who had paid all our expenses, to cherry-pick the best parts and sit in bars drinking the rest of the time. On a few occasions I walked alone while the others caught a train or a bus, but at least my conscience was clear. I had walked it all, and so could honestly write about it all.

In the course of one of the days I walked with Peter and Don Philpott and our conversation turned to the subject of outdoor magazines and why there wasn't a specialist magazine for hillwalkers and backpackers. There were a couple of general camping magazines on the go and the popular *Climber and Rambler* magazine which, despite its name, was dedicated virtually entirely to rock climbing. Holmes McDougall, the publishers of *Climber*, had recently brought out the first issue of the *Great Outdoors* but it looked as though that was going to be a magazine for low-level ramblers. We felt there was room in the market for something aimed at those of a slightly harder edge, those who took their hillwalking and backpacking seriously, a magazine-of-record that would also campaign for access rights, better lightweight equipment and even green issues. We decided there and then that, since there was no magazine of this type on the market, we should publish one. We settled on the name too – it was to be called *Footloose*.

At that time, Peter had left *Practical Camper* magazine to set up his own little publishing empire in Newcastle, and *Footloose* would be part of that group. Don was fairly committed to his work with the Press Association in London so he took on the title of contributing editor, using his writing skill and wider contacts to find new and innovative articles and features. I was to be the editor, putting the whole thing together before taking it all to Newcastle to be typeset and designed. Initially we would publish every two months and, if things went well, we would publish on a monthly basis. In many ways, it was a bold thing to do and, from today's perspective, rather risky, but the heady days of the early eighties were very different from present times. People were willing to take risks and often encouraged to just go for it. We spoke to a number of potential advertisers and they all felt the outdoor market could easily cope with another magazine. Peter was well known in the industry and I was being recognised as an up-and-coming writer, one of a new generation of outdoor journalists.

Gina and I regularly chatted about our future prospects. While she enjoyed working together in the hostel and being there for our two young sons, she was keen to go back to nursing at some point. It was what she had trained for, what she was very good at, and it was important that she too should feel fulfilled in her work life.

Working for SYHA had been great but by the time we agreed to publish *Footloose* we knew it was time to move on again. I was pretty confident that I could get enough writing and instructing work to sustain my little family so we began looking around for somewhere to stay. We still had money saved from selling our house in Neilston so with that, and some more from cashing in a couple of insurance policies, we managed to scrape together a deposit on a little bungalow in the nearby village of Kincraig.

We left the employ of SYHA with a heavy heart. It was a lovely organisation and we enjoyed the work although, to be honest, after eight years I was beginning to turn into a kind of Basil Fawlty character. It was definitely time to move on and move on we did. Despite our sadness at leaving SYHA we were excited, optimistic and utterly thrilled to be moving into our own little home in one of the most beautiful areas in the Scottish Highlands.

THE village of Kincraig lies midway between Aviemore and Kingussie with its scattering of houses lying on the shores of Loch Insh, essentially a broadening of the River Spey where the river eases itself across the floodplain of the Insh Marshes, or Insh Meadows as they were previously known.

The village was originally called Boat of Insh and before the modern bridge was built across the Spey, just where it leaves the loch, you had to cross by ferry. The original ferryman's house is still there, nowadays a private dwelling.

Kincraig has a wonderful setting, deep in the shadow of Creag Mhigeachaidh, an outlier of the Feshie hills that boasts the highest natural tree line in the UK. When we moved into the village in May 1982 there was a small shop, a hotel with a bar and another with a highly acclaimed restaurant, and a rather fascinating church. Insh Kirk is owned by the Church of Scotland and its position, on what was once a promontory, is thought to be the oldest continuous Christian worship site in Scotland. Legend suggests that it was originally used for pagan worship and when St Adamnan, the first biographer of St Columba, arrived, he felt inspired to build his own cell there. The present church was erected in 1792. It possesses a very ancient cast bronze bell, possibly dating from the time of St Adamnan, and a stone basin set in one of the windows, probably the font of the earliest church. It stands on Tom Eunan, or Adamnan's

Mount (Eunan being a diminutive form of the saint's name).

Inspired by the village's fascinating history, I did a bit of research, digging out some of the legends and folk tales of the area. One especially intrigued me. It was called the Swan Children of Lir. The legend suggests that the King of Lir in Ireland had two children, a son and a daughter. When they became teenagers his wife suddenly died and he took another woman as his wife. The King's new wife was something of an enchantress and was very jealous of the love the King had for his two children so she cursed them and turned them into swan-children: half people, half swan. The youngsters were destined to fly between Scotland and Ireland for two hundred years, and one of the places they visited in Scotland was a lonely lochside where there were many other swans. An old priest would come down to the shore every morning and ring a bell, summoning the swans to worship and, after prayers, he would feed them. Local legend has it that the old priest was St Adamnan and that Loch Insh was where the Swan Children of Lir would spend each winter. The wonderful thing about this story, as I soon discovered, was that Loch Insh and the neighbouring Insh Marshes are the principal wintering places in Scotland for migrating whooper swans.

Another interesting local church (the twin kirk of Kincraig) is Alvie Church, which stands on the shores of nearby Loch Alvie. It makes a captivating and photogenic scene, set against the backdrop of the rising Monadh Liath, with the light of the low sun casting reflections across the still waters, the shores fringed with birch. It's the archetypal Highland scene, but how many folk are aware of the gory remains that were found in that wee kirk? The Church of Alvie dates from 1380 when a chapel was built on the site of an earlier religious cell attributed to St Drostan. In the late nineteenth century, the building was partially renewed and refurbished and, in the course of the excavations, a grim discovery was made. Below the floor no fewer than 150 skeletons were found lying 'head to head'. The skeletons were re-interred in the burial ground beside the church and a granite stone with an inscription on it was erected over them:

'Buried here, are remains of 150 human bodies, found October 1880, beneath the floor of this church. Who they were, when they lived, how they died, tradition notes not.

Their bones are dust, their good swords rust, their souls are with the saints, we trust.'

Who were these people? How did they die? Were they the fallen of some great battle that history has not recorded? Were they perhaps Jacobites in hiding and for some reason never freed from the hiding place that became their tomb? It seems we will never know for sure and the tiny, quaint and innocent little kirk will forever hold its grim secret.

In the course of my local research, I discovered something about another local relic, the Argyll Stone, a gigantic boulder situated high on the Sgurans ridge above Gleann Einich. The Marquis of Montrose, during the Covenanting wars, was chased by the forces of the Duke of Argyll over the Sgurans and down onto the Muir of Alvie where a fierce battle took place, possibly sometime in the mid seventeenth century. Montrose escaped with a few followers and I wondered if the dead of that battle ended up in Alvie Kirk? It's an interesting thought, a distinct possibility as the Alvie Kirk would have been the consecrated ground closest to the battle on the Moor of Alvie. Some other curious old records claim that, in 1729, Ann Down and Kate Fraser of Kannachil were severely reprimanded for 'prophanation of the Lord's Day in going to the woods for pulling nuts' and in the following year John Meldrum and Alexander McIntyre of Dalnavert got into trouble for 'prophaning the Lord's Day by fishing upon the water of Feshie'.

It didn't take us long to settle in Kincraig, which we decided must be the friendliest village in Scotland. From the day we moved in, we were overwhelmed by kindness and generosity. Strangers would leave little baskets of fresh eggs by our front door and villagers would drop in to introduce themselves and ask if they could help in any way. We didn't have any direct neighbours, as our house was in a fairly recent development of less than a dozen houses beside the Dunachton birchwoods. Only four of those houses had families living in them permanently, the rest were holiday houses or second homes, the curse of the Highlands. Today, 20 per cent of houses in the Cairngorms National Park are second homes, a scandalous state of affairs that effectively means young local folk are priced out of the housing market. It's hardly surprising that many local born and bred folk distance themselves from 'incomers', or 'white settlers' as we were known. There was a strong feeling at the time that people from England or the central belt of Scotland could afford to pay huge amounts of money for property, effectively putting local folk at a distinct disadvantage when buying a house. There was also a suggestion that we white settlers wanted to change the Highlanders' ways to a more urban, faster-paced lifestyle.

When we lived in Aviemore this wasn't an issue as the majority of folk who lived there had moved to the village for work or for the skiing. In Kincraig a sizeable proportion of the small population were retirees, mostly from affluent backgrounds. To make matters worse, the Highland Council, in its wisdom, built a small council estate that was physically separate from the main village. As a result, the two communities rarely mixed. The village community used the church hall as a community hall, but the folk from the council estate wanted a proper village hall in their own part of the village. To their great credit, they campaigned for a long time and eventually their wish was granted, and today the whole village makes full use of the modern, well-appointed village hall.

My first experience of all of this 'white settler' business occurred one warm summer's evening just before we moved into our house in Kincraig. A hillwalking pal, Jeff Faulkner from Aviemore, was a carpenter who put up some shelves for us. When we had finished for the night I suggested we grab a pint of cold beer before heading back to Aviemore. We popped round the corner to the Suie Hotel where I thought there was a public bar. There was, and it was a dark and gloomy place. The barman sat behind the bar reading a newspaper. As we approached he looked up with the greeting, 'What are ye wantin', hairy face?'

Rather taken aback by the welcome I asked if we could have two

1. With my Grandfather and Grandmother
and parents

2. On an early summer
holiday at Dunbar, birthplace
of John Muir, although I
didn't know it at the time.

Photograph by J. & S. Sternstein
GLASGOW W.

3. King's Park Secondary School photo, c1963, I'm in the back row,
third from the left.

4. My first love, long jumping. I became Scottish Junior Champion in 1968.

5. Learning to shot put with John Anderson.

6. A very special day over 45 years ago.
Cutting the cake with Gina.

7. Lomond Mountaineering Club, c1975. I'm at the back,
fifth from the left.

8. During a wonderful Cairngorm to Ben Nevis backpacking trip in 1975.

9. Cameron the Youth Hostel warden at Aviemore SYHA.

10. Gina with Gordon and Gregor cross country skiing.
They're never too young to learn.

11. Seventies climbing pal Jeff Faulkner near the summit of A'Mhaighdean.

12. Long time friend and colleague, Roger Smith, leaving Ben Macdui with Braeriach in the background.

13. On the Robert Louis Stevenson Trail in France with old pal, Peter Lumley.

14. My good friend, mountain guide John Lyall, as we climbed
January Jigsaw on the Buachaille Etive Mor.

15. A favourite shot of Gina at Carnmore
below A'Mhaidghean.

16. On the Matterhorn summit as part of the celebrations of the
125th anniversary of the first ascent by Edward Whymper.

17. Family outing to Yosemite in 1997.

18. Gina, Gregor and me on the summit of Mount Whitney, at the end of the 221 mile John Muir Trail in California.

19. Getting all nostalgic in a favourite howff in Glen Coe,
a place I often frequented in my rock climbing days.

20. Of all the great mountaineers and naturalists I have met, none was more encouraging than my old friend, Tom Weir (with thanks to D.C. Thomson Ltd).

21. The redoubtable Chris Brasher, athlete, journalist, mountaineer, and one of the greatest characters I've ever met (Richard Else with permission).

22. With Chris Townsend after we had completed the GR20 over the mountains of Corsica.

pints of lager? As he poured our drinks he seemed to mellow a bit and asked us if we were up for the fishing?

'No,' I replied. 'I've bought a house here and we were doing a couple of jobs in it before returning home to Aviemore.' He looked at me under thickset eyebrows. 'And where is this new hoose o' yours?' he asked. 'Oh, just around the corner,' I replied, 'opposite the Ossian Hotel.'

He glowered at me again and said with some disdain, 'Oh right, millionaire's row, eh?'

I had heard that description before so I laughed and said something like, 'Apparently, although I don't know any millionaires who live there.'

'And whit do you dae fur a living?' he asked.

'I'm a writer,' I said with some pride. 'I write books, articles for magazines and I write a weekly column in the *Strathie*.'

By this time I had his full attention. He put down the lager, came over to me, stared at me full in the face and said, 'Are you that bugger McNeish?'

7

KINCRAIG EXPLORATIONS

I was aware that not everyone approved of my articles in the weekly *Strathspey and Badenoch Herald* newspaper, a column I went on to write for thirty-two years. I wrote about my experiences on the hills and the local wildlife, but gradually had become more critical of other land users, particularly the huntin', fishin' and shootin' fraternity. This was at a time when many locals still tugged the forelock to landowners and many were still directly or indirectly employed by the lairds. On the face of it my weekly offerings were pretty innocent, but my mild criticisms didn't always win me friends.

I certainly didn't win many friends when I took a strong local stance against the development of the Cairn Gorm ski grounds. The Cairngorm Ski Company wanted to extend the ski area into Lurchers Gully and the corries neighbouring Coire Cas where the main development was. To my mind there was nothing more unsightly than a commercial ski area in the summer months, when the lack of snow exposes the associated environmental carnage and detritus. The thought of the wonderful Northern Corries, Coire an t-Sneachda and Coire an Lochain being subjected to this commercial destruction was more than I could bear. Week after week I wrote against the plans and, while the contributors to the letters column castigated me and demanded I be sacked, I had many supporters. None more so than Dave Morris, who at the time was the local officer of the Nature Conservancy Council (Scotland). Dave was shortly to leave the NCC and become director of Ramblers Scotland and he and I were to work on many environmental campaigns in the future but, for the moment, he managed to convince the local planners that the ski development proposals should be the subject of a public inquiry.

At the inquiry, I was called as a witness to speak against the proposals on behalf of cross-country skiers and ski tourers who used the relatively unspoiled Northern Corries to get away from the razzamatazz, noise and crowds of Coire Cas. My public evidence didn't do me many favours or win me many friends amongst the Aviemore ski supporters and on one occasion, when I took a group of youngsters to Cairn Gorm for a skiing session, a senior official of the development appeared in the car park and at the top of his voice shouted, 'Hey McNeish, get off my fucking mountain.' I didn't think it was the cleverest approach considering all the youngsters I had with me. Despite that little altercation, he and I became friends and Gina eventually nursed him when he spent his final years in St Vincent's Hospital in Kingussie where she worked as a staff nurse.

Despite my controversial newspaper column, we made many friends in Kincraig. We had never experienced being part of a small community before. In Aberdeen, the hostel was virtually isolated within the city. In Aviemore we had made many friends but the unsociable hours we had to work meant that we couldn't really become involved with the community. In Kincraig we settled down to what we considered to be rural bliss. Gordon and Gregor entered the tiny Alvie Primary School, where the head teacher, Mrs Grant, made them both very welcome. They made lots of friends and were soon involved in various after-school activities while Gina managed to get some part-time work as a home help, before becoming a staff nurse in St Vincent's Hospital dementia unit.

I was in my element. Every so often I had to pinch myself. This was exactly the lifestyle I had dreamed of, climbing hills and mountains, watching wildlife and writing about it. I soon developed a routine: Gina and I would see the boys off to school then I would wander out with our two labrador dogs, Bess and Jasper. We would ramble through the neighbouring birchwoods or along the shores of Loch Insh and I would think about my programme for the day – what I would write about or who I had to contact. More often than not I would settle down somewhere with my binoculars and watch waders, or the whooper swans, or tiny weasels hunting rabbit holes. This became the foundational material for my weekly columns and articles.

I also didn't have to travel very far to get into the mountains. The Glen Feshie hills were on my doorstep as were the rolling tops of the Am Monadh Liath and short journeys by car would take me to the start of walks that led into some remote areas of the Highlands, not just the Cairngorms.

The view of Ben Alder down the length of Loch Ericht from the A9 often stirred me on journeys to the south. Much of the time the same view can be dull and grey, as if the waters of the loch merged with the very edge of the world, but when the sun shines on the snow-fringed tops of Ben Alder and the air is clear it's as though the hill is only a couple of miles away. But it isn't.

Ben Alder is a remote hill, a big bastion of a hill that demands a long walk-in, and I reckon it's all the better for that. It turns an ordinary hillwalk into an expedition and gives the mountain an air of isolation, of seriousness. A friend of mine was badly frostbitten during a winter weekend there and two others severely underestimated its remoteness and had to be helicoptered out. You don't mess around with Ben Alder.

The hill's north-eastern extremities can be reached by mountain bike – a long haul along the seemingly endless miles of bulldozed track on the shores of Loch Ericht, past Ben Alder Lodge to Culra bothy; but a far better option if you have the time is to walk in from the north, from Kinloch Laggan, up the length of the River Pattack.

The Pattack is a grand river of intense character. Bubbling, swirling, crashing under a canopy of pines with waterfalls, just north of the Linn of Pattack, which are probably the most impressive in the area, a powerful aquatic display of thundering, crashing waters crowned by an almost permanent rainbow. Throughout the length of the river, other, smaller falls add interest, and tiny coves, bays and pools beckon you for a swim. A good track follows its meandering course through stands of proud old pines until higher up, closer to Loch Pattack, the countryside widens to give good views of Ben Alder, Geal Charn, Beinn a' Chlachair and the Matterhorn-like shape of the Lancet Edge of Aonach Beag.

A short distance from Culra bothy a stream runs down from the high corrie that holds Loch a' Bhealaich Bheithe and joins up with the Allt Chaoil-reidhe which pours down from the Bealach Dubh between Ben Alder and the Lancet Edge. Beyond the loch, a path crosses the craggy Bealach Breabag with another sneaking off westwards to reach the prominent ridge that skirts the rim of the impressive Garbh Choire. After half a mile or so a high-level lochan, the Lochan a' Garbh Choire reflects the scudding clouds and indicates the point to leave the corrie edge and cross the huge, flat plateau, to the summit cairn and trig point at 1,147 metres/3,766 feet. In misty weather, accurate navigation is essential. Ben Alder is a vast, high plateau containing about four hundred acres of ground above the 1,066-metre/3,500-feet contour. Cairngorm-like, it's surrounded by fine corries, particularly those that show their sculptured faces to the east.

My usual descent route from the summit heads north-west via Meall an t-Slugain and down to the Bealach Dubh where an excellent footpath runs back to Culra. There has been some exceptional footpath work carried out on the track and the bothy book at Culra contains many compliments to whoever has sweated and navvied so hard. Ben Alder Estate has a long-standing reputation of kindness and welcome to walkers. It's certainly much appreciated.

I soon came to know the head stalker on Ben Alder Estate. Geordie Oswald was a wonderful character, a real friend to hill-goers and shooters alike. I once interviewed him for a BBC Radio Scotland programme and asked how many stalks had been spoiled by hillwalkers. He gave a surprising answer. 'Not once,' he said with a grin. 'I've never, ever had a stalk spoiled by walkers because I know where the walkers go. I make sure I take the shooting clients somewhere else.' Simple.

On another occasion walking with Geordie, we stopped for a bite to eat. 'What's in your sandwiches, Geordie?' I asked. I was interested in calories and protein and what outdoors folk eat in the hills to sustain them. Geordie's answer once again surprised me.

'Jam,' he proclaimed. 'I've had jam in my sandwiches every day for thirty-five years. 'It makes the bread nice and sappy.'

Another area I became very familiar with when we lived in Kincraig was Glen Feshie. This magnificent place has often been described as the 'jewel of the Cairngorms' and it wears that description with some justification. Lying in the north-west of the Cairngorms National Park, the pine-skirted slopes of the glen rise steeply to the deer-haunted plateau of Am Moine Mhor, a vast Arctic tableland which, in turn, rises to the big Munros of Braeriach, Cairn Toul and Beinn Bhrotain. The area has a long history of people living and working in and around it, and was greatly favoured by Queen Victoria. The natural beauty and mystery of the glen inspired the artist Edwin Landseer and such inspiration is not surprising. There is a sense of timelessness at work here. It's an intriguing thought that some of the older pines, the so-called 'granny' pines, are between 250 and 300 years old so thirty-odd generations of these trees take us back to the end of the last ice age.

These gnarled and knotted old trees are rock hard and anchored deep. Their orange-red trunks contrast vividly with bottle-green foliage and you can feel their antiquity in the rough bark. Nature has woven an immaculate carpet of lichens and mosses on the woodland floor. Juniper and heather live alongside bilberry and cowberry, and wintergreen chickweed and orchids open in the sunlight of summer. It's a beautiful environment that has benefited enormously from positive estate management in recent years under the direction of Conservation Manager Thomas MacDonnell. Red deer numbers have been reduced, browsing sheep have been moved out, and the results have been absolutely astonishing. Today the glen is glistening with new growth and is alive with birds: crested tit, tree pipit, dipper, common sandpiper, skylark, wryneck, jay and crossbill in or near the woodlands, and golden eagle, peregrine, dotterel, ptarmigan, red and black grouse, dunlin, greenshank and ring ouzel on the hills and moorlands. In addition to red and roe deer, the mammals include mountain hare, brown hare, otter, badger, fox, wildcat, weasel, stoat, water vole, red squirrel and moles. Pine martens are resident and wildcats have been seen in the lower glen.

Above Glen Feshie lies the vast sprawling plateau of Am Moine Mhor, or the Great Moss, a vast expanse of stony ridge and green hollows of turf and moss, drained by a profusion of sparkling clear streams. A high tableland like a vast raised moor, it's a favourite feeding place of red deer and reindeer and a haunt of Arctic-type birds like ptarmigan, snow bunting and dotterel. Lying as it does, virtually on my doorstep, it didn't take long to familiarise myself with its lonely solitude: green rather than grey, tending to the gentler end of harsh, a soft pearl in a crown of hard diamonds. Its billowing acres flow south from the Sgurans and the head of Loch Einich over Mullach Clach a' Bhlair to upper Glen Feshie. Bounded on the east by the huge swells of Monadh Mor and Cnapan Mor, its peat-hag ridden heartland is gnawed deep by the River Eidart, a tumultuous watercourse fed by some of the highest streams in the country.

One of the books that inspired me as a youngster was V. A. Firsoff's *On Foot and Ski in the Cairngorms*. Since moving to Kincraig I had read about the old Foxhunter's Path that climbs the hill from the old croft at Achlean in Glen Feshie to the broad col between Sgor Gaoith and Carn Ban Mor. At the top of the path the Am Moine Mhor rolls on, lochans sparkling like all-seeing eyes in the sun.

Within days of arriving in Kincraig I decided to visit this remarkable place with a simple plan: to climb the two remote Cairngorm Munros of Monadh Mor (1,113 metres/3,651 feet), and Beinn Bhrotain (1,157 metres/3,795 feet), returning to Glen Feshie by my outward route – the old Foxhunter's Path to Achlean. It was a big day: about sixteen miles of hard walking. I knew a shorter route was possible from the east, from White Bridge in Glen Dee, particularly when you can ride a mountain bike from Linn of Dee to the slopes of Carn Fiaclach Beag, but I guessed the sense of remoteness of these two hills would be well and truly heightened when you have to cross Am Moine Mhor first.

Below Sgor Gaoith, Loch Einich fills a deep cliff-girt hollow. Directly opposite, across the deep trench, wind-scoured corries pockmark the massive dome of Braeriach, the UK's third highest mountain. Beyond lies the square-cut profile of Cairn Toul, the fifth highest hill in the land. Easing itself south from these great landmarks, the Great Moss forms an addendum to the high tops of the Cairngorms, an afterthought, as though the great landscape architect had finally run out of ideas. The result is an area that is neither moorland nor mountain, but a mixture of both, a high level shallow basin in the cusp of Carn Ban Mor, Mullach Clach a' Bhlair and the relatively diminutive top of Tom Dubh, at 918 metres/3,011 feet. Beyond Tom Dubh's dumpy profile lie the great whalebacks of Monadh Mor and Beinn Bhrotain.

Despite a chill wind, I wandered across the Great Moss in a rather desultory fashion, watching meadow pipits feed their fledglings and listening to the roaring of the red deer rut. On a whim, I climbed to the summit of Tom Dubh and was surprised to find a family of reindeer, the youngsters all spindly legs and boundless energy.

From Tom Dubh I climbed the stony slopes of Monadh Mor, to its long whaleback ridge and followed a footpath to the summit cairn. The highest point is about halfway along the ridge. From here the path continues to a subsidiary top before descending steep slopes to a high bealach known locally as Cadha nam Fiann, the pass of the fair-ones. From there, steep boulder-covered slopes finally lead to Beinn Bhrotain. The local name of this high pass is intriguing and has led the mountaineer and ecologist, Dr Adam Watson, to question the assumed translation of the great corrie that falls down from the pass into Glen Geusachan below. Most authorities suggest that Coire Cath nam Fionn means the corrie of the battle of the Fingalians, the warriors of the legendary Celtic hero Fionn Macumhail, but if the corrie is named after the bealach above it, as would seem likely, then it's simply the corrie of the pass of the Fingalians, and nothing to do with a battle. I suspect the Fingalian link is authentic enough as Beinn Bhrotain is the hill of Brodan, the jet-black hound of Celtic mythology.

Long walks like this were important to me. Exploratory expeditions, they allowed me to peep over horizons and gasp in astonishment at the diversity of landscape that exists within a few miles of where I now lived. In years to come I would visit the Great Moss and its tops numerous times but the initial sense of discovery you get when you first visit an area is very special and can never be repeated. At this stage in my outdoor career I found myself discovering lots of new areas. We had sold our old car and bought our first campervan, the first of many over the years. We would load it up, Gina and I, the boys and two dogs, with all our gear, and trundle off to territories new. Ardnamurchan was a great favourite, as was Torridon and Kintail, but it was our first excursion north of Ullapool that really blew us away.

As we drove north from Ullapool, around the head of Ardmair Bay, we couldn't help notice the landscape changing dramatically, the result of the effects of the geological feature known as the Moine Thrust. West of this line there are fewer rolling hills, no high-level plateaux or mini-mountain ranges. Here the mountains are individual, stark and contrasting. The Torridonian sandstone that they are made from forms a wondrous array of shape and form, the result of millions of years of erosion – some still have their protective caps of quartzite. It's no wonder this whole area has been designated the North-West Highlands Geopark, the first geopark in Scotland. To get the most dramatic impression of this landscape we drove west down the winding road below the craggy outline of Stac Pollaidh to Achnahaird and, just beyond the Brae of Achnahaird, bundled out and gazed back at the rosary of isolated mountain shapes: the hills of Coigach, Stac Pollaidh, Cul Beag and Cul Mor, Suilven, Canisp and Quinag, some of the most dramatic mountains in Britain, and not one of them a Munro.

We camped at Achnahaird where the crofter allowed camping on the big sloping fields that looked inland towards the mountains. It was a wonderful spot to spend a few nights. During the day we beachcombed at Achiltibuie, scrambled on the sea cliffs at Reiff and took long walks along the rugged shoreline of the Rubha Mor peninsula, where we could gaze across the sea towards the dim outline of the Western Isles. But it was the view of those mountains of Coigach, Inverpollaidh, Assynt and Sutherland that really captivated us and remained longest in our memory. As the sun dipped low in the north-west they would turn from yellow to gold to orange and then flame-red, as wondrous a sight as you'll see anywhere in the world. It was some years before I fully familiarised myself with all these montane gems, but that early campervan trip laid the foundation for a long and wonderful love affair with the North West, with Inverpollaidh, Assynt and

Sutherland, the ragged coastline, the haunted lochs and most of all the small, but magnificently formed hills. Let me take you over them . . .

Ben Mor Coigach lies just north of Ullapool, beyond Ardmair, where an extensive wall of weathered Torridonian sandstone commands the northern shore of the bay, a relic of one of the most ancient land masses in the world. Below the sandstone lies a platform of crumpled Lewisian gneiss, said to be well over a thousand million years old, toughened by heat and pressure deep within the earth's core. The long sandstone wall runs slightly south of west to north-east, from Garbh Choireachain to Speicin Coinnich, and is collectively known as Ben Mor Coigach. The hill's protective cap of Cambrian quartzite has long since gone, like many of its neighbours, but the bare bones of this venerable relic still rise straight from the sea to almost 762 metres/2,500 feet: a mile-long wall of seamed buttresses, gullies and cliffs, a living archive of this spinning rock we call earth. While that seaward wall is impressive it's really only a front, a craggy facade that hides an intricate, complex system of peaks, ridges, corries and lochans.

Coigach is a gem of a wild area. Unspoiled and challenging, it expresses itself more fully as you drive further north on the A835. Ben Mor Coigach, at 743 metres/2,437 feet, is the highest summit, but the other main peak of the area, Sgurr an Fhidhleir rises to a sharp and dramatic point about a mile along a broad north-west ridge from Ben Mor. It's a high eyrie of a summit, the culmination point of a huge blade of rock that rises from the bare, soggy moors close to the reflective waters of Lochan Tuath.

The traverse of these two hills brings together all the finer characteristics of a walk that blends sea and mountain in a distinctive combination you only find on Scotland's western seaboard. Indeed, it's perhaps not too fanciful to imagine the traverse of Ben Mor Coigach's long south-west ridge beyond Ardmair Bay as a high-level promenade to Tir nan Og, beyond the shimmering ocean of the Celtic twilight. Add to that the opportunity of gazing across at Stac Pollaidh, one of Scotland's most unlikely mountain icons, and beyond its serrated skyline to the equally unlikely shape of Suilven, and you begin to realise that this is a very special area indeed, perhaps God's own country?

Some years ago, there were huge erosion problems on Stac Pollaidh. Some 30,000 people were visiting it every year, although comparatively few reached the actual summit, which requires a bit of scrambling skill. I remember the erosion problems well; people followed a nasty and dangerous route right up the south face from the roadside car park, culminating in a horrible scree-filled gully in which one woman had sadly fallen and died from her injuries. Following the fatality, the Footpath Trust, a partnership involving Scottish Natural Heritage, Ross and Cromarty Enterprise and the Highland Council, took on the work of extending the path around the west shoulder of the hill, offering a circular route around the mountain which would offer a better descent than the stone-filled gully. Since then the hill has become possibly even more popular.

Stac Pollaidh could be described as the 'perfect miniature'. Drive over the road from Drumrunie and see it appear beyond a tree-lined lochan. On first viewing it makes you gasp. It's impudent in its other-worldliness. Rising from the surrounding moorland it thrusts its jagged crest into the sky with a cocky bravado, dominating everything around it despite its small size. A good footpath circles the hill at about half-height before a subsidiary path lifts you to a high bealach which is the highest point for most folk. To stand on the true summit, to the west of the bealach, calls for a measure of commitment as it is an exposed and rocky scramble, which calls for some skill in route-finding. Most folk are happy enough to sit amongst the rocky pinnacles of this narrow saddle to eat their lunch and soak up the views towards Coigach or west to the Hebrides.

Look north from Stac Pollaidh and one mountain dominates the landscape of Inverpollaidh. I believe Suilven is the uncontested showpiece of Sutherland. From Elphin in the east it can look like the Matterhorn, rising from its bedrock plinth of Lewisian gneiss to a narrowing spire, but from the Lochinver coast, its western sentinel, Caisteal Liath, forms a huge rounded bastion of quartzite-capped sandstone. From Stac Pollaidh, or Cul Mor in the south, its shape changes again into a long, drawn-out sugarloaf, with an obvious depression in the middle: the Bealach Mor, the only break in its fortress-like defences.

You can climb Suilven by several different routes: from Inverkirkaig in the south-west, from Lochinver in the north or from Elphin in the east. Take your choice. My own preference is to be dropped off by car in Elphin, and picked up at the end of the day in Lochinver, a wonderful through-route of some sixteen wild miles. This route also offers the adventurous opportunity of a scrambling ascent of the mountain's eastern prow, Meall Beag. This east-west traverse of Suilven is a day you'll never forget.

Just beyond a bridge over the Ledmore River, just north of Elphin, a stalker's path runs along the north shore of the Cam Loch. About halfway along the lochside, just beyond the crossing of the Abhainn a' Chroisg, the path begins to fade and its faint outline can be difficult to follow through the heather as it bears north onto the long ridge of Meall na Braclaich. Once on the rounded crest, the route becomes clearer and the great spire of Suilven lies ahead. To the north, the long trench of Lochan Fada reflects the slopes of Canisp and to the south, across the waters of the Cam Loch and Loch Veyatie, lies the craggy outline of Cul Mor. As you approach Suilven its dominance gradually fades into something less portentous, the angle of its eastern slope lessens and it's with some relief that you realise that while still steep, it's eminently climbable. By threading together a variety of ledges you can scramble up to the broad summit of Meall Beag surprisingly easily, but don't relax too quickly – the main difficulties still lie ahead. Suilven doesn't submit its crown quite so easily.

From Meall Beag the ridge narrows appreciably until you are greeted by a deep crack in the sandstone strata. Step across this fissure and continue until you reach a sudden and sheer 100-foot drop with no obvious point of descent. This is a very serious obstacle, but it can be turned by descending steep ground on the north side of the ridge to where a faint line can be found traversing west into the dank and gloomy bealach below Meall Mheadhonach. From this dripping recess a faint path takes a zig-zag route up the steep slopes of Meall Mheadhonach from where more steep, rocky slopes eventually give way to grassy slopes dropping to the safety of the Bealach Mor. As if to offer some assurance, an ancient drystone wall crosses the ridge at this point, pointing the way of the eventual descent route down a steep gully. If a wall can be built down the gully, it shouldn't prove too difficult to scramble. Easy grassy slopes now lead to the summit of Caisteal Liath, a rounded dome of a place with breathtaking views of mountain, moor and sea. Enjoy the panorama, a visual feast from the mountains of Assynt, the delectable outline of Quinag, the great massif that runs from Seana Braigh to Beinn Dearg, the mountains of Inverpollaidh and the coastal hills of Coigach. The descent route follows the wall down the northern gully of the Bealach Mor: pass the western outflow of Loch na Gainimh and find a stalker's path which crosses the Abhainn na Clach Airigh and continues down the glen towards Glencanisp Lodge and the track to Lochinver.

To the north of Suilven lie the long boulder-covered slopes of Canisp. A Scottish Mountaineering Club guidebook of the thirties describes the 2,779-feet mountain as 'uninteresting' but relents slightly by suggesting, 'as it is in the midst of so many striking and shapely hills it forms a fine viewpoint.' Mmm . . . it's exactly because it is such a fine viewpoint that Canisp is anything but uninteresting.

The ascent of Canisp is simplicity itself. From the head of Loch Awe on the A837 Ullapool to Durness road the hill rises in a long, slightly curving ramp to its summit whose slopes then fall precipitously on three sides. It's a long and steady pull from the road, over swampy, grassy ground leading to drier, shattered screes and slabs of Lewisian gneiss, some of the oldest rock in the world. Keep well to the left of the ridge and enjoy the drama of the Inverpollaidh landscape as it unfolds below you. As this low-lying landscape opens up, its topography becomes more and more astonishing. The bumps and hillocks and ridges are underscored and pockmarked by dozens of pools and lochans, and several long and linear lochs, angled in exact parallels, slash their watery course across the mottled landscape. On the far edge of this watery wilderness the spired peaks of Cul Mor dominate the curiously primeval outline of Stac Pollaidh and as you climb higher the fortress-like shape of Suilven dramatically appears out of the west, rising on its rocky plinth from the shores of

Loch na Gainimh to a series of castellated turrets and spires – one of the most impressive landforms in Scotland.

On one early spring visit, over the bump of Meall Diamhain and onto the final summit slopes, our eyes were led beyond Suilven, beyond the immediate coastline, to the distant Trotternish ridge of Skye and beyond to the blue hills of Harris, shimmering on the far horizon. Further north, beyond the mass of peaks and ridges that is Quinag, lay the conical outline of Ben Stack and the snow-covered ridge of Arkle. To the east, snow sparkled on Conival and Ben More Assynt and further south row upon row of mountains glinted white below a long layer of shredded cumulus.

Just beyond the summit cairn of Canisp lies a large stone-built shelter and it was good to settle down for a few minutes out of the wind and grab something to eat. I couldn't sit still for long though, aware that this hill, while lacking in any kind of spectacular features, is one of the finest viewpoints in the country. I wanted to gulp it all down, as much of it as possible, to store it in the camera of the mind, ready to be projected, re-focussed and enjoyed any time I wanted.

The final hill on this long montane rosary is Quinag, a mini-mountain range that has become a great favourite of mine over the years. Approaching Kylesku from the north, the first glimpse can be intimidating. On dour days of scudding cloud she can look distinctly menacing, the main backbone of the mountain shy and retiring, hidden away by the perspective of the land behind steep, barrel-shaped buttresses of terraced rock. From the Lochinver road, in the west, that retiring ridge becomes the dominant feature of the mountain, a three-mile wall of Torridonian sandstone with a splintered quartzite crest. In the fiery light of a winter sunset she can look fierce and distinctly threatening, but given a long summer's day, this old girl of the far north-west shows her kindly side and all her threats melt away. With a high-level start, obvious paths and wide-ranging views, the ridge-walk to her three Corbett summits makes one of the best high-level excursions in the north.

Shaped like an elongated euro sign, with those steep buttresses forming the ends of the two upper prongs, the mountain's saving grace, as far as walkers are concerned, is that lower prong, which, unlike the other two, fades out into a long and gentle ridge and offers easy access to the hill's backbone. Unusually for a Corbett, Quinag boasts three summits: Sail Gorm (776 metres/2,545 feet), the highest point on the top prong of the euro; Sail Gharbh (808 metres/2,650 feet) on the middle prong and Spidean Coinich (764 metres/2,506 feet) on the southern one. Indeed, it's this southern top that is supposed to resemble the spout of a bucket, giving the hill the name Cuinneag, Gaelic for a narrow-mouthed water stoup. For years we knew the hill as Queenaig, giving it a royal and female association. Old habits die hard and I still think of the hill as a 'her'. Pronounce it 'coon-yak'.

A parking space on the A894, at an elevation of almost 250 metres/820 feet, makes a good starting point but don't be tempted by the footpath that appears to run up into the Coire Chornaidh. We met a couple on the summit of Spidean Coinich and their guidebook had told them to follow a path into the upper corrie from where they could climb on to Spidean Coinich. They looked a little shaken by their experience! A far better way to reach Spidean Coinich is to follow the gently curving east ridge over grass and quartzy slabs to a small rocky top. Beyond this, steeper rocky slopes lead to the rounded summit. A steep descent down a narrow ridge is the highlight of the day – high above the watery wastes that form the hinterland of the Eddrachillis Bay coast.

On the other side of the ridge the dark waters of Lochan Bealach Cornaidh reflect the steep slopes of Sail Gharbh, which, in a few hours, will be your final top of the day. The ridge then drops to the broad Bealach a' Chornaidh from where a well-used path zig-zags up to the ridge just east of a knobbly top. Skirting the top itself, the path traverses its north-east slopes and descends to another bealach before climbing the long ridge out to Sail Gorm, the second summit of the day. With the waters of Loch a' Chairn Bhain and Kylesku below your feet, the whole of the north stretches past the Schiehallion-like form of Ben Stack to Arkle and Foinaven and distant Cranstackie. From Sail Gorm you have to retrace your steps to the Sail Gharbh ridge but it's no hardship, with views of massive Suilven and the Inverpollaidh hills illustrating why this is a landscape without equal.

It's an easy stroll out to the third summit, Sail Gharbh, before descending back to the low point on the ridge where the best route of descent is to simply drop down the steep slopes to Lochan Bealach Cornaidh. A rough path down the corrie makes a grand end to the day – a downhill stroll amid the truly regal surroundings of Scotland's far north-west.

8

WEIR'S WAYS

When I arrived home after one particular visit to the North-West, Gina told me I'd had a visitor. 'Who was it?' I asked, and she replied with a twinkle in her eye. 'A wee man and his wife. He was wearing a red bobble cap and his nose was the same colour as the bobble.'

I knew immediately who she was referring to: Tom Weir and his wife Rhona. They had been staying at the Scottish Ladies Climbing Club hut at Milehouse near Loch Insh, a little hut that neighbours the late Clive Freshwater's Loch Insh Watersports Centre. Clive had told them I had just moved to Kincraig. Inclement weather had prevented them heading to the tops so they had decided to come and say hello. Fortunately, Gina had the good sense to tell them to come back in the evening for some supper, and what a glorious evening it was. Tom was highly enthusiastic and encouraging about my writing and we became firm friends. In many ways, he became a much-valued mentor, especially when, years later, I found myself following in his footsteps on my own faltering route into television. But during that precious evening I was more than content to simply sit at the feet and listen to a great man whose life had been dedicated to conserving the wildlife and landscape of Scotland, a life that had been compared to that of Scotland's greatest ever export, John Muir.

A mutual friend, Bob Aitken, while suggesting he didn't particularly believe in reincarnation, had pointed out to me on one occasion that there were only a matter of days between the death of John Muir and the birth of Tom Weir. Indeed, the two men lived for wild places and wildlife, both men sang the praises of wild land in their prolific writings and influenced their conservation. I suspect it had never entered Tom's head that he could be the reincarnation of anyone, never mind the great John Muir but, coincidentally, just a couple of years ago when Tom's widow Rhona invited me to unveil a statue of Tom in Balmaha on the shores of his beloved Loch Lomond, she said a curious thing. 'I've been watching your television programmes,' she said with a grin, 'and I'm beginning to think you must be a reincarnation of Tommy.' I couldn't have received a bigger or finer compliment.

The truth of the matter is that Tom Weir was undoubtedly a one-off and, as he inspired a generation, including me, he in turn had been inspired by the writings of the Highland naturalist Seton Gordon and the mountaineer Frank Smythe.

Through his books, television programmes, radio shows and, in particular, his 46-year-long monthly column in the *Scots Magazine*, Tommy shared his experience and passion for Scotland with countless others, both young and old. At one time, in the sixties, I thought I might be the only teenager in Scotland to have a subscription to the *Scots Magazine*, which I bought purely for the delight of following Tom Weir's 'My Month'.

He had been born and brought up in Springburn in the north of Glasgow, and left school at 14 to work as an apprentice grocer in Cowlairs Co-operative Society. During this time, he was a member of the Springburn Amateur Boxing and Wrestling Club, learned to play the drums and later formed his own band. His sister, Molly, went on to find celebrity status as an actress with *Life with the Lyons* as the canny Scots lass of the Ben and Bebe show. Meanwhile Tom took an evening course in writing at Glasgow University and joined the Glasgow YMCA Camera Club where he made full use of the club's darkroom to learn how to develop film and enlarge the negatives. It was probably a notice in a local newspaper that had the biggest impact in Tom's career. 'Do you have an aim in life?' it asked. 'If so what are you doing to achieve it? The Pelman system of mind and memory training could help you.'

In Tom's own words he 'paid for a course that did me far more good than I ever expected'. Tom completed his Pelmanism course and harboured ambitions as a freelance journalist or, more pointedly, 'wanted to be a naturalist and writer on Scotland like Seton Gordon'. His sister Molly taught him shorthand and how to type

126

and, according to Rhona, charged him two and sixpence per lesson.

After World War II service in the Royal Artillery, Tom worked as a surveyor for the Ordnance Survey before beginning a full-time career as a climber, writer and photographer. He led the kind of life that most folk could only dream of (Rhona once said he was the only married bachelor she had ever known), but that's not to say it was an easy life. As someone who has followed a similar course for over forty years I'm well aware of the difficulties of making a living as an outdoors writer and broadcaster. Tom had the advantage of a wife who worked full-time as a schoolteacher and once told me that he found it difficult to make ends meet until television came along. It was television that gave Tom his biggest audience and allowed him to promote his beloved Scotland in a way that he had never thought possible. That successful television career began with a series of short five-minute slots about the Scottish countryside but his first producer, Russell Galbraith, soon realised that he had discovered a gem of a broadcaster. The short slots soon became 30-minute programmes and *Weir's Way* was born.

Tom was a natural broadcaster. I always reckoned his greatest skill was his ability as a storyteller. He could captivate an audience, and loved to tell his tales. Indeed, one of his early television producers, Dermot McQuarrie, told me that the problem with working with Tom was that he was almost too knowledgeable. Dermot described filming Tom as he interviewed a crofter in the Western Isles when making a film about Bonnie Prince Charles.

'And this was the house where Prince Charles Edward Stuart and Flora MacDonald sheltered before setting sail for Skye when the Prince was on the run from the Duke of Cumberland's forces after the battle of Culloden,' said Tom to the crofter. The crofter looked at Tom and muttered 'aye!' There was little more he could add, but it didn't take Tom long to learn the skills of interviewing and he had a wonderful way of putting people at their ease. He was completely unthreatening, a friendly wee man with a red bobble cap and beery nose (although he rarely drank alcohol), who simply liked to blether about Scotland. But Tom wasn't always comfortable in his role as a popular broadcaster. At first he was very apprehensive. He had only the vaguest notion of what he should do but that difficulty was apparently resolved for him. He had a phone call from a rather brusque director who told Tom exactly what he wanted. 'We'll begin with you working at your typewriter, show your house and where you live, then you'll tell us what these programmes are going to be about. We only have a few hours to shoot each story, so we've got to work fast.' Tommy described it as 'very good fun, slap-happy stuff.'

'There was no forward planning,' he later wrote. 'A telephone call one day would tell me the camera team was available the next, so I always had to have a story up my sleeve, and would read it to the director as we motored to the location. Over a few months we shot about a dozen films, much of it in the cold grey of a normal Scottish winter. Uncomfortable yes, but it didn't worry me unduly, the truth being that I didn't think the film would ever be shown. I regarded the experience as an apprenticeship, which might be useful to this old dog if I could learn a few new tricks.' When Tom was given the broadcast dates he wanted to run away and hide. He described them as 'home-spun', and in a sense they were. Simplicity was the key, Tom either talking directly to the camera or chatting to a variety of country folk, two television skills in which he excelled.

From the comfort of this digital video age it's very easy to be critical of the broadcast quality of the programmes, but it's important to remember that the film cameras used in the mid-seventies were extremely bulky and heavy in comparison with the tiny lightweight video cameras that are used today. I frequently go off to film a television walk with only one other person, a camera operator who also records sound. In Tom's day there would have been a whole team of people: a camera operator, a focus puller, a sound recordist, a director and probably a secretary and a runner too. Not only was the equipment heavy and complicated but it required large batteries to keep it all working, batteries that required charging every night.

Tom Weir's personality made up for any misgivings about broadcast quality, and even after a thirty-odd-year gap between the last of his shows and today he still sounds enthusiastic and knowledgeable, friendly and interesting, the key points that made his programmes so successful. They were broadcast between 1976 and 1987, starting with compilations of the short initial films he had made for Russell Galbraith, and followed by rather more ambitious half-hour *Weir's Way* films 'which had their own continuity, made on the very best filmstock'. No scriptwriters were employed, Tom wrote the storylines himself – tales of Rannoch Moor and Glen Coe, historical events and the opening of the West Highland Way, amongst others.

Weir's Way was hugely popular and more programmes, but this time with a nautical flavour, followed on. *Weir's Aweigh* saw Tom visit Scotland's remoter islands, beginning at Tayvallich on Loch Sween as gateway to the Sound of Jura, then west to Barra, Mingulay, Eriskay, Vatersay and back east by the Garvellachs and the whirlpool of the Corryvreckan. Most of the sailing was done on Graham Tiso's yacht with Graham, an old friend, doing the skippering. The whole series was filmed in just two weeks.

Finally, Tom went off to trace the footsteps of Charles Edward Stuart, the Prince in hiding. This was a massive journey that began on Culloden Moor and visited Knoydart, Glen Shiel, Glen Moriston, Glen Affric and Ben Alder, before setting off to the Hebrides once again, tracing the complicated route through the Hebrides before returning to the mainland and Loch nan Uamh, from where the beleaguered Prince eventually returned to France.

One of the highlights of *Weir's Way* for me was when Tom interviewed the outdoors pioneer and Clydeside crane driver Jock Nimlin and Sir Robert (Bob) Grieve, who at the time was Chair of the Highlands and Islands Development Board. The three men sat beside a crackling fire on a bank by Loch Lomond and chatted naturally about their love of wild places, about outdoor politics and their own very different careers. It was magical television, and it was an extremely simple format.

There was little doubt that Tom was immensely proud of Scotland and believed it should be an independent nation. In his final book, *Weir's World – An Autobiography of Sorts*, he wrote:

'I am in the position I think, to make comparisons with other countries. The only thing I am disappointed in is that we don't run our own affairs as does Norway. We have the resources, and history shows we have the people. England has its own problems for its fifty million or so to contend with. With only five million Scots we can manage ours, and I think the same goes for Wales. I hope I shall live long enough to see it happen, and another age of enlightenment dawn.'

Tom Weir wrote about a country that was changing fast. A land that had come through the war; a country that enjoyed the fruits of a socialist union that had created a welfare system and a national health service that were the envy of the world; a country in which people were leaving the glens to live and work in towns and cities; a nation where people had more time to spend on leisure pursuits and where the hills, once silent, now echoed to the voices of burgeoning numbers of hillwalkers, climbers and tourists.

During that first meeting at my home in Kincraig, Tom suggested that his generation had enjoyed the best of Scotland's hills and mountains. 'I treasure memories of spending time with families like the Macraes of Carnmore in Letterewe or the Scotts at Luibeg in the Cairngorms. The glens are emptier now that they have gone. The hills weren't so busy then and people weren't rushing to climb Munros and Corbetts.'

Tom never did climb all the Munros, despite being an excellent all-round mountaineer. He said he had been to the top of most Munros, but preferred to climb only those he liked best, enjoying the whole experience of the sky, the lochs, trees, birds, flowers, animals: the spiritual as well as the physical. Indeed, one of his favourite hills was a mere 142 metres/465 feet in height. Duncryne, close to his home in Gartocharn, is known fondly as the Dumpling. 'I used to climb Duncryne every day,' he once said in an interview, 'sometimes even at midnight.' He was asked if this was his favourite place in Scotland. 'No,' he replied, 'that honour goes to Glen Lyon. It is a beautiful place. I call it 'the three L's' – the loveliest, the longest and the loneliest. I like to walk there because of the loneliness.'

Although Tom and Rhona Weir lived in Gartocharn for most of their married life, they weren't averse to moving elsewhere. Indeed, on the occasion they came to visit me they were thinking of moving to Kincraig – Tom was captivated by the diverse birdlife in Strathspey and Badenoch and the Arctic plateaux of the high, rolling Grampians.

When I was first offered some work on television I spoke to Tom about it, looking for advice. 'Make sure you have a good film crew,' he advised me after complaining that the crew he had been filming with stopped work at 5p.m. on the dot, no matter where they were. 'And make sure they're fit enough to keep up with you on the hill,' he added with a grin.

Tom Weir's successes were impressive: an OBE, president of the Scottish Mountaineering Club, followed by the prestigious Lifetime Achievement Award from the John Muir Trust, but Tom wasn't always the avuncular, genial character that appeared on television. He had opinions, and strong opinions too, and he was a prodigious campaigner when it came to fighting for Scotland's wild places. He could be a wee terrier when he wanted to be.

Along with his great friend, W. H. (Bill) Murray, they fought a scheme to dam upper Glen Nevis for hydro-electric purposes and Tom later fought a similar proposed development for the wonderfully wild corrie above Craig Royston on Loch Lomondside. He was also a fierce and proud defender of the rituals and heritage of his beloved Scottish Mountaineering Club as I would find out to my cost.

Few mountaineers or naturalists will ever exhibit a greater passion for the wild places of Scotland as Tom Weir did, and his television programmes are fondly remembered for his unbridled enthusiasm and his ability to communicate his love of the bens and glens. Even today, a decade after his death, he is still warmly and fondly remembered by many people and the DVDs of his television programmes still sell well. When I first heard some people wanted to erect a statue of him I wondered what he would have thought of the idea? To find out I asked his wife, Rhona.

'I think he would have been delighted,' she bubbled enthusiastically into the phone. 'He would have been thrilled that people remembered him because he loved people and I think his legacy was this – he was good at inspiring people. He had a great rapport with people. And I think he left behind something rather special. He always believed that anyone, from any background, could achieve anything if they had vision.'

Tom had vision in plenty. From humble beginnings in tenement life in Springburn he went on to travel far afield. In 1950 he took part in the first post-war Himalayan expedition. In 1952, he was one of the first to explore the mountains of Nepal and northern India. He also climbed in Greenland above the Arctic Circle, in Norway, Morocco, Iran, Syria and Kurdistan, but his heart was always in the Scottish hills and glens. And that's how he'll always be remembered. As Scottish as the heather below his boots.

Supporters for the Tom Weir statue included broadcasters Stuart Cosgrove, Martel Maxwell, Tom Morton, Mike Harding and Muriel Gray and Christina McKelvie MSP and on a dark and dour December day at the end of 2014 a huge crowd of Tom Weir fans gathered in Balmaha to see the statue unveiled. Almost everyone wore a red bobble cap, knitted specially for the occasion. Folk singer Jimmie Macgregor and I were to do the honours but we had a wee chat beforehand and agreed that Rhona should be on stage with us to actually do the job. She did it magnificently. When I asked her to say a few words to the gathering she said she was delighted to see so many people were wearing woollen hats. 'Tom always thought wearing a warm hat was important,' she said. 'You lose most of your body heat through your head and that can lead to hypothermia. And I can let you in to a wee secret today,' she said with a cheeky smile. 'Tommy often wore his woolly hat in bed.'

While Tommy's public persona was that of a benevolent uncle, he had a much more serious and curmudgeonly side to his character. He could be determined when he wanted, an attribute that stood him in good stead when fighting conservation battles. As a proud member of the Scottish Mountaineering Club he delighted in its history and heritage. On one outing we had together on the hills of

Moidart, he asked me why I wasn't a member of 'the club'. I told him I wasn't particularly a club person, I wasn't a team-player and enjoyed my own company on the hill but he insisted that I should join. 'I'll propose you,' he said, 'and we'll find someone to second you.'

I didn't think much more of it but one day Hamish Brown rang me with a bit of gossip. It had been the weekend of the SMC Annual Dinner, a Masonic-type affair that was proud of its tradition of being a male-only event. Indeed, the SMC at that time didn't allow female members, a rule that Hamish fundamentally disagreed with. Every year the club sends out invitations to the chairmen of 'kindred clubs' and, unbeknown to the organisers of the dinner, the Chair of one of England's most prominent mountaineering clubs happened, for the first time, to be a woman.

The invitation was for the 'Chair' of the club and a friend, and there were red faces all round when two females appeared to take their place of the top table of this traditionally male-only function.

I was amused by the story and, at Hamish's suggestion, wrote an article suggesting that perhaps the SMC should haul itself into the twentieth century and open their membership up to some of the excellent female mountaineers of the nation.

A few days after the story appeared my telephone rang. It was Tommy. 'I've just read your piece about the club,' he said. 'Remember I said I would nominate you for membership? Well forget it,' and he rammed the phone down on me. He didn't speak to me for two years.

In the course of various meetings and days out with Tommy, I got to know his producer at STV, Dermot McQuarrie. When Tom eventually decided to stop making television programmes, Dermot suggested to the great and good at STV that I should replace him, but they had other ideas. A cheeky blonde-haired lassie with her own production company called Gallus Besom had got there before me and Muriel Gray's wonderful series, *The Munro Show*, changed hillwalking in Scotland in a way that I could never have done. Muriel ably demonstrated that you didn't have to be a burly bloke with a beard to enjoy the hills. The hills and mountains were for everyone, male or female, fit or not-so-fit, young and old. I reckon that between Hamish Brown and Muriel Gray, hillwalking in Scotland was changed forever.

My own broadcasting career would come later, but it actually began in a small way when I was interviewed by a radio producer called Murdoch McPherson from BBC Scotland. Murdoch was Head of Sport at BBC Radio Scotland and a former Church of Scotland minister, but I was never sure if his heart was in mainstream sport. He also edited a live Saturday morning radio show called *Leisure Trail*, an hour-long programme that covered everything from gardening to mountaineering. The show was presented by a motoring correspondent of the *Glasgow Herald* called Ross Finlay, but Murdoch loved nothing better than to take time from his sports editing duties and head off to the countryside to interview someone for *Leisure Trail*.

He came to visit us in Kincraig where we took a walk through the birch woods to record a piece about a book I'd just written, *Backpacker's Scotland*, published by Robert Hale. It was a good interview and we chatted long into the evening about mountains, wildlife and man's place in the great outdoors. I must have impressed Murdoch in some way because a few days later he rang me up and told me that Ross Finlay was taking a short break from the programme. Would I like to stand in? It was an opportunity I couldn't turn down. It would mean travelling to Glasgow on a Friday, staying overnight with my mother and going across to Broadcasting House in Queen Margaret Drive for 6a.m. The programme ran from 7 to 8a.m. so there wasn't much time for rehearsals. Essentially, I had an hour to have a look at the script and chat to the various regular contributors: gardeners Sid Robertson and Jim McColl, angler Roderick Wilkinson and Jimmie Black, who read out amusing extracts from the local papers.

It was a great team and we had a lot of fun but things changed as soon as the 'live' light went on. It seemed as if the Reverend Murdoch McPherson had a Jekyll and Hyde character. On first appearance, he was the nicest guy in the world, but as soon as we were on air he became nervous and ill at ease, often rude and impatient.

Bearing in mind this was the first time I had presented a live radio show he showed me no mercy. In the middle of my first telephone interview he roared at me through my headphones to tell me the question I'd just asked was stupid. Fortunately, the interviewee couldn't hear him. By the end of the show I was a nervous wreck. I had to finish by announcing a trail for the Saturday afternoon sports programme when the highlight of the afternoon would be the women's Wimbledon tennis final between Andrea Jaeger of the US and Martina Navratilova of Czechoslovakia.

As soon as I saw the script I had a horrible feeling I was going to screw up on the pronunciation of the Czech player's name and by the time I reached the end of the programme, thanks to Murdoch's constant interventions, I was as nervous as a kitten. But I had nothing to lose so I went for it with a feigned confidence.

'And before we go let me remind you that this afternoon's *Sportsound* will feature the Wimbledon women's tennis final between the American Andrea Jaeger and the current champion Martina Nat ... Nat ... Natratilova! And we'll be with you again next week at 7a.m. here on BBC Radio Scotland for another wander along the leisure trail. Bye bye for now ...'

No sooner had the theme music stopped than Murdoch stormed into the studio shouting, 'My God, she's only the greatest tennis player in the world and you can't even pronounce her bloody name.' The others thought it was very funny but I was convinced that I had completely fluffed my chances. In those days, the BBC canteen didn't open until nine on a Saturday so we had an arrangement where we would all troop across Great Western Road to the Grosvenor Hotel at the corner of Byres Road where we were treated to a slap-up breakfast. By the time we sat down at the table Murdoch had asked if I was okay for next week.

Interestingly, it was during that meal that Jimmie Black let it slip that Ross Finlay was taking a break from the programme due to nervous exhaustion. He couldn't cope with Murdoch's mood swings. Ross never did come back to the show and I inherited his role by default. I presented the programme for a few years until Murdoch resigned from the BBC to pursue a career in public relations. Tragically he died a short time later, after falling down a flight of stairs in the office where he had gone to work.

When Murdoch McPherson resigned, the BBC decided to drop *Leisure Trail* and in some ways I felt quite relieved. Driving to Glasgow on a Friday, staying there overnight so I could be in Broadcasting House early the next morning, and spending all Saturday morning driving home again, I felt I was running short of time. I was spending a lot of time on *Footloose* and had been asked to organise the activities at an outdoor centre in nearby Newtonmore. Craigower Lodge was a privately-owned centre and the owner, Ian McAllister, had a background in catering. While visiting him about doing some instructional work I realised that he had absolutely no knowledge of outdoor activities. We had a long chat and he asked me if I would run them for him. It also involved a little bit of admin work, hiring instructors and spending a bit of time in the off-season drumming up business in schools, mainly in Glasgow, Edinburgh and Aberdeen. Against my better judgement, I said I would give it a go and we agreed a fee.

I wasn't all that confident I would have the time to deal with all the bits and pieces of work I had committed to and I was well aware I had a young family and how vital it was that I spent a good amount of quality time with them. I was also aware that the life of a freelance instructor-cum-outdoor writer would be a feast or a famine existence and, when an opportunity for work came along, you had to accept and worry about how you would deal with it later. That's how it was and I'm sure every freelancer can sympathise. Despite my concerns, I soon settled in to an exhausting but reasonably satisfactory regime. I would get up at six, grab a coffee and write until about eight thirty. I'd then have a bite of breakfast and head off to Craigower Lodge where I'd teach hillwalking skills, skiing or orienteering until five fifty. I'd get home about six, spend an hour with the boys, then write again until about nine thirty or 10p.m. Somewhere deep inside a voice kept telling me this kind of routine wasn't sustainable, but I did manage to keep it going for about three years.

Footloose wasn't exactly setting the heather on fire, even after we changed it from bi-monthly to monthly, which certainly increased my workload. During one of our regular management meetings, Pete and Don Philpott suggested I hire an assistant editor. I wasn't earning a lot of money for the work I was putting in and wasn't at all sure we could afford another regular outlay, but I approached a potentially good writer from Lancashire who had contributed a number of features for us. He worked in one of the outdoor shops in Manchester and was as keen as mustard. When I asked him if he would be interested in writing regularly for us, and in the position of deputy editor, he jumped at the chance. His name was Chris Townsend.

Chris was a long-distance backpacker and a fellow member of the Backpackers Club. We met up at one of the Camping and Outdoor Leisure Association shows in Harrogate and I was impressed by his enthusiasm and dedication. He had a degree in English from Lampeter College in Wales but wanted to spend as much of his working life as possible in something associated with the outdoors. In many ways, he was a mirror image of myself.

I soon found myself working flat out. As well as editing *Footloose* and working at Craigower Lodge, I was also writing a weekly column for my local newspaper, the *Strathspey and Badenoch Herald*, which paid me the grand fee of £20 a week. Any spare moments went to writing a book on backpacking skills. An Irishman by the name of Turlough Johnston, who lived in Sweden, had approached me and asked me to write *The Backpackers' Manual*, a book he wanted to publish in several languages. Working on the freelance theory that you could never afford to turn down a job I accepted the offer but soon began to feel highly pressured. What was worse was the fact that I wasn't getting out on the hills. Here I was teaching others how to do it, and writing about it, promoting it to all and sundry, but not actually having the time to get out there and do it for myself.

One of my neighbours happened to notice that I was under a bit of pressure. Jock Lamb had been a Territorial Army Colonel and he had dealt with management issues all his working life. He was now retired and was the session clerk in our local church. He popped in to see me and very apologetically suggested that he had been in a similar situation when he was younger and although working flat out may seem to be the best thing I could do for my young family it was far more important to spend as much time with them as I could, while I could. As he gently shared his wise advice I knew, deep in my knower, that he was right. Something had to give and I didn't want that 'something' to be my relationship with my family. I greatly appreciated Jock's wisdom and kindness but, at the time, didn't know what to do about it.

Gina and I discussed the matter at length and she admitted that she was concerned about me. She knew I needed to get on the hill on a regular basis to revitalise and refresh me, to keep me grounded, and she felt I should give up one of the jobs I was doing. The problem was this: although I had several jobs on the go I didn't earn a lot of money from any. Losing even one meant a large hole in our income. Eventually, I decided I would stop editing *Footloose*. It took up a lot of time and I wasn't earning a lot of money from it. It was my baby though, and it was a real wrench to let it go, but I knew that Chris Townsend, who had become a close friend, was more than capable of taking on the editorship. I phoned Peter Lumley in Newcastle and told him I was resigning. Peter took it calmly and understood the problem. He told me we wouldn't make a big deal out of it and he and his wife Kate would come up to Kincraig the following week with the necessary legal papers for me to sign away my shares in the company. 'Book a table at the Ossian Hotel,' he said. 'We won't make a wake of it.'

I thought I would feel relieved but I wasn't. More and more I grew worried about earning a living. A few weeks later, Ian McAllister announced he was going to sell Craigower Lodge and I realised that freelance working is like walking on eggshells. There is a very slim divide between success and failure and it's often the decisions of other people that can drop you over the edge. My idyllic world had grown a few shades darker. Every morning I would wake with a black cloud hovering over me. In the course of the day, the cloud would sink and threaten to envelop me. I began to lose confidence in my writing and without income from both *Footloose* and Craigower Lodge I found myself scrabbling around, looking for any kind of job. I took on a role selling advertisements for the local paper, the

Strathie, and realised almost immediately that I was no salesman. Then suddenly, out of the blue, fate lent a hand. I had a telephone call from Roger Smith, the editor of the *Great Outdoors* magazine in Glasgow.

To this day, I can't remember why Roger phoned me. *Footloose* and the *Great Outdoors* were competitors and, although Roger was still a good friend, we didn't have a lot of contact. In the course of our conversation, he took the opportunity of asking how things were with *Footloose*. I told him I had resigned and was looking for work. There was a momentary silence on the phone before he asked me to hang on for a moment while he transferred the line. Within a minute or so another voice came on the phone. 'Hi Cameron, my name is Duncan Kirk and I'm the managing director of Holmes McDougall Ltd. Roger tells me you've resigned from *Footloose* and might be looking for a similar role. As you know we also publish *Climber and Rambler* Magazine. We're hoping to employ a deputy editor. Would you be interested?'

Was I interested? Most certainly I was. We arranged to meet at the company's office in St Vincent Street in Glasgow the following week. Could my life be about to change again?

9

ACCIDENTS AND RESCUES

I had been an avid reader of *Climber and Rambler* for years. The magazine was originally published in Castle Douglas by Ron Butchart, its first editor, before being bought by Holmes McDougall, part of the huge Lonrho group. Butchart died and the editorship was taken on by a Lancastrian school teacher and climber called Walt Unsworth who, virtually single-handed, turned it into a commercial success.

The name of the magazine was causing some concern with the publishers. Walt Unsworth used to joke that *Climber and Rambler* sounded more like a rose growers' magazine and with the publication of sister title the *Great Outdoors*, considerations arose that perhaps there should be clearer boundaries between the two. However, while TGO tended to cater for all walkers, with an initial emphasis on low-level walking, Walt was adamant that he didn't want to lose the more serious hillwalking content of C&R. The company decided to re-design the title, change the contents slightly, and hire a deputy editor to assist. Walt was in his mid-fifties and was also developing his own successful publishing house, Cicerone Press, concentrating on walking and climbing guidebooks so, in effect, the company was also looking to the longer-term editorship of the magazine.

I hit it off with managing director Duncan Kirk from our first meeting. I was 35 at the time and Duncan only a few years older, but he had that kind of corporate business confidence that I lacked, plus a great ability to put you at your ease. Our first meeting started on formal lines but soon turned into a light-hearted and banter-filled conversation that went on for a couple of hours. In the course of that interview-cum-blether Duncan explained that company rules insisted that the post be advertised, so I would have to go through the full interview procedure. The next stage in that process would be a meeting with Jim Warnock, the Holmes McDougall personnel manager (this was before the days of so-called human resources), followed by a final interview involving Duncan, Jim and Walt Unsworth himself.

To cut a long story short, I had a successful meeting with Jim and was told by Duncan that I was through to the shortlist. Also through to the final interview were the Scots mountaineer Mal Duff and rock climber Mark Hutchinson, who worked for the British Mountaineering Council. That deciding interview was to be held at the Camping and Outdoor Leisure Exhibition at Harrogate in November. I felt reasonably confident, but harboured a number of fears. Neither Mal or Mark were writers and neither of them had edited anything but, on the other hand, Mal was one of the UK's best-known Himalayan mountaineers with a number of important first ascents to his credit. Mark Hutchinson was an excellent rock climber who knew the workings of the British Mountaineering Council inside out and was very well versed in the politics of the sport. That could be important.

So ensued a month of fretting and worrying. I prayed as if there was no tomorrow, and worked through every possible scenario that could be thrown up in an interview. I was fully aware that I hadn't rock climbed seriously for a few years and enlisted the help of a good friend in Kincraig to drag me up a few climbs, in the Cairngorms and elsewhere, to help me get back into it again. John Lyall was the son of our parish minister in Kincraig and worked for the Forestry Commission but, like me, he was keen on making a career from hills and mountains. He eventually became a UIAA (International Climbing and Mountaineering Federation) Mountain Guide, and one of the most respected in the business.

I had been attending the annual Camping and Outdoor Leisure exhibition in Harrogate for several years and, although the event was ostensibly about manufacturers selling their new designs to retailers, the exhibition was really much more than that. As my friend Jim Perrin succinctly described it, it was the 'tribal gathering' of the outdoors industry. Every year the great and good of the outdoors would turn up in the rather genteel Yorkshire town. It was here I first met great mountaineers like Don Whillans, Chris Bonington and Doug Scott and, on one memorable occasion, the hero of Everest, Ed Hillary. It was in the cavernous halls of the Harrogate Exhibition Centre, and later in the bars of the town, that I first met Chris Brasher.

I generally attended this commercial orgy of outdoor gear, this gathering of the clans, largely for the social side, but the 1985 exhibition now had a very serious aspect as far as I was concerned. In the early afternoon of a dark and wet November day I put on my brand-new sports jacket, collar and tie, all bought specifically for the interview, brushed what hair I had (more than I have now) and wandered round to the very grandiose Cairn Hotel to await my fate. It may have been nerves but I was convinced that Walt Unsworth wasn't very keen on me becoming his depute. Duncan was supportive and Jim was even-handed, but I felt that Walt was ever-so-slightly hostile. I had already reckoned that Mark Hutchinson, being a rock climber and fellow Mancunian might get his vote. I suspected, correctly, that Mal Duff was only in there to add some credibility to the importance of the title. I think everyone was aware that Mal was unlikely to give up his expeditions and the magazine certainly couldn't afford an editor who vanished to the Himalayas for six weeks on an annual basis, no matter how fine a mountaineer he was.

Unlike the first two rounds of interview, I didn't enjoy this one. I was tense and nervous and it must have showed. Convinced I had fluffed it, I was relieved when Duncan finally brought the proceedings to an end and said he would meet me at three o'clock in the foyer to tell me the outcome. It was a long wait. I wandered around the town for a while and tried to eat some lunch but I didn't have much of an appetite. I managed to avoid everyone I knew until just before three when I returned to the Cairn. Only a handful of people were in the foyer and, on the stroke of three o'clock, Duncan marched in, face impassive, and came over to where I was sitting. He sat down opposite me, held his hand out and said one single word: Congratulations!

The rest of the exhibition went by in a blur. The company held a reception in the evening where I was unveiled as the new depute editor and I remember being wakened about two in the morning by a banging at my hotel room door. It was Mike Parsons, at that time the owner of Karrimor. 'Come to offer my congratulations,' he said. 'I think you should come down to the bar and buy us a drink.' A crowd of friends and acquaintances were gathered and since I was the only resident I had to order the drinks and pay for them. I was beginning to realise that being depute editor of *Climber and Rambler* magazine might be a costly business.

The following day I had a brief meeting with Walt who frankly admitted to me his choice would have been Mark Hutchinson, but he was nevertheless quite happy with my appointment. I appreciated his honesty. We agreed to meet the following week at Harmony Hall, his rather grand home in the south Lake District, where he both edited the magazine and looked after Cicerone, his publishing business. Over the next year or so we worked fairly well together, overcoming the obvious obstacles of him living in Cumbria and me in the Scottish Highlands. We met once a month at Harmony Hall. I would get there early in the morning, having spent the previous night in Glasgow, and we would work on the magazine in the morning. Walt then insisted I take him out for lunch. 'I'll sign your expenses,' he always said with a great grin on his face. We worked very hard on re-designing the magazine, working out a new logo and a new name. After much discussion we eventually decided to drop the word 'Rambler'. We felt it was old fashioned and gave an outdated impression of what the magazine was all about. *Climber* magazine was born.

Walt spent very little time in the Glasgow office and, because I was there two or three days a week, I found myself representing the magazine at meetings. Often I had to make decisions on behalf of the editor, something I wasn't very comfortable with. It didn't take a sixth sense to know that this was unsustainable.

About a year later, on my return from a holiday in Romania, there was an answerphone message waiting. It was Duncan, asking me to telephone him as soon as I got home. While I was away he'd had a meeting with Walt and suggested he should stand down as editor of the magazine. In return Walt was offered a role of consultant editor for a two-year period. I was to take over with immediate effect. I was surprised and delighted at the same time. I had guessed this might happen eventually but . . . so soon? I wasn't altogether sure I was ready. I had been learning a lot from Walt, but Duncan assured me Walt was delighted with the arrangement, particularly because it allowed him to spend more time developing Cicerone Press, 'with a little bit of pocket money from the company for a couple of years'.

The editorship of *Climber* magazine had one downside. Duncan insisted I had to live closer to the office. Appreciating my desire for as much independence as possible he said he didn't expect me to sit inside, in Glasgow, all day and every day, but he felt it was important that I should be available within an hour or so. He suggested moving to somewhere within a thirty-mile radius of the city.

To be honest, my initial delight at becoming editor was considerably dampened. Ten years earlier I had moved away from Glasgow because I wanted to live close to the hills and here was I having to move back again, albeit to a dream job. Gina and I discussed the situation at great length, weighing up all the pros and cons. We loved living in Kincraig and it would break our hearts to move from our little bungalow, but we decided the move needn't be forever and we would try and find somewhere to live in the countryside near Glasgow. On the plus side, it was not only a dream job for me but a steady income, with a company car and a pension.

We eventually decided to buy a house in the Stirlingshire village of Fintry, in the northern shadow of the Campsies. Tom Weir suggested it would be a fine place to live as driving over the Crow Road from Lennoxtown to Fintry was like coming ' . . .oot o' the warld, and intae Fintry'. Tom and Rhona lived in Gartocharn on Loch Lomondside, a short drive away.

Fintry is certainly a bonnie village, nestled as it is below the crags of Dunmore with its Neolithic fort. The community is a lively one and the village has its own sports centre and rugby team. There was a good primary school where Gregor would attend while Gordon would attend Balfron High, three miles away, a school with an excellent reputation. Gina managed to get a part-time job in a community hospital in Stirling and I could get into the Holmes McDougall office in an hour or so. It all looked so promising.

I had begun climbing again with a variety of companions including my Kincraig friends John Lyall and Steve Spalding, both excellent rock climbers, and Peter Evans, the Welsh deputy editor of the *Great Outdoors*, who actually preferred climbing to hiking. Peter and I had shared some wonderful days on the Etive Slabs, on Buachaille Etive Mor and, one particular epic, Ben Nevis. It was a sunny summer's day in August and we tramped up beside the Allt a' Mhuillin to the foot of the mountain's North-East Buttress. The route we wanted to climb wasn't difficult but it was long and had some route-finding issues. We decided to walk in wearing trainers and climb in our rock shoes but, just below a feature called the Mantrap, the crux move of the climb, it began to snow. We couldn't believe it. Snow in August? Our smooth-soled climbing shoes were not designed for snow so we completed the route in trainers before battling off the summit in a snowstorm. I suspect we were both highly motivated by the thought of the banner headlines if we'd had an accident or become stuck. 'Editor of *Climber* magazine and deputy editor of the *Great Outdoors* caught out on the Ben – ill-equipped!'

I was enjoying climbing again. Rock climbing and winter mountaineering were my first loves when I was a member of the Lomond Mountaineering Club and it was good to catch up with some of the former members now that I was close to Glasgow. As editor of the country's leading climbing magazine I had to expand my horizons south of Scotland: routes in the Lake District with Tom Prentice, who had become my deputy editor, and a very memorable day climbing at Tremadoc in North Wales with one of our contributors who was to become a close friend, Jim Perrin. Our Lake District correspondent, Bill Birkett, was to become another close friend, as were Glenn Rowley and Tim Greening of Keswick. The two lads had met at university and decided during a gap year that they would form a trekking company. They called it Karakorum Experience and they employed a wandering Aussie by the name of Rex Munro as their first trek leader. Glenn and Tim were giving a slide show in Glasgow to promote their new business and invited me along to report on it. It was the beginning of a long friendship during which I would work for them as a trek leader, a role which took me to Nepal, Pakistan, India, Guatemala, Jordan, Morocco, Russia, Turkey, Kenya and Tanzania.

That was in the future. Despite enjoying my dream job and being able to spend a good amount of time in the hills I was aware that being a full-time magazine editor for a corporate publishing company had its downsides. The nine-to-five routine, advertising meetings, finance meetings and planning meetings all smacked of what I had turned away from. Essentially, what I wanted to do was climb, wander the hills and write about it, and I found myself trying to avoid all these other distractions.

One night, completely out of the blue, I took a phone call from a BBC Scotland radio producer by the name of Christopher Lowell. Chris was originally from Wales but had worked in BBC Aberdeen for some time. He had produced a six-part series of short radio pieces with the angler and hillwalker Bruce Sandison called *Tales of the Loch* and he had read some of my stuff. He wondered if we could discuss a possible series of *Tales of the Hills*? Within a couple of weeks he came to Fintry, complete with his trusted Uher tape-to-tape recorder and we sat in a field below nearby Culcreuch Castle and recorded the whole series in one afternoon. At the time he suggested there might be a couple more radio projects in the offing and would get back to me. A week or so later he phoned to tell me that BBC Scotland wanted to revive the old *Leisure Trail*-style Saturday morning outdoors programme. The controller of BBC Scotland at the time, John McCormack, was keen to spread out a range of programmes across the various BBC studios in Scotland and it had been decided that the new weekend leisure programme, to be called *Weekend Break*, would be produced live from the Beechgrove Gardens studio in Aberdeen.

Chris suggested that I present the show and that since I had to travel north to Aberdeen on the Friday, to enable me to be in the studio for a 6a.m. start the next morning, would I like to present and record another programme on the Friday afternoon? Kill two birds with one stone, so to speak. The show was one very close to Chris' heart and was to be called *In the Country*. It was to be Radio Scotland's flagship environmental programme.

These exciting opportunities came at a time when I was becoming a bit restless again. I loved what I was doing and enjoying my climbing but, despite all its natural attractions, I couldn't quite fall in love with Fintry. I badly missed the Highlands and the slower, more deliberate way of life. Fintry, even though it was sheltered from Glasgow and its far-reaching environs by the physical swell of the Campsie Fells, was really no more than a dormitory village. I felt uncomfortable and wanted to move back to Strathspey and Badenoch where neighbours were never strangers and where I felt I had a place in the community.

Despite living in the south, I still wrote my weekly column for the *Strathspey and Badenoch Herald* and had mentioned to Ken Jones, the paper's editor, that I was homesick for the north. Out of the blue he offered me a job as the paper's reporter based in Kingussie and I, rather hastily, agreed. By this time Duncan had moved to pastures new and the company's advertising manager Mike Ure had been promoted to managing director. When I submitted my resignation letter he appeared surprised and concerned but, when I told him the reason I was leaving, he shrugged his shoulders and told me that as far as he was concerned I could live wherever I wanted, provided I could do the job effectively. I already had a company car so he offered me a fax machine to make working remotely that bit easier.

By May 1988 we had found a house in the Badenoch village of Newtonmore, sold the house in Fintry, and moved back to my beloved Highlands. It was the best move we ever made, although for the next 22 years I was to be a one-man contributor to global warming as I drove the 130 miles from Newtonmore to Glasgow and back two and sometimes three times a week. Mike turned out to be a very supportive and understanding boss and appreciated how much I valued my independence. I wasn't a nine-to-five magazine editor. Nor was I a company man or a good team player, but Mike knew that I lived the outdoors twenty-four hours a day and that I was committed to the job. He trusted me, and I'll forever be in his debt for allowing me to develop professionally as well as recreationally, albeit in my own rather maverick way.

Mike was also very supportive of what could have been construed as a secondary career. I had taken up Chris Lowell's offer of the two radio presenting jobs with Mike's approval, and he was equally supportive when I later became involved in television presenting. Mike reckoned that the better known I became, the better it would be for the magazine; the higher my public profile, the higher would be the profile of *Climber* magazine. Unfortunately, that wasn't always the understanding of various assistant and deputy editors, who tended to have an unfair share of the magazine workload dropped on them from time to time, but I did go out of my way to give them as much opportunity as possible to get out on the hills and develop themselves as I had done. I owe a huge amount of gratitude to Tom Prentice, John Manning and Emily Rodway for their patience and understanding during the years they worked with me, as I certainly wasn't the easiest editor to work for, considering the time I had away making television programmes.

Combining my role in the country's leading climbing magazine with presenting two national radio programmes raised my profile considerably and this high profile soon elevated me into the role of 'expert', that the media would turn to for comment whenever there was a mountain accident. No sooner had I taken up the role of editor than news came through from Pakistan that there had been a terrible accident on K2, the world's second highest mountain, in which five climbers died, including Al Rouse and Julie Tullis. It was the most tragic accident I had to report on during my five years as editor of *Climber*, and my first big mountaineering news story. Indeed, it was more than that because there was an emotional tie – Julie and Al were friends. Instead of gathering what information I could as a journalist to present a sad but factual story, I soon realised that I was far too emotionally involved. This was not going to be easy, especially as reports coming out of Pakistan were sporadic and often conflicting.

I decided to get in touch with Terry Tullis, Julie's husband, whom I had met a few times, who kindly and generously gave me of his time in awful circumstances. He said he hoped to speak to Julie's companion on the mountain, the veteran Austrian mountaineer Kurt Diemberger, by satellite phone and in fact got me an exclusive interview which I ran in the next issue. This gave Diemberger the opportunity to explain the circumstances of Julie's death and, to a certain extent, the others. At one point it seems that Al Rouse, although conscious, couldn't be moved and the other climbers had to leave him behind in his tent, to save their own lives. It was a decision for which the survivors, particularly Diemberger, would be later criticised, especially by those who had never had to make such a tough decision.

A year after the tragedy Jim Perrin brought Kurt to stay with me in Newtonmore where he was going to interview Kurt to inform an in-depth story. Over the weekend we went for a walk in the Cairngorms. It was a slow process and other walkers would be forgiven for thinking I was in the company of a very old and infirm man, but it was harrowing to watch him shuffle along on feet that had endured the searing pain of frostbite, supported by a single ski pole. Even an easy and fairly flat ramble to the Lochain Uaine, the Green Lochan, in Ryvoan was too much, and when we stopped for a rest he poured out the litany of thoughts and recriminations that had been churning in his mind for fifteen months. On 4th August 1986, Kurt and his climbing partner Julie Tullis stood on the summit of K2. It was Julie's dream mountain and, for Kurt, another high point in a long and successful mountaineering career, but their descent from the mountain disintegrated into an epic fight for survival that Julie and four others lost. Kurt barely survived.

He was in deep mourning for Julie and the other four, but it was as if in trying to convince me, he was trying to convince himself that he had done all he could to save their lives. His own physical injuries had been bad enough (as well as frostbite to his fingers and toes he suffered a lung embolism and, on his way home from Pakistan, caught malaria) but the mental anguish he was suffering was almost unbearable. Other than some criticism that Kurt had perhaps pushed Julie beyond her capabilities, the mountaineering world did not blame the veteran mountaineer for the death of his friends. His own survival was no less than miraculous, but Kurt took every opportunity to recount what happened and what he thought had gone wrong. Over and over again. It was as though he was seeking some kind of absolution.

Over three decades later, history has not held Kurt Diemberger accountable for what happened on K2. I don't think anyone ever did blame him but, like many others who have faced such tragedy, he seemed to be trying to convince himself that mountains were worth dying for, that his aims and ambitions were worthy of paying the ultimate price. The cost of survival was a burden of guilt.

In his award-winning book about the expedition, *The Endless Knot*, Kurt described that awful period in his life. 'The darkness, the all-encompassing dreariness,' he said, 'lasted for a long time after the return from K2 – as if the storm, like a bad spell, had not fully worked itself out. There were gaps in memory ... full of fantasies; there were heroic poems, and clichés. There were invented "rescues" – when in fact nobody unable to climb down by himself could have survived. The most extreme opinions clashed together. But that time is over, it was a fight, but it was necessary for the truth, for all those who will climb in the future. Luckily, I learned to know a different side too: friendship, people who really helped me and had to bear a lot ... it takes a long time to clamber out of an abyss like that.'

Clamber out he did. After a long period of recovery, Kurt continued to climb and to travel. I guess he can't help himself. He's simply been feeding the rat.

'Losing my friends was not all there was to it, I also lived with them up there,' he later wrote. 'They found their *life* up there. I couldn't, not now, change the way I live. I have been going to the Himalayas for thirty years; I cannot imagine any sort of future that doesn't involve going back there. I have to be with the big mountains – even if now only rarely do I get up to the summit.'

It's a remarkable testimony to Kurt's tenacious endurance that he first climbed an 8,000-metre Himalayan peak, Broad Peak, with the legendary Hermann Buhl in 1957. That was the first time a summit of that height had been climbed without bottled oxygen and with no high-altitude porters. Such frugal alpine-style tactics were extremely unusual at a time when mountaineering expeditions were put together like military campaigns with scores of porters, large teams and heavy logistics. It was many years before such Alpine-style climbing, what Buhl called '*Westalpenstil*', became the norm. Three years later Diemberger made the first ascent of Dhaulagiri (8,167 metres/26,794 feet), at the time considered the most technically difficult of the Himalayan giants. In climbing that mountain he became the only person (apart from Buhl) to have made first ascents of two of the world's highest peaks, but it was some 18 years before he climbed another 8,000-metre peak, and that followed the emergence of a young Tyrolean climber by the name of Reinhold Messner, who was to become the greatest mountaineer the world has known.

The appearance of that younger challenger acted as an irresistible spur to Kurt. Now in his forties, he climbed Everest, Makalu, Gasherbrum 2 and Broad Peak for a second time. In between, there were adventures in Greenland, North America, Africa and other areas of the Himalaya, most notably in the Hindu Kush where he climbed Tirich Mir West IV (7,338 metres/24,074 feet) and Tirich Mir main peak (7,706 metres/25,282 feet) and five other virgin peaks. But it was the world's second-highest mountain that had always acted as a magnet to Diemberger, attracting him three times to its icy flanks before he finally managed to climb it during that fateful expedition of 1986. Thirty-two years later, aged 66, he took part in an Italian expedition to Nanga Parbat in Pakistan where he soloed to 6,000 metres/19,685 feet on the Kinshofer Wall.

Mountaineering at that sort of standard is an extremely high-risk activity and it's been said that the sport's dead heroes outnumber the living. Names like Ian Clough, Nick Estcourt, Mick Burke, Pete Boardman, Joe Tasker, Dougal Haston, Al Rouse, Paul Nunn and many, many others are probably better known than those of the many who have survived. Indeed, it could be argued that only Chris Bonington and Doug Scott remain as British mountaineering's household names. That makes Kurt Diemberger's 40-plus years as a top mountaineer even more remarkable, his enduring qualities more staggering. His physical and mental characteristics have set him apart as a great survivor; mountains are an essential part of his life, not combative opponents that he must conquer, but friends that he wants to be amongst as often as he can. Having said that, he will never come to terms with what happened on K2.

'Up on our dream mountain I lost Julie, lost my climbing companion of so many years, sharer of storms and tempests, joys and hopes on the highest mountains of the world. How often did we count the stars together, or look for faces in the clouds? Life somehow goes on. The mountains, like dear friends, have always helped me before. Whenever it was possible.'

Many people can't understand sentiments like those. Unless you have experienced the existential joy of mountains and mountain climbing, it's asking a lot to expect people to appreciate that, even in the face of death, love for such places is rarely extinguished. But such love has to be embraced with respect for all the various aspects of the mountain, including potential dangers.

During the winter of 1979/80 I was avalanched in Coire Laogh Mor in the Cairngorms. I came down several hundred feet and thought I was drowning in the snow. The impact of the avalanche was so powerful that my hat, gloves, rucksack and even my wrist-watch were all ripped from me. When the snow stopped moving I was buried up to my chest but fortunately my head and arms were free. I managed to extricate myself and other than a few bruises and a badly damaged ego I was fine. However, it was a long time before I could cross a snow slope again without fear. I read everything I could about avalanches, soaked up every bit of information because I never wanted to experience such a thing again. Did I think of giving up the hills? Of course not. The incident made me want to know the hills better, to understand them better, to treat them with more informed respect, just as you would with any lover you've had a tiff with.

The closest I've come to losing my life was an accident while hill-running (of all things). I'd decided to have an afternoon run to the summit of Creag Dhubh, a lovely 756-metre/2,480-feet high hill that overlooks the village. As I approached the summit on a fine and clear late September afternoon I remembered that I had to collect Gregor from rugby practice at five thirty. I checked my watch and saw it was only four thirty. I had an hour to jog down the hill and drive back to the house before meeting him, but something happened and to this day I have no idea what it was. I may have tripped, I just can't remember, but the next thing I recall is trying to climb over a wall at the foot of the hill and onto the Newtonmore to Laggan road. I tried to jog along the road thinking to myself that this run seemed a lot tougher than usual. Fortunately, I was spotted. One of my elderly neighbours was in her car when she saw me limping along. She stopped but (she later told me), was reluctant to give me a lift in her brand-new car because of all the blood that was dripping off me. Fortunately, another neighbour, Dave Fallows, also stopped and had no hesitation in pushing me into his car and phoning for an ambulance in what was, for the time, a new-fangled mobile phone.

We got back to Cherry Glen, my house, just before the ambulance arrived and I was whipped off to Raigmore Hospital in Inverness. Gina, who had been visiting relatives in Stirling, turned onto our road as the ambulance left, complete with flashing blue light. She had no idea I was inside. Whatever happened obviously involved a long fall down steep ground. I was covered in cuts and bruises, required 40 stitches in my head, had broken my left ankle and snapped the end of the radius bone in the arm, just above my wrist. And I couldn't recall a thing.

The consultant who operated on me told me this lapse of memory wasn't unusual, it was the mind's way of protecting me and to this day I'm not sure what happened. I've gone back to the area and looked around and can only think that perhaps I slipped while crossing a stream, before sliding down a series of short crags. Dave Fallows picked me up at 7p.m. so I reckon I must have lain unconscious for an hour or perhaps ninety minutes before stumbling down the hillside to the road. I rather like the notion that a couple of angels picked me up, carried me down to the roadside and left me for my neighbours to find.

I guess I was lucky, and my consultant told me at one point that ten years earlier he wouldn't have had the technology to save my wrist. A decade earlier my right hand would have been amputated.

Not everyone is as lucky. It's always cruel when we hear of people dying in the mountains but while every single death is a tragedy for families and loved ones, the hysterical ranting from some sections of the media is neither helpful nor welcome. The barrage of ill-informed comment from certain journalists who know next to nothing about our love of mountains, about mountain safety or mountain rescue, has incensed outdoor folk for years. One journalist in particular made so many factual errors on a radio phone-in that the accident statistician from the Mountain Rescue Committee of Scotland phoned in to correct her. Despite that, the same journalist later went on to an evening television programme and spouted the same misinformation.

I don't want to dwell on poor reporting or knee-jerk reactions, but it's worth examining some of the suggestions these journalists and others come up with. There are three general issues that raise their head after every spate of mountain accidents.

One: Mountaineers should be made to take out insurance.
Two: The mountains should be closed off during and after bad weather.
Three: Mountain rescue teams should be professional.

Perhaps I can take the last point first. Here in Scotland our civilian search and rescue teams are professional in every sense other than they don't receive payment. There is a certain amount of funding from the Scottish government – about £300,000 to Scotland's 27 rescue teams, and the teams raise the rest of the cash they need themselves, much of it from donations. These teams are made up of experienced mountaineers and they understand why people go to the mountains in winter. They believe the present system of search and rescue in Scotland works well and besides, who would pay for 'professional', paid mountain rescue. Presumably those who had been rescued, as in some Alpine countries, and that would mean taking out insurance. But what if someone wasn't insured? Would they still be rescued? Would they receive a court injunction demanding a rescue fee? Under the present set-up, where we have volunteer, highly-skilled yet unpaid rescue teams, who would claim the insurance money? Where would it go? The present system of search and rescue in Scotland seems to suit everyone very well. Why change it to appease the baying of a handful of tabloid journalists?

The other hoary old chestnut is to close the mountains in bad weather. I wonder how you could do that? Tie red tape all round the base of our mountains? Call the military to stand guard and stop us setting foot on the hills? Change Scotland's much-envied Land Reform Act to make it a trespass to walk in the hills between the months of December and March? Who would be responsible for deciding the weather was bad enough to close down the hill?

What about the tens of thousands of people who see a walk or a climb in the winter mountains as an antidote to the prescribed, over-regulated society we live in, a society largely created by those same journalists who see personal freedom as some form of self-destruction?

The mountaineering and mountain safety organisations in Scotland are not unaware of these dreadful accidents. I know that David Gibson, the boss of Mountaineering Scotland, person-ally feels the pain of every parent or loved one of those who have perished. Mountaineering Scotland and the Scottish Avalanche Information Service are always trying to think up fresh ways of getting their messages across. The Scottish government has always supported mountain safety and has financially backed the likes of the Scottish Avalanche Information Service and Geoff Monk's excellent Mountain Weather Information Service. As patron of Mountain Aid, a charity that supports mountain rescue in Scotland, I certainly do what I can to help further the cause of education and mountain training. This is all positive stuff, and that's what required. We need such positive action, not negative calls to ban people, to charge them for being rescued, by making insurance compulsory or by suggesting that those who encourage people into mountaineering are irresponsible.

Any death in the Scottish mountains is awful. It's nothing less than tragic but bear in mind that each year there are some seven million participation days, when all those people went to the hills, got themselves a little bit fitter, cleared their mind of all the rubbish our over-sanitised society has thrown at them, and came home refreshed and rejuvenated by the natural world. We have to put these very sad and unfortunate accidents into perspective. Most hillwalkers, climbers and scramblers get untold joy from the hills. And what is that joy? Why do people like me want to climb the Scottish hills in winter?

Anyone who has watched any of my television programmes will be aware of my love affair with the mountains and wild places of Scotland, those areas that have been my lifeblood for more years than I can remember. I'm proud we can boast of some of the most beautiful and diverse landscapes in the world. From the rolling hills of the Borders to the arctic landscapes of the Cairngorms, from the mist-shrouded islands of the Hebrides to the wild grandeur of the North West Highlands, few would argue that this little country of ours is one of the most beautiful in Europe. One of the great benefits of that natural beauty is that it attracts visitors from all over the world and, in particular, those visitors who come outside the normal tourist season, during the winter months when snow turns our mountains into a magical playground for hillwalkers and climbers. Under cover of snow every gully and corrie is picked out in stark shades of black and white and mountain slopes appear as curved and sensuous lines against the blue of the sky. In such conditions many people want to immerse themselves in their grandeur, soak in the peace of them, take from them something of their timelessness and implacable nature. On a personal level, being amongst mountains makes me very happy.

Whenever there is a mountain fatality I'm asked by the media just what it is that attracts me and thousands of others to the mountains in winter, that draws us from our warm and comfortable homes into the cold, sometimes dangerous world of high, rugged winter landscapes. Why are people like me willing to take the risk of being lost, avalanched, stormbound or involved in an accident and is it worth the risk? Or as one journalist suggested, 'Isn't Scotland in danger of becoming a sort of outdoor Dignitas for healthy, fit people?' I obviously can't answer for anyone else, so what I'm about to write is personal, my reasons for climbing hills in winter as well as the other seasons.

In short, I could boil it down to three things: love and appreciation of natural beauty; a desire for escapism; the regular need of a natural drug fix.

I'm aware that the society in which I now live is very different from the society I was brought up in. In those far-flung days there was less fear, less political correctness and less regulation. Today we seem to live in a sanitised, prescribed society where health and safety considerations give the impression that we should all be bubble-wrapped and protected from ourselves. We live in a grossly over-regulated country where knee-jerk reaction and a persuasive media regularly shape and bend public opinion. Many people, perhaps most people, live in a permanent regime of nine-to-five repetitiveness with only weekends and an annual holiday to break the monotony. It's perhaps not surprising that an increasing number of them are discovering a need to break that regime from time to time, to escape the monotonous regularity of it all, to find respite in a landscape that has a more lasting reality, a world of heather and rock, big skies and the opportunity for some kind of adventure. Mountaineering, particularly in winter, offers all of that in an environment that is not yet wrapped up in rules and regulation. This sense of escapism is important, and that's why so many of us become hooked on what appears, at first sight, to be a completely pointless exercise: expending a lot of effort to climb to the top of a mountain, only to turn round again and come back down.

I believe there is a sense of true 'wildness' on our high mountains. Signs of man's presence are minimal and in winter, under cover of snow, that perception is heightened, when even the footpaths vanish from sight. It's then that we experience the fleeting nature of man's time on this planet against the more lasting reality of nature. Mankind, our successes and failures, somehow seem insignificant against the age-old, slowly evolving world that gives us sustenance and life. These words may seem very grand and worthy but it's probably the core reason for my own love of mountains. There is also the challenge, the adventure, the risk factor and the cerebral exercise in learning the skills that minimise the risks.

Our winter mountains are not only beautiful, they are potentially dangerous places. So are our cities, our road networks and our own homes. We wouldn't handle bare electrical wires; we wouldn't knowingly walk out in front of a bus; we avoid certain city streets late on a Saturday night. We make every attempt at minimising the risks involved in everyday living, and yet people still die from electric shocks, from road accidents and from alcohol- and tobacco-related illnesses. In fact, one of the biggest killers of Scots is lack of exercise, resulting in obesity and diabetes. Winter mountaineering is like everything else: you learn to recognise the risks and you try to manage them. You find out what skills you need to cut that risk to a minimum and you learn those skills. In terms of mountaineering we learn how to navigate in bad weather; we learn how to use an ice axe and crampons; we learn about avalanches and how to avoid them and we learn how to listen to our natural instinct for survival.

In the world we live in today those base instincts rarely surface. Our bubble-wrapped society protects us from too much risk but, expose yourself to the bare elements of nature and they will appear, like the embers of a small fire. We have to breath those embers into a full flame to hear those base instincts, intuition if you like, that protected our ancestors from sabre-toothed tigers and marauding mammoths. Such protective instincts are there, lying dormant in every one of us. We just have to fan them into life, and we can do that by going to the mountains. I appreciate that accidents do, and will continue to, happen. I will continue to try and minimise the risks I face when I go to the hills and even after five decades of climbing mountains I'm very aware that I'm still learning. What I do know with certainty is that the feelings I experience on top of a winter mountain are like a drug. I am addicted, completely and utterly. Let me explain.

There is considerable physical effort involved in climbing a mountain and this exercise releases endorphins in our body – a kind of feel-good natural drug. The excitement of tackling risk and challenging situations releases another natural drug called adrenaline, which heightens our awareness and sensitivity. Add that to the sheer pleasure of being in a remarkably beautiful environment and a sense of achievement and the resultant mix is highly potent. A natural high like no other I know, a sensation that can last for days. Yes it's addictive, but it's a healthy addiction and I for one will continue to encourage others to share that addiction with me.

During the vast majority of Scottish winters some people die in the mountains. Such deaths are tragic, but consider those deaths against the hundreds of thousands of people who are refreshed and rejuvenated by winter mountaineering, inspired and re-equipped to go back to their normal everyday world. We certainly need to continue to educate and train people, we need to continue to warn people of the dangers of the hills, but we also need to put the accidents into some kind of realistic perspective. Going to the hills is not a route to your own death, as one journalist suggests. No, it's the route to life in all of its glorious fullness.

10

JOB SWAP

On one glorious autumn afternoon in 1989 I was rock-climbing with Peter Evans on the Etive Slabs, on the eastern slopes of Beinn Trilleachean above Loch Etive. When seen head-on from Ben Starav across the waters of the sea loch, these boiler-plate slabs hang from the mountain like a grey curtain, and they contain some of the most surreal rock climbs in the country. Etive slab climbing is friction climbing, tiptoeing upwards through a steep ocean of granite, relying on the sandpaper roughness of the rock. It's not climbing for the faint-hearted.

Peter and I climbed a lot together and that afternoon tackled two of the Etive Slabs classics, Hammer (HVS) and Spartan Slab (VS). The climbing was magnificent: the warm sun had dried the crag of early morning drizzle and we delighted in the rough nature of the rock, tiptoeing up ridiculously steep granite relying virtually solely on the friction of our boots. It's fair to say that Peter was a better rock climber than I was and on that particular day he ably demonstrated his prowess. As we romped down the hill after our second ascent, which Peter had led, I congratulated him on his performance. In what was to become a somewhat prophetic utterance, he joked that perhaps he was in the wrong job. Maybe he should be editor of *Climber* and I should be editor of the *Great Outdoors*?

Walking back to the car along the lochside I mulled this over. While I loved editing *Climber* magazine, there were several issues evolving in the climbing world at that time that I didn't go along with, issues that made me uncomfortable. Indoor climbing was one of them. Climbing walls were being built all over the country and many climbers were treating them like gymnasia. Others had virtually given up climbing outside and, along with this explosion of climbing walls, inevitably came competition climbing. I had already attended a major competition in Leeds and it had bored me rigid. It was like watching paint dry. I knew the British Mountaineering Council was very keen to embrace this new activity and was pushing for climbing to be recognised as a future Olympic sport, which it now is, but I argued against the idea whenever I could. The only real ally I had on the Public Relations Committee of the BMC was the late Ken Wilson, the book publisher who was generally regarded as the conscience of British climbing.

Ken and I fought vociferously against climbing competitions, arguing that climbing was an outdoor activity. Hearing the birds sing, dealing with the weather, feeling natural rock against your fingertips were all vital attributes of the sport. The only person you should compete against was yourself, but our arguments were to no avail. The BMC could obviously see government aid and subsidy coming their way if the Olympic Games embraced climbing.

I was convinced that Olympic approval would mean professionalism and had seen what happened when track and field athletics went down that route. I certainly wasn't keen on having to report on indoor climbing competitions in what I had always considered to be an outdoors magazine. Perhaps Peter's throwaway comment about swapping jobs would be worth considering.

As we drove south I mentioned the subject again and, while admitting he had merely been joking, Peter did say he'd have a think about it. A few days later he told me he'd be up for it. We went to see Mike Ure our publisher who gave the idea his blessing and so I became editor of the *Great Outdoors*. I had the most curious feeling that I had come home.

Peter and I swapped jobs in 1990. The *Great Outdoors* magazine had been losing circulation, thanks to a glut of copycat titles that had been unashamedly published by bigger and wealthier publishers. In an attempt to stem the flow, I introduced some new writers and columnists, bringing in my old pal Chris Townsend as gear editor and another dear friend, Jim Perrin, as a regular essayist.

It's exciting to take over a new title but it also takes a little time for readers to catch on to what you are doing. Although the *Great*

Outdoors was ostensibly a magazine that catered for walkers from Cornwall to Cape Wrath, I wanted it to be a hillwalking and backpacking title, a return to my own outdoor loves. With the exception of the Lake District and North Wales there are few mountains and hills to speak of other than in Scotland, so that's where I wanted the emphasis of the magazine to be.

Let's face it, you couldn't find an editor with a more Scottish name then me, the magazine was published in Scotland and Scotland was where the real hills, mountains and wild land are to be found. To emphasise my point, there were now other magazines available that would cover walks in the Cotswolds, the South Downs and other areas of the south. My editorial emphasis would be towards Scotland, the Lake District and North Wales.

I was also aware that Munro-bagging had reached a new level of popularity and that folk of all ages and backgrounds were ticking off Scotland's 3,000-feet mountain summits. I had always been keen on the idea of finishing my round of the Munros before I turned forty but I just missed that particular deadline. Not long after my birthday, on a very wet and cloudy day, Gina and I set out for Ben More on the Isle of Mull, my final Munro the first-time round. We were heading for a celebratory walk, but it was a rather curious celebration.

Wet and miserably cold, we huddled behind the windbreak on the summit of Ben More, sipping champagne and pretending we were enjoying it. Gina just wanted to get down and into a dry set of clothes and another couple, whom we had met on the hill and encouraged to come to the summit with us, were terrified we would leave them in the mist. It was my party, my final Munro, and I was determined to live every moment of it, but a resolute wife usually has her way and I reluctantly agreed to put the celebrations on hold. A warm restaurant in Tobermory would help improve the champagne, and it did, but it had been an unholy quick raid to a holy island to climb a hill. I knew deep inside that I hadn't done Ben More justice.

I've been back to Mull several times since, and I've shown more respect to its one Munro, the highest of our Hebridean mountains outside Skye, and Britain's last volcano. Scientists say that about thirty-five million years ago the Hebridean archipelago was dotted with active volcanoes pouring out masses of molten lava. What is now Ben More was the last of these and its great western lava flows created the wonderful cliffs of the Ardmeanach peninsula, the cliffs of Gribun, the island of Ulva and the amazing columnar rock architecture of the island of Staffa.

More hillwalkers save Ben More as their final Munro than any other, but their reasons have little to do with the mountain's volcanic past. Because of access difficulties you have to make a weekend of it, and if you're going to make a weekend of it you might as well make it a celebratory one. It can be costly too. Come to think of it, if you're going to make a weekend of it you may as well make it a week as there's plenty of other mountain games to play on Mull.

Positioned near the west of the island, Ben More is a fair distance from the ferry terminal at Craignure. You can either take a car on the ferry from Oban, and drive to the starting point, or take a local bus to Salen from where you still have a seven-mile walk to the foot of the hill at Loch na Keal. A bike would be useful, and cheaper to transport on the Oban–Craignure ferry.

As its name suggests, Ben More lords it over the island. This 'big hill' can be seen from all points of the Mull compass and radiates ridges in a number of directions from its summit cone, the best of which is that which connects with neighbouring A'Chioch, a superb rocky highway that involves a steep descent to a rock-girt bealach, then an even steeper, rocky scramble that leads directly to Ben More's summit.

Most walkers tackle Ben More from the B8035, on the south-eastern shores of Loch na Keal. The lovely Abhainn na h-Uamha, complete with tantalising pools and waterfalls, wanders down the length of Gleann na Beinn Fada from the obvious saddle in the ridge between Beinne Fada and A'Chioch. From the saddle, steep and rocky slopes lead to the summit of A'Chioch. The route to Ben More then continues to the south-west as a superb rocky ridge, involving a steep descent to the bealach. Crags fall away to the north-west and there are a couple of big gaps in the slabby wall (which can be easily avoided). A steeper, rocky scramble leads directly to the summit of

Ben More at 966 metres/3,169 feet. This final climb looks steep and difficult from the bealach but don't be discouraged, it's easier than it looks.

I suspect that's the case with many of the Munros. I recall creeping along a narrow ridge in the mist of the Skye Cuillin, cautiously aware that a steep ramp of loose scree would indicate we had come too far. That ramp would carry us upwards to the top of Sgurr Dearg but that wasn't the Munro summit we were after. Our summit lay on the top of an unlikely finger of rock that poked its head above Sgurr Dearg: the Inaccessible Pinnacle. I had first climbed this Munro at the age of 16, but then I was safely cosseted between two outdoor instructors from Glenmore Lodge. On this particular day, some thirty years later, I had a small group of friends relying on my skill and experience. I didn't want to let them down by failing to find the start of the scramble. We found it sooner than expected, helped by various shouts from above – mostly calls of encouragement, although some of the cries had a terrified edge to them. My own little group coped superbly well, with only one person calling for a rope about halfway up.

I wonder how many hillwalkers have climbed every hill other than the Cuillin summits? It's for very good reason that Hamish Brown, in his fine book, *Hamish's Mountain Walk*, recommends aspiring Munro-baggers to climb these mountains while they are still young and fit. The Cuillin Munros don't get any easier with age. Other Munros that require a bit of rock scrambling skill include the Aonach Eagach in Glen Coe and An Teallach, if you choose to follow the crest of the Corrag Bhuidhe buttresses. But you don't have to, a footpath bypasses the buttresses on their west side. A similar situation exists on Liathach if you choose not to follow the crest of the Am Fasarinen pinnacles.

I guess I've been lucky. Even before my youth hostel days I had spent years rock climbing and even reached a reasonable standard during my years as editor of *Climber* magazine, so technical routes on the likes of the Cuillin and the Aonach Eagach were more of an attraction than an obstacle. Indeed, I would often seek out the scrambling routes on Munros as something of a relief from the interminable, and often busy, Munro-baggers' paths. Good examples of this would be the Buachaille Etive Mor by Curved Ridge, a long, scrambling route on the north-east face of the mountain or Ben Nevis by the North-East Buttress (which takes you direct to the summit). So, which Munros would I regard as the most difficult? This is a question I'm repeatedly asked and it's a very difficult question to answer because it depends on a number of factors including remoteness, inaccessibility, the weather and indeed, how I was physically feeling at the time.

A good example was my first ascent of Meall Dubhag in the Cairngorms. This hill was chopped from the Munros list away back in the seventies and I approached it on a dark and dour day as a Hogmanay celebration. We had been partying all week and I took myself off to the Moine Mhor above Glen Feshie to clear my head, partly in preparation for the next bout of New Year festivities. To say I wasn't in particularly good fettle would be an understatement and I struggled up the old Foxhunter's Path from Achlean to the dip just south of Carn Ban Mor, which incidentally was also a Munro at the time. It was an easy, almost flat, stroll to Carn Ban Mor but as I turned south again I became aware of a veil of cloud that was quickly covering the vast high-level expanse of the Moine Mhor. I also sensed the wind picking up and I hurried along wishing I had a bit more energy. I was halfway between Carn Ban Mor and Meall Dubhag when the storm hit me. It came with such a violent ferocity that it shook me and within a minute or so I was blinded by spindrift. Eventually I realised that the only way I could escape was to crawl as close to the ground as possible and so began what was to become a long crawl on my knees, trying for the life of me to follow a compass bearing.

It was the first of only a very few occasions in a long hillwalking career that I thought I was going to die in the mountains. I crawled and half-stumbled for a good forty minutes or so before some sixth sense suggested that I was going downhill. I had missed the summit of Meall Dubhag and was crawling innocently towards the edge of the steep-sided Coire Garbhlach, the long and twisted glacial corrie that bites its way into the massif of the Moine Mhor.

Concerned that I might stumble through a cornice, I turned-tail and climbed back uphill, still battered and rocked by the wind. When the dim shape of an ice-encrusted cairn eventually came into view the relief was immense and I almost cried. I could now take a proper bearing and head virtually due west, downhill all the way into the safety of Glen Feshie. Thirty minutes later I stumbled out below the cloud and, while the wind was still intent on knocking me over, could finally see where I was going. It was the hardest Munro I'd climbed, but at least it cleared my head.

Other Munros tend to be more awkward than difficult, particularly those out-and-back affairs that we so often leave for another day. Two of them stand out in my memory because I eventually had to make special efforts to climb them when I was 'tidying up' the remaining Munros on my first round.

Beinn Fhionnlaidh sits in isolated splendour above the south shores of lonely Loch Mullardoch and its cairn lies one and a half miles north of Carn Eige. The latter is most usually climbed along with Mam Sodhail from Glen Affric in the south or from Gleann nam Fiadh in the east. However you climb them, Beinn Fhionnlaidh lies out on her limb, with a descent and re-ascent of about 350 metres in both directions, as if to taunt you. It's so, so easy to leave that long out-and-back for another day, citing any number of reasons: weather, tiredness, lack of time or just honest-to-goodness procrastination. In fact, it took me three rounds of Carn Eige and Mam Sodhail before I eventually conquered this procrastination and climbed the hill. On two occasions I was with others who didn't happen to be Munro-baggers. The first couldn't understand why I wanted to climb a hill that was way out on a limb, and with the second group the weather was so bad I just wanted to get down and off the hill as quickly as possible. I eventually climbed it as part of a big three-day-round climbing all the hills that circle Loch Mullardoch.

It was on that backpacking trip that I climbed the other infamous out-and-back: Mullach na Dheiragain, the north-east Munro top of Sgurr nan Ceathreamhnan. The main Munro is remote enough, rising steeply between Glen Affric and the western end of Mullardoch, but the out-and-back to the Mullach puts Beinn Fhionnlaidh into the shade. That long ridge rolls on for about four and a half miles into the West Benula Forest with the Munro summit about halfway along. It's enough to make you consider climbing it from Iron Lodge in the north-east, but that would necessitate a long bike ride from the road-end at Killilan before even starting.

Backpacking has been my saviour on so many multi-Munro sorties, especially on subsequent Munro rounds. I learned valuable lessons after my first Munro round and it was as I became older and a tad wiser that I realised the value of multi-day trips taking in big ranges like the Mullardoch Munros; the Cairngorms; the Grey Corries, the Aonachs and the Mamores on a big round from Ben Nevis; the south Glen Shiel ridge and the Sisters of Kintail ridge; and the Ben Lawers summits.

It would be silly to write about the difficulties of Munro-bagging without mentioning winter. Under cover of snow and ice and when temperatures barely rise above freezing, the climbing of our Munros changes dramatically from pleasant tramps on the hills to nothing less than pure mountaineering. Extra skills are required, more equipment is necessary, and a different mindset and greater degree of fitness and flexibility also help keep you safe. Relatively straightforward Munros take on a new character. Mile upon mile of wading through calf-deep snow can exhaust you; the cold and the wind strip you of warmth and energy; simple slopes can become avalanche-prone and the consequences of a simple slip can be fatal. And sometimes, just sometimes, the snow can act as an impassable barrier.

A number of years ago I tried to climb three Munros above Loch Cluanie in Kintail: Carn Ghluasaid, Sgurr nan Conbhairean and Sail Chaorainn. The first two summits came and went fairly easily but the ridge between the latter two was heavily snowed-up and corniced on either side. At one point between the tops the ridge narrows considerably and, on this day, it looked like an Alpine arête. I tiptoed along carefully but was sending down huge slabs on either side of the ridge. The snow was soft and deep and I certainly didn't like the way it broke off. Feeling distinctly uncomfortable

I eventually gave up, descended steeply down towards the Allt na Ciche to where the snow cover looked less avalanche-prone, and then climbed up again more or less directly to the summit. Then I had to do the whole thing in reverse. I was a weary Munro-bagger by the time I got back to my car but not as weary as when an old friend of mine and I almost got stuck on one of Scotland's easiest Munros.

Laggan's Geal Charn suffers the ignominy of being labelled as one of the most boring Munros and, for those who 'climb it as a quick excursion from the road' as one guidebook suggests, it's perhaps not surprising that the mountain fails to throw up any treats. Time-saving Munro-raids are often unmemorable affairs and every hill, if you give it the courtesy of your time, will display its potential. Even Geal Charn can offer a very exciting ascent, as we discovered.

During the nineties, I had the benefit of a regular hillwalking buddy. I met John Hood, originally from Essex but now living in Newtonmore, through our local church and he was keen to climb some hills. He had read somewhere about the Munros and decided that he was going to climb them all. We went out together a couple of times and found that we got on very well. He was fit and strong and eager to learn and for the next decade he and I climbed hundreds of hills together until, eventually, he and his wife Ann decided to move to Cumbria to be closer to their son and grandchildren. To this day, we meet up whenever we can and share some good chortles about some of our days on the hills, including this one.

John had already climbed Geal Charn by its more popular western route, from Garva Bridge, but I managed to convince him that a long snow-plod up Glen Markie to the east of the hill could bring rewards. This route follows an ancient drove road up the glen for about two and a half miles before crossing the Markie burn and climbing into Geal Charn's redeeming feature, the grand cliff-girt corrie that lies above Lochan a' Choire. Our original intention was to climb the slopes north of the lochan and so avoid the crags that form the corrie walls. We would then head south-west across the plateau summit slopes to the cairn, returning to lower Glen Markie by the south slopes of Geal Charn's neighbour, Beinn Sgiath. That was our plan, but the words 'best laid' and 'gang awry' come to mind. In short, we were beguiled by the mountain's glistening raiment into something rather more challenging. As we crossed the iced-up flow of the Markie burn, the steep east prow of Beinn Sgiath reared above us, steepening in its final hundred feet or so into what looked like a good sporting snow climb. We'd had enough of snow plodding, it was time to use our ice axes!

Initially the climb was hard work. The snow was deep and unconsolidated but was broken here and there by rocky outcrops. These fins of rock, we soon discovered, made an easier passage than the snow. Higher up on the slope, great flows of green ice hung from the rocks, forcing us back onto unconsolidated snow again and as we reached the topmost section, just below a thirty-foot cornice, we realised that we had reached a point of no return. Neither of us wanted to down-climb the icy rocks but the potential for a safe upwards ascent depended very much on how solid the cornice was. If it was soft and unconsolidated like the snow below we could be in trouble. A fall from here, over steep and rocky ground, could have serious consequences, but a short traverse led to the foot and I managed to ease my way across to it, virtually hanging from my ice axe which I had hammered into a patch of frozen turf. With the toes of my boots on a couple of rocky niches I gently eased the ice axe from the turf and swung it into the snow above. The solid thud as it planted into the snow was incredibly reassuring and, moments later, I was kicking my way up and over the slight overhang onto the plateau above. The first thing I noticed was that I was shaking slightly.

Meanwhile John was having his own adventure and I was relieved when an ice axe appeared over the cornice rim and whammed into the snow beside me. 'So much for your sporting route,' he muttered darkly as he hauled himself over the edge. The rest of the day was an anti-climax as we trudged across Beinn Sgiath and onto Geal Charn's broad plateau. From the summit, we returned to the corrie rim and followed it north to where long slopes led down into the corrie and the route back to Glen Markie. As we waded through knee-deep snow by Piper's Burn, more words of Munro guru

Hamish Brown came to mind. 'You cannot exhaust the potential of even the dullest hills in Scotland,' he once wrote. The potential is always there, we just have to look for it. Often enough that kind of potential is only a thin crack away from difficulty and danger but that's when the straightforward pursuit of Munro-bagging becomes something altogether more adventurous and rewarding.

Another question I'm often asked is which is my favourite Munro. The truth is I have a number of favourites including An Teallach, Beinn Alligin, Beinn Eighe and Ben Macdhui but, for a number of reasons, not all of them purely aesthetic, I could easily plump for A'Mhaighdean in Wester Ross. I reckon this is possibly also Scotland's remotest Munro.

Despite recent discussions in the Scottish Parliament about land reform, I found it interesting that the legislators decided to leave the access provisions of the 2003 Act exactly as they were. Despite constant challenges from a handful of recalcitrant landowners, those access provisions have been extremely successful: legal rights that the Scottish public can be proud of as being amongst the finest and most progressive access legislation in the world. While fellow writers like Tom Weir and in particular my old friend Rennie McOwan from Stirling campaigned for a very long time to see Scotland's de facto access rights become formalised, much of the foundation of the land reform provisions was laid down during discussions at Letterewe House on the shores of Loch Maree in Wester Ross. Indeed, the Munro of A'Mhaighdean was central to those early discussions. That's partly why it's my favourite Munro.

The vast deer forests of Strathnashealag, Fisherfield and Letterewe have long been known as the Great Wilderness. The hills unashamedly expose the bare bones of the earth, folded into complex patterns, and a series of long sinuous lochs betray the evidence of geological faults, subsequently carved out by the grinding of massive glaciers. These scoured-out basins form the grain of the land but excellent tracks weave their way through glens and up over the bealachs at their heads, giving good access to the summits, and what summits they are. The heart of this Great Wilderness is dominated by the Torridonian sandstone peak of Ruadh Stac Mor and the grey quartzite peak of A'Mhaighdean, arguably the remotest of all Scotland's Munros. And if these are the remotest Munros, then neighbouring Beinn a' Chaisgein Mor, at 856 metres/2,808 feet, could well be amongst the most remote of the Corbetts.

It seems a hillwalker had cycled into Letterewe and left his bike at Carnmore when he went off to climb A'Mhaighdean (967 metres/3,173 feet). On his return he discovered his bicycle tyres had been let down by an estate employee. The erstwhile owner of the estate, multimillionaire Paul van Vlissingen, had stated he didn't welcome walkers and a number of notices around the estate made this very clear. This event created some consternation amongst outdoor organisations but it was a hill-going member of the aristocracy who actually took the initiative. John Mackenzie has a series of titles including Earl of Cromartie and Chief of the Clan Mackenzie, but amongst climbers he was known as the author of the Scottish Mountaineering Club's guide *Rock & Ice Climbs in Skye*. He was incensed that access to the Letterewe estate with its famous crags like Carnmore might be in jeopardy and said so publicly. A story appeared in one newspaper stating that John intended leading a clan march onto van Vlissingen's land in protest about the Dutchman's attitude.

That march never happened but what did follow were two years of detailed debate involving not just Mackenzie and van Vlissingen, but also representatives of numerous bodies including the Ramblers and the Mountaineering Council of Scotland. These discussions eventually produced The Letterewe Accord, which guaranteed walkers certain rights and, for the very first time anywhere in Britain, a landowner acknowledged that recreational users had rights to roam over their land. This Accord document was very important in the following discussions that eventually produced the current access provisions of the Land Reform (Scotland) Act.

I'm not sure if A'Mhaighdean will go down in history as the mountain that was central to the access debate but it will probably continue to be recognised as our remotest Munro, if for no other reason than master Munro-man Hamish Brown says so (he describes A'Mhaighdean as 'the least easily reached') and his assertion has been backed by Irvine Butterfield in his book *The High Mountains of Britain and Ireland*. Irvine reckoned that the roads at Kinlochewe, Poolewe and Dundonell are all about nine miles equidistant but A'Mhaighdean is notable for something else: a host of writers have suggested that it has the finest viewpoint of all the Munros. The view out along the length of the crag-fringed Fionn Loch to Loch Ewe and the open sea is simply unforgettable, across a landscape that is as close to 'wilderness' as anything we have in this country.

I'm very aware of the emotive context of that word, particularly when we are describing a landscape that is primarily remote and empty of people, but the poet John Milton once defined wilderness as 'a place of abundance', a paradoxical definition which American philosopher and poet Gary Snyder suggests catches the very condition of energy and richness that is so often found in wild systems:

> '...all the incredible fecundity of small animals and plants, feeding the web. But from another side, wilderness has implied chaos, eros, the unknown, realms of taboo, the habitat of both the ecstatic and demonic. In both senses it is a place of archtypal power, teaching and challenge.'

I like that last sentence of Snyder's, because it is especially relevant in this particular area. It's not known as the Letterewe Wilderness for nothing. The high-level route from the bothy at Shenavall around Beinn a'Chlaidheimh, Sgurr Ban, Mullach Coire Mhic Fhearchair, Beinn Tarsuinn, A'Mhaighdean and Ruadh Stac Mor is not only a genuine mountain challenge but it takes you into a landscape that ticks most of the wilderness definition boxes. I've climbed A'Mhaighdean a couple of times as part of that long rosary of Munros; once on my own and another time with an old ski instructor pal, Jeff Faulkner from Aviemore. Jeff and I climbed An Teallach from Dundonnell and carried our heavy backpacking gear over the steep-sided Corrag Bhuidhe buttresses. We then descended steep ground to Shenavall where we spent the night. A river crossing heralded the next day's hill bashing, and a long day it was traversing Beinn a' Chlaidheimh, Sgurr Ban, Mullach Coire Mhic Fhearchair, Beinn Tarsuinn and

A'Mhaighdean. We camped between the Maiden (A'Mhaighdean can be translated as 'the maiden' although Peter Drummond, in his excellent *Scottish Hill and Mountain Names*, points out that in both Scots and Gaelic cultures a maiden is also the last sheaf of corn cut during the harvest. There are many Highland traditions associated with this last stook when, after a good harvest, it would be dressed to look like a young girl. You certainly notice a likeness to a sheaf when you look at the summit from the west) and her northern neighbour Ruadh Stac Mor, before climbing the latter Munro first thing in the morning. And then it was the long walk-out to Poolewe . . .

I've also climbed A'Mhaighdean from the marvellous oak woods of Loch Maree where there was once a thriving iron smelting industry; from the cathedral-like grandeur of the Fionn Loch below the steep crags of Beinn Airigh Charr, Meall Mheinnidh and Beinn Lair and from the empty quarter around lonely Lochan Fada before returning to Kinlochewe from the narrow gorge of Gleann Bianasdail. But even the simplest route, the most direct route to A'Mhaighdean and Ruadh Stac Mor, is a classic, a memorable walk-in (you could use a mountain bike) and an ascent through a landscape that is as wild and formidable as any.

The long walk-in is a fine way to court this particular maiden. The walk-in from Poolewe allows you time to ease yourself gently into this marvellous landscape, by way of Kernsary and the Fionn Loch. Stay in a tent or use the bothy at Carnmore. Whatever way you approach these hills the undoubted highlight is the ascent of A'Mhaighdean from Carnmore.

On one memorable ascent, Gina and I walked in from Poolewe and camped close to the causeway between the Fionn Loch and the Dubh Loch. A'Mhaighdean's 'stook-like' summit dominated the view from the tent door. Nearby, the house at Carnmore was locked up and I recalled Tom Weir's stories about the family, the MacRaes, who once lived there. Over the years Tom got to know them quite well and was always made welcome. That was probably in the fifties. The house is now used by estate guests. The nearby bothy is always available but be warned, it's a little less than basic. We certainly felt more comfortable in our tent and a memorable camp it turned out to be. The sunset, reflected on the waters of the Fionn Loch, was as spectacular as any I've seen, a slowly changing kaleidoscope of rich reds and yellows and purples fading to a delicate pink. We lay outside the tent, dram in hand, desperate to tease out every last second, before the midges drove us inside to our sleeping bags.

While a superb stalker's path traverses the steep slopes of Sgurr na Laocainn from Carnmore and makes a tortuous route into the mountain's north-east corrie we chose to scramble up the steep, stepped north-west ridge. The stalker's path took us as far as Fuar Loch Mor where we skirted the loch's western bank and took to the rock. There was plenty of good, steep scrambling but all the real difficulties can be avoided. In essence, this was a stairway to heaven, a heaven with some of the best views imaginable.

I truly believe the view from the summit of A'Mhaighdean is the best in the country.

For such a rocky looking mountain, the bald bluff summit comes as a bit of a surprise, but it makes for a fairly easy descent towards the high bealach above Fuar Loch Mor where a scramble takes you up steep broken slopes surprisingly easily to the summit of neighbouring Ruadh Stac Mor and its beautifully crafted stone trig point.

Back at the bealach, a superbly built stalker's path eases its way downhill below the skirt of red screes which form the base of Ruadh Stac Mor, past the brooding Fuar Loch Mor and down over the high gneiss-patched moorland to the track beside Lochan Feith Mhic-illean. We followed this path back to Carnmore and the long, but beautiful, return to Poolewe below the crags of Meall Mheinnidh, Beinn Airigh Charr and Spidean nan Clach. Although it's certainly a long walk, this 'normal' route to A'Mhaighdean and Ruadh Stac Mor shows that no hill in Scotland is truly remote.

I was to edit the *Great Outdoors* (later to be known as *TGO* magazine) for twenty years, two decades that were to become a balanced blur of travel, both at home and abroad, and office work. I loved editing the magazine; loved the creative process of producing a new, brightly illustrated issue every month from nothing; loved finding and encouraging new writers and photographers and I thoroughly enjoyed working closely again with old friends like Chris Townsend and Jim Perrin whom I had formerly worked with at *Footloose* and *Climber*.

We had a great team. John Manning from Yorkshire was my deputy editor, an excellent journalist and keen outdoors guy. At one point he took a year's sabbatical (a posh way of saying he took a year without pay) and hiked the Pacific Crest Trail from the Mexican Border to the Canadian Border, a life-changing event that gave him the space to consider his own future and what he wanted from life, and another great example of how the outdoors can influence and shape our lives. John eventually met and fell in love with Steph and together they moved to a cottage in the Yorkshire Dales and had two lovely Yorkshire children. I was thrilled that John fulfilled his dreams after doing so much to help me fulfill mine.

I hired my old compatriot Chris Townsend as our equipment editor, a *TGO* role he still holds. Chris is one of the most honest people I know and certainly the most experienced gear tester and outdoor market analyst in the country. He is also one of the world's most respected and prolific long-distance backpackers. I thought that was quite a good combination for an equipment editor. In all the years we worked together he never let me or the magazine down.

I had first met Jim Perrin when he was deputy editor of *High* magazine and I was deputy editor of *Climber and Rambler*. We were oppos in competing titles, but we got on well and when I became editor of *Climber* I 'poached' him from *High*. I considered Jim to be the finest writer in the country on outdoor matters, bar none. Formerly one of the country's leading rock climbers, he turned his attention to writing about wider countryside issues and eventually authored some hugely influential books like *Menlove*, the biography of the mountaineer John Menlove Edwards, and *The Villain*, an equally incisive biography of the Lancashire climber Don Whillans, one of the UK's finest ever mountaineers. I'm delighted that Jim is still a mainstay of *TGO* although he now lives predominantly in south-east France.

Another member of the team in those days was Mike Harding. It's difficult to describe Mike because he has achieved so much in his life but essentially, he's a folkie, like me, and a keen walker and trekker. Wikipedia describes him as an English singer, songwriter, comedian, author, poet, broadcaster and multi-instrumentalist. He's also a photographer, traveller, filmmaker and playright. Some folk accused me of pandering to the personality cult when I brought Mike onto the magazine but I was well aware of his enthusiasm for hiking, particularly in the Himalaya, and he was a fellow trek leader with KE of Keswick. He had also served a term as president of the Ramblers' Association. I felt his humorous contributions to the magazine gave us something our competitors lacked: the opportunity to occasionally look at ourselves and have a bit of a giggle at what we saw.

As much as I loved editing *TGO* I still railed against working in a corporate environment. I spent much of my time fighting budget cuts and silly 'advertorial' ideas and I was determined that the magazine should have a high level of commercial honesty. I had seen too many magazines go down the route of appeasing advertisers to the detriment of their own integrity and had no intention of treating our readers as some kind of market fodder. I was certainly aware that many outdoor folk buy the climbing and walking magazines to read the gear reviews and evaluations, a service that helps them choose their own kit. Outdoor gear is not cheap so it was vitally important that our appraisals of gear, whether it be fleece jackets, mountain tents or dehydrated food, would be to as high a level of accuracy and integrity as possible, even if a bad review meant we might lose an advertiser. Interestingly enough, in my entire career we only lost one, and that was because we disagreed with their methodology of fitting crampons.

I remember writing up a review of a Regatta jacket. It wasn't a bad jacket but there were one or two design problems that let it down. I explained the issues in my review. The day after the review was published the company's PR person rang me to say their MD had just read the piece. 'What did he say?' I asked. 'Bastard,' she replied. We didn't lose Regatta as an advertiser, the company took our advice and changed the design. That was how we wanted to work. We didn't criticise equipment fabrics or design just for the sake of it but in more of an advisory mode. It was entirely up to the manufacturer if they wanted to take the advice or not.

Unlike the way many modern magazines operate, under my reign at *TGO* the editorial, advertising and marketing departments all came under the editor's jurisdiction. I had the last say on everything and anything that affected the content of the title. Well, most of the time. As you can imagine this attitude led to a few power struggles and I had threatened the company with my resignation on numerous occasions. Fortunately, no one ever called my bluff although I suspect one or two publishers came close to it. Mike Ure was to be my immediate boss for a good few years and he fully understood my role, a role that was substantially different to that of any other editor in the company.

I was, in effect, a full-time employee but lived the life of a freelancer, writing a weekly column for one of our sister newspapers, the *Sunday Herald*, writing books and spending my official holidays leading treks for Tim and Glenn's company, now known as KE Adventure Travel. I worked extensively from home, using fax machines then various kinds of word processors and then computers to allow me to work remotely. I became fascinated with the digital world and the opportunities it promised for publishing. As a result, *TGO* became the first outdoor magazine in the country to have its own website. With my radio experience, I became interested in the potential of podcasts and so I became the first magazine editor in the country to introduce a regular podcast on our website. Those audio podcasts were later to become a series of video-podcasts featuring videoed hillwalks that I called *Five-Minute Mountains*.

The magazine prospered and so did I, professionally and recreationally. Now into my forties I was as fit as a flea and into my second round of the Munros. I would complete the Corbetts, the 220 Scottish mountains between the heights of 2,500 and 2,999 feet, the little brothers (the wee Ronnies) of the Munros, and finish my second round of Munros before the end of the millennium, following on with a third round of the Munros before I turned sixty. Life was still pretty sweet.

11

Overseas Climbs and Trails

By the time Gordon and Gregor had left school and gone to university (Gordon to do a media studies course in Aberdeen before going to Glasgow University to do an English degree and Gregor to Glasgow School of Art to study graphic design), Gina had become my regular hillwalking companion. In the space of a few years she became a highly seasoned and experienced backpacker and trekker. Together we twice hiked the 220-mile John Muir Trail in California, backpacked round the Tour of Mont Blanc and the walkers' Haute Route between Chamonix and Zermatt and picked out high-level walking routes across the Sierra de Tramuntana, the mountains of Mallorca, from Andratx to Port de Pollenca, a route across the limestone peaks that very few people had ever tackled.

In addition to these self-contained backpacking routes, Gina accompanied me when I led treks for KE Adventure Travel to Manaslu, the Annapurna Circuit, to Everest Base Camp, to the Annapurna Sanctuary in Nepal and to the volcanoes of Guatemala, as well as a couple of treks in Jordan and a memorable traverse of the Atlas Mountains in Morocco. As a trek leader on a 3–4 week trip it's always great to have your spouse along and, as a practising nurse, Gina's presence was always really useful. It was a real delight to share these wonderful trekking experiences with her. I reckon she has plastered more blistered heels than anyone alive!

During my editorship of *TGO*, one of the highlights of the job was climbing some of the world's most beautiful and iconic mountains: the Matterhorn, the jewel of the Alps, to celebrate the 125th anniversary of Edward Whymper's first ascent; Mount Rainier in the Pacific North-West of the US with Lou Whittaker (Lou led the first American ascent of the North Col of Mount Everest in 1984 and his brother Jim was the first American to stand on the summit of Everest back in 1963); Kilimanjaro, the highest mountain on the African continent along with Mount Kenya; Mount Ararat, the biblical mountain of Noah and Elbrus, the highest mountain in Europe.

Two of the most memorable expeditions of that period were to Corsica and Jordan. The Corsican GR20 (*Grande Randonnee 20*, one of a nationwide network of great trails in France) begins in the mountain village of Calenzana, near the coastal resort of Calvi in the north-west of Corsica. It finishes at Conca, in the south-east of the island. As in so many other mountain areas of the world the Corsicans, for many centuries, carried out the practice of transhumance: herding their sheep, cattle, goats and pigs onto the higher, cooler pastures for summer grazing. In doing so they created a plethora of mountain paths and trails and built dozens of *bergeries*, or summer farms, many of which lie in the most delectable situations imaginable.

Conceived in the seventies by the French alpinist Michel Fabrikant, the GR20 is regarded as a mountaineer's route, but actually poses very few technical difficulties. It follows high and exposed ridges but few are as awkward as our own Cuillin of Skye or even the narrow granite ridges of Arran. There are certainly some sections, like the steep-sided slabs in the Spasimata Gorge or the descent into the Cirque de la Solitude, that are potentially dangerous, but in situ chains and ladders take the sting out of the technical difficulties. The route offers a real sense of mountain wilderness, but a system of mountain refuges, or huts, allows you to sleep in a soft bed and have a hot meal every night. Although not quite a sheep in lion's clothing, the GR20 is not, ostensibly, as tough as its reputation would have us believe. The route actually makes full use of many of the ancient mountain trails, and passes close to many of the *bergeries* where you can buy brocciu (ewe's cheese) and figatellu (liver sausage or saucisson, the dry chorizo-like charcuterie of the mountains). I can't think of a better hiking lunch to wash down with cold, clear water from a mountain spring.

An *haute route*, or high-level route, the GR20 also passes close to the summits of some of Corsica's highest peaks, weaving back and forth across the central spine of the island in a crazed, serpentine course. The deep blue of the Mediterranean is rarely out of sight for long, especially on the southern section of the trail. The common assumption is that the route simply climbs to a high mountain ridge and follows it south for a hundred miles, but the reality is considerably more complex. The island of Corsica is not made of a single mountain range but a number of ranges, each thrusting its steep-sided and forested flanks across the breadth of the island. This, in effect, means that the long-distance walker faces a corrugated route of considerable ups and downs with a total ascent of some 12,500 metres/41,000 feet. Mount Everest is slightly over 8,839 metres/29,000 feet.

My companion on that expedition was my old friend and colleague Chris Townsend. Resolute and seasoned backpackers, Chris and I decided to camp at night, rather than endure the sounds, smells and stuffy atmosphere of the mountain refuges. We preferred the scent of a mountain breeze wafting through our tent doors and the privacy that a tent offers, but Corsica's Parc Naturel Regional insist you can only camp at designated areas around the huts. Wild camping is not permitted. Since most of the mountain refuges were positioned high in the mountains we had wonderful views from our tent doors, but the downside was exposure to any winds that rolled down the steep chutes above us at night.

The rugged nature of the trail can be demonstrated by the fact that it took us thirteen days to walk the route, the length of which is anything between 100 and 120 miles. An average distance of ten miles a day is not very impressive in itself, but each day involves a climb of Munro-height and more, and I have never walked on such a sustained rough and rocky trail. Never. Anywhere.

Our abiding memories of walking the GR20 would principally be of a high and sustained mountain walking route, in which there are few 'easy' days to allow the body to recover. Having said that, the delectable blend of mountain and sea views, the long days of good weather, the scent of laricio pines in the hot sun, the delight of peeling your socks off and plunging your feet into a mountain stream, the camaraderie amongst mountain walkers of all nationalities and, perhaps above all else, the marvellous sensation of simply being amongst glorious mountains for almost two whole weeks, gave all the difficulties of the route a different perspective.

Jordan is a country I became very fond of, having led two treks to the Wadi Rum desert before the current Middle East crisis. It is a place immortalised by the writings of T.E. Lawrence, or Lawrence of Arabia, as he became known.

'Rum the magnificent,' he wrote, 'vast, echoing and godlike. A processional way greater than imagination … the crimson sunset burned on its stupendous cliffs and slanted ladders of hazy fire down its walled avenue.' When I was later asked to lead a new trek between the Dana Nature Reserve, near the country's capital of Amman, and the rose-red city of Petra I grabbed the opportunity with two hands. We later christened this route across the Hashemite Kingdom of Jordan 'the Inca Trail of the Middle East'.

On one of my earlier visits I had discussed other trekking opportunities with local guides and, on one memorable evening sitting by a flickering desert fire, with the English adventurers Tony Howard and Di Taylor, who have probably done more for Jordanian adventure tourism than Moses himself. They had highly recommended the rugged trek between Dana and Petra, entering the ancient city by its mountainous back door. Unlike the ancient city of Petra, Dana is small and unpretentious – almost sleepy. Its Nature Reserve covers over 115 square miles of deep valleys and rugged mountains, which extend from the top of the Jordan Rift Valley down to the desert flats of Wadi Araba. As you'd expect in such diverse landscapes, the wildlife is also incredibly diverse with about six hundred different plant species, almost forty species of mammals and nearly two hundred species of birds.

My little trekking group and I arrived in Dana village, the site of an interesting social experiment in which the RSCN (Royal Society for the Conservation of Nature) has tried to rejuvenate a dying community by protecting the natural environment. In the fifties and sixties, the majority of the inhabitants moved out of their Ottoman stone cottages to find jobs in nearby, more modern villages but, in the early nineties, a group of twelve women from Amman formed the Friends of Dana, a project to revitalise the fabric of the villages. With help from the RSCN, the World Bank and the UN, electricity, telephones and a water supply were extended to the village and 65 old stone cottages were renovated. Today the village is a classic example of low-impact tourism. A number of families have moved back into their traditional homes and other buildings have been used for housing natural history research students. Fairly recently a guesthouse was opened in the village and there is a camping ground at nearby Rummana.

From the green oasis of Dana we had descended into a landscape that was wild and desolate but a good track carried us along to our first night's camp at Wadi Feinan. It had been a long and very hot first day.

From Wadi Feinan we had a day of very rough and tough walking, crossing the edge of the flat Wadi Araba on a surface of classic 'hamada': dry, rocky desert with very little sand. High mountains lay before us, to be crossed next day, and the sun beat down on our little band as we slowly made our way towards them, stopping whenever possible below the branches of bleached, desiccated trees, desperate for just a hint of shade, just as travellers to this region had done for thousands of years. We eventually set up camp in the dry canyon of Wadi Barwas where, after supper and a magnificent desert sunset, we fell asleep under the star-laden sky, dreaming of pints of cold beer.

The next four days were spent in the deep-set canyons of the Shara mountains, climbing up through high passes, descending into lovely, verdant green valleys before negotiating scrambling routes over dry, rough sandstone slabs. We camped high too, enjoying spectacular sunsets across the flat Wadi Araba to the Negev desert. Nights were cold but dry enough to allow us to sleep outside under the stars. By day we hiked through sensational sandstone landscapes, passing through ancient Byzantine and Nabatean settlements, taking time to watch spiralling vultures and dashing hawks, or disturbing curious blue lizards from crevices in the rocky ground. All the time we were aware we were walking in the footsteps of the prophets, the heroes of the Old Testament, the wise men and women on whose writings and philosophies our whole western civilisation has been based. No matter your feelings about religion, no matter whether you think the Old Testament stories are folklore or accurate historical records, you just couldn't help be aware that this was where it all happened. This land, and its near neighbour Israel, was the cradle of Christianity, Judaism and Islam.

It was near here, at Tell al-Kharrar, that the prophet Elijah ascended directly to heaven. Not far away lies Bethany beyond the Jordan, where Jesus was baptised by John the Baptist, and beyond that lies one of the oldest cities in the world – Jericho. John the Baptist met his death at Herod's hilltop palace at Mukawir after Salome's demand for his head on a platter was sanctioned by the king, and close by lies Bab adh-Dhraa, one of the contenders for the site of biblical Sodom. You might even want to take shelter from the heat of the sun in Lot's cave, where Abraham's nephew sought refuge with his family from the destruction of the twin towns of Sodom and Gomorrah.

After several days hiking, the wide dusty trail narrowed and became steeper. Signs of man's ancient handiwork became more and more evident. Sections of ancient walls now lined the route and steps, carved from the red sandstone and worn smooth by the passage of countless footsteps, climbed the steeper sections. The upthrust of sheer, rocky walls forced us outwards to where the path was no more than ledge above a vertiginous drop. Beyond lay a rocky ridge and, beyond that, the flat expanse of the Wadi Araba evaporated into a hazy outline that was Israel. Directly ahead of us, across a great cleft in the mountains, rose the sheer crags and buttresses of Jebel Haroun, topped by a tiny building, one of Jordan's holiest sites, the supposed resting place of Aaron, the brother of Moses.

For the past five days we had walked across the ancient biblical lands of Edom, Moab and Ammon, passing Byzantine and Nabatean ruins and age-old Bedouin encampments. We had taken tea with Bedouin shepherds, slept under the desert stars and gazed at mountain panoramas of red sandstone. Now we were approaching the climax of our journey, on a pathway slabbed with drainage channels cut from the rock. Massive square-cut vats hinted at ancient reservoirs and then, around a corner in the crags, we were treated to a sight that simply took our breath away.

The Monastery of the age-old city of Petra is the first of the great rock-carved monuments you come across when you approach Petra, as we did, through the back door, from the ancient city's mountain backdrop. The name of the monument is something of a misnomer, more likely it was a temple dedicated to a former Nabatean king, Obedas I, who reigned in the first century BC and was posthumously deified. Its purpose isn't of great significance to those who approach it from our direction. It is the sheer size and scale of the structure that almost defies description; even the doorway is higher than a normal house. In fact, the Monastery boasts a huge facade about fifty metres square, carved, like everything else in Petra, from the red sandstone mountain itself.

We spent the rest of the day exploring the ancient city, officially one of the Wonders of the World, with the glowing satisfaction that we had walked here across the biblical lands; across rough and red hot rocky 'hamada' terrain, over mountain passes, along sky-high ridgelines and through sandy wadis. If truth be told, we felt rather smug in our sweat-stained trekking gear amongst the fashionably dressed tourists who had driven to Wadi Musa, the local town, and entered the city through the tourist trinket shops and the noisy and very busy entrance (*siq*). We could proudly compare ourselves with the nomads, the traders, the armies who have visited this amazing place ever since the industrious Nabateans challenged the might of Rome, growing wealthy on the profits of trade.

Petra, standing between Egypt, Arabia and Syria, became an important centre for all kinds of traders, adding to the traditional commodities like copper, iron and Dead Sea bitumen with the spices of the southern Arabian coasts: myrrh, balsam and frankincense. Even before those heady days, when the settled population could have been as many as 30,000, local legend claims that it was near here that Moses found water for the peripatetic Israelite tribes by striking a rock. The water that gushed forth was Ain Musa, the Spring of Moses, which supplied precious water for the city of Petra for many hundreds of years.

Another country that managed to get under my skin and has me returning time and time again is Nepal. I've tackled half a dozen treks there and loved every one. A trek in the Himalaya, the vast Asian region that boasts the highest mountains in the world, is on the must-do list for most of us who climb mountains for fun. Since Nepal opened its borders to tourists in 1948, the numbers visiting the land of Shangri-La has risen dramatically, and the Nepalese people, hospitable and welcoming to a fault, have perfected the art of not only making trekkers feel welcome, but making them want to return.

My love affair with trekking started in the early nineties when I took part in the very first *TGO* Readers' Trek, organised for the magazine by KE Adventure Travel. With Pete Royall as trek leader we hiked over the Darkot Pass in the Hindu Kush of Pakistan and I was hooked.

Early on in the trek we came across an ancient fort that appeared to be in the middle of nowhere. It was obviously inhabited and a tall and very elegant man-servant came out as we approached, offering us a grassy area within the fort where we could camp. It was delightfully shaded and we eagerly accepted the offer. No sooner had we erected our tents than he appeared again and in broken English told us that the lord of the region was in residence and would like to meet us. We were delighted, and lined up as though we were about to be inspected by royalty.

A few minutes later a very elderly, wizened and stooped old man swaddled in white robes appeared and walked along the line shaking our hands. When he reached me, he said in very good English, 'And where do you come from?' 'Scotland,' I said mouthing the words deliberately in case he didn't quite understand. 'Ah, Scotland,' the old fellow repeated. 'Where about in Scotland?' 'New-ton-moar,' I slowly mouthed. 'Ah, Newtonmore,' says he, 'near Kingussie. I have a good friend in Kingussie: Colonel Sanderson, we fought in the war together and I am going to Scotland to visit him next month.' You could have blown me over with a feather. Here was me thinking we were in the very back of beyond, close to the Wakhan Corridor that borders Pakistan and Tajikistan and this old fella knew one of my neighbours at home in Scotland. It's a tiny world indeed.

After the Hindu Kush came a long trek round the back of Manaslu into the Annapurnas with my great friend Rex Munro, an Australian who years earlier had given up a well-paid engineering career in Australia to became KE's first official trek leader. I assisted him on a handful of treks before leading one on my own, and learned a huge amount, particularly in how to handle porter crews and the occasional truculent trekker. I just loved the guy. That trek around Manaslu also started my long love affair with the landscapes, culture and people of Nepal.

After that first trek to the Hindu Kush I led over twenty treks for KE Adventure Travel in parts of the world as diverse as Guatemala and Turkey, including a handful of trips to Nepal, but more recently I've been keen on travelling to the old Himalayan kingdom without the responsibilities of leadership. I think it's important to emphasise that I thoroughly enjoyed my years as a trek leader. I loved the camaraderie, met some terrific people and made lots of new friends. I enjoyed passing on nuggets of information and advice picked up over the years and I've been fortunate in that I had relatively few problems to contend with. Mind you, when problems do arise they can be mammoth, like when Gina broke her ankle at 17,000 feet on the Thorung La, a high, snowy pass on the Annapurna Circuit, or when I had to get a dozen people back to the UK from Jordan when volcanic ash grounded most of Europe's aircraft in early 2010. On another occasion, a trekker suffered an epileptic seizure and our Moroccan porters thought he had become possessed by demons, but generally speaking I've had less than my fair share of problems.

Independent trekking was unfamiliar to me until I retired from the magazine and stopped trek leading, when Gina and I and Richard and Meg Else, my television producers and close neighbours in Newtonmore, decided to go to Nepal for a proper holiday. It's worth pointing out that no matter what people think, leading a trekking group is not a holiday. The role comes with many responsibilities, worries and concerns and, although it's a great way to earn a few crumbs, it is rarely restful and stress-free.

We chose Langtang and Gosaikund as our trekking destinations, largely because Richard and Meg had never trekked in Nepal before and I wanted them to experience a journey that was dramatic but relatively risk free. The route allowed us to reach our high point of just over 15,000 feet in several days of easy walking. Langtang is only a few hours' drive from Kathmandu and our return from Gosaikund took us to within fifteen miles of the capital. With no connecting or internal flights to worry about, transport is less potentially troublesome than treks out of Lukla (Everest), Pokhara (Annapurnas) or Jomsom (Mustang). Langtang is also well served with lodges, so we wouldn't have to carry any camping or cooking equipment. Indeed, we had to carry very little because we hired an excellent guide, Dorje, and a couple of very strong and competent young porters, Sonam and Dawa, who carried our trek bags for us, shared Tibetan songs with us in the evening, and taught us a lot about Tibetan culture. Not only did these lads make our trek much easier physically, they enriched it in an untold number of ways with their enthusiasm, friendliness and humour.

The lads came from Syabru Bensi, at the foot of the Langtang valley, where we began walking. We had organised everything through a Kathmandu company called Himalayan Expeditions, whom I'd had previous dealings with. Over the years I'd got to know Bikrum Pandey and his extremely efficient manager Satish so I knew I could trust them to provide us with a good crew and ground arrangements. Those arrangements included booking us into a good hotel in Kathmandu, the Shankar Hotel, at the beginning and end of the trek, picking us up and returning us to the airport, and transporting us to Syabru Bensi.

The Langtang and Gosaikund trek is not a difficult one, but it is remarkably beautiful. The landscapes are less extreme than in the Khumbu or Everest region or in the Annapurnas where the big mountains appear to be pretty distant. In Langtang the mountains tower above you and although there are no 8,000-metre giants, they still rise to an impressive 7,000 metres/23,000 feet. What I enjoyed most about trekking in Langtang was the variety of the landscapes we passed through. The first couple of days were on a trail that climbed up through sub-tropical jungle to rhododendron and bamboo forests, with langur monkeys swinging in the trees and vultures soaring high above us on the thermals. At one lodge someone claimed they saw a red panda, which is not unlikely since the forest hereabouts is a prime habitat. The jungle feel soon evaporates though, as the trees give way to Alpine scrub followed by bare rock and ice, glaciers and snow-covered jagged peaks, the kind of landscape everyone imagines when you mention the Himalaya.

The Gosaikund section of the trek is equally diverse. Ethereal bamboo forests, like Tolkien's Fangorn forest, the deep, dark woodland that grew beneath the southern Misty Mountains, took us up to the misty mountains of the Gosaikund lakes, holy lakes made to look more impressive and mysterious by a fall of unseasonal snow. After a night huddled round the lodge's wood burning stove we made our way over the snowy and starkly beautiful Laurabina La at 4,600 metres/15,100 feet, to begin our long descent back to Kathmandu through the Helambu region, an area that bridges the Hindu culture of the south from the Tibetan culture of the north. Here you return to medieval times where huge water buffaloes still pull the plough in the fields and Brahman women wear traditional dress. Culturally it is more authentic than Langtang or Gosaikund and is more agricultural than tourism-oriented.

The highlight of our trek, literally, was the ascent of a little peak called Kyimoshung (4,620 metres/15,517 feet), above Kyangjin Gompa, a village at 3,900 metres/12,800 feet, at the head of the Langtang Valley. This took us almost within touching distance of Langtang Lirung (7,234 metres/23,733 feet), only a few miles from the Tibetan border. From the prayer flag-covered summit, the view across the glaciers to the face of Langtang Lirung is very impressive with curtains of snow and ice falling from the steep face. To the south-east, Cherko (Tsergo Ri) lies immediately beside the magnificent Kangchenpo (6,387 metres/20,955 feet), nicknamed Fluted Peak by Bill Tilman in the fifties. Other peaks in this massive amphitheatre included Pemthang Ri, Langshisha Ri and Dorje Lakpa.

Our porters had brought ash and new prayer flags to the summit with them, and, as they strung up the flags, they chanted, rubbed ash on our foreheads and sang Tibetan prayers. They had us join in with them and it was a deeply moving experience, forging an even stronger bond between us. In that high and magnificent eyrie, surrounded by mountains and glaciers, snow and ice, I felt curiously at peace with myself and the world. If I had a group of trekkers with me I would have been bustling around, taking the group photographs and generally checking that no one was suffering from the altitude. It was a joy to have so little responsibility.

The next section of our trek was back the way we had come, taking a single day in descent for the four days it had taken us to climb to Kyangjin Gompa. We didn't descend all the way back to Syabru Bensi though. Instead, we cut through a dense forest of oak and pine, traversed a large cirque and climbed to a magnificently situated village called Thulo Sybaru. We stayed in the Peace Lodge and enjoyed the best hot shower of the trip, followed by fresh organic Italian coffee. After a week of instant coffee and tea our caffeine cravings were well satisfied.

From Thulo Syabru we climbed through the Fangorn forest I mentioned earlier, with mists drifting through the trees to Sing Gompa where we spent the night. Next day we climbed again, into the sunshine on a spectacular footpath that dropped savagely on one side. It didn't take long to reach the huddle of lodges that form the high-level village of Gosaikund, and we knew it was going to be a cold night. It was, and it snowed overnight, transforming the colourful village into shades of black and white. The holy lakes of Shiva lay sullen and iron-grey.

Tradition says that Shiva left his holy mountain, Kailash, to come to the foothills of the Himalaya and meditate. Meanwhile, other gods, in search of *amrit*, the nectar of immortality, accidentally extracted a poison that could kill everyone in the world. They begged the Lord Shiva to do something about it so he selflessly drank the poison, which did no more than burn his throat. In some discomfort he thrust his trident into the ground where three springs of water formed to allow him to ease his parched throat and, in this way, the holy lakes of Gosain, Bhairab and Saraswati were formed.

Every year pilgrims visit Gosaikund during the festival of Janai Purnima, when they believe Shiva returns to the world and lies at the bottom of the lake in the form of a large rock. Such tales add a cultural dimension to the experience of walking amongst the most impressive mountains on earth. Add to that the extravagant hospitality of some of the poorest people in the world and it's no wonder so many people form an emotional attachment to this tiny Asian country, sandwiched between the super-powers of China and India. It is no wonder so many of us want to return, either with a trekking group, or as infatuated individuals.

Gina and I returned to Langtang two years later, this time with our oldest son Gordon and his partner Hannah. It was their first experience of Himalayan trekking and they loved it but, catastrophically, the following year a huge earthquake hit Nepal with devastating consequences. Almost 9,000 people died and over a quarter of a million people were injured. Countless families lost their homes and 250 people were registered missing in the Langtang area alone. It was a disaster on a colossal scale and it will take years for Nepal to recover. As a result of the earthquake, Langtang village was demolished and swept away by avalanches and mudslides. It's reckoned there could be dozens, if not hundreds, of villages in Nepal that suffered the same fate. Gone. Demolished. Wiped out as if they had never existed. Only the memories remain.

For me those memories are of sitting in the sun after a hard day's trekking sipping Everest beer; or around the table in a tea-house, swapping songs with our host and his family; or lying on the hillside above the village hearing the faint calls of yak herders from the pastures below; or sampling yak cheeses in the village cheese factory. Happy, joyful memories.

On that trek with Gordon and Hannah we met a young man called Pertemba Tamang, with whom we shared tea and some songs. For Pertemba memories of Langtang are not so joyful. His brothers and mother died in the earthquake, and his home was demolished by the snow and the ice and the mud. His yaks, his only hint of wealth, were all killed and, with that, his future appears to be dead too. He has nothing left, absolutely nothing, and he is one of many, many thousands.

12

ON THE EDGE

It's a curious thing, but occasionally fate intervenes in your life in a way you'd never expect. After years of presenting radio programmes, I dabbled slightly in television. An independent production company called John Gau Productions invited me to front a six-part series for Channel 4, appropriately titled *The Great Outdoors*, and I was keen to become more involved in similar programmes. Never in my wildest dreams did I think that opportunity would present itself in a crumbling Soviet hotel in the shadow of Europe's highest mountain.

Glenn Rowley of KE Adventure Travel had invited me to join him leading a trek around Elbrus, a journey that took us into some of the most remote areas of Russia and the Caucasus Mountains. We ate curds and yoghurt and drank illicit booze with Ukrainian shepherds, sang Beatles songs with local farmers and embraced the opportunity of exploring a landscape that for much of my life had, because of the Cold War, been out of bounds. It wasn't easy travelling but, as the American author James Michener once said, 'If you reject the food, ignore the customs, fear the religion and avoid the people, you might better stay at home.'

Once we had circumnavigated the mountain we climbed it. A dormant volcano, Elbrus forms part of the Caucasus Mountains in Southern Russia, near the border with Georgia. It has two summits, the higher rising to an impressive 5,642 metres/18,510 feet. The east summit is 23 metres lower.

Considering its height, Elbrus is not a technically difficult climb, more of a long and strenuous snow and ice plod. The changeable weather is the biggest problem and in 2004 alone there were 48 deaths on the mountain.

Our circumnavigation of the mountain showed us that this was a very poor area. Poverty was rife and most folk depended on subsistence farming. There were one or two hotels in the valley below Elbrus but they were Stalinesque-type buildings and very run down. They were also comparatively expensive and if you wanted any kind of semi-luxury goods, like a beer or two, you had to resort to inducements. Bribery was how normal business was done. Curiously enough, two items that were cheap and freely available were caviar and champagne. Vodka was also easy enough to get hold of.

As it happened we weren't the only British group on the mountain. Chris Bonington turned up with a small film crew. They were filming Chris' attempt on the Seven Summits, the rich man's form of Munro-bagging. I had known Chris for some time and also knew his camera operator, Jim Curran from Sheffield. The third member of the party was the crew's director/producer, Richard Else, a name I recognised as belonging to the man who had cajoled the curmudgeonly Alfred Wainwright, author of a series of Lake District guide books, on to our television screens. Richard was about to play an important part in my continuing career, although I could not know it at the time.

Once we had all climbed the mountain and safely descended back to the hotel we enjoyed a bit of a party with our local guides and Chris's team. Champagne flowed like water and we all threw back glass upon glass of cheap vodka. The cries of 'nostrovia' became louder and louder. It was only later that someone explained that 'nostrovia' is not a drinking toast at all. It's normally used as a reply to thank someone for a meal or a drink. As we became drunker our guides plied us with more and more vodka. Eventually Glenn, who realised it might be a long night, muttered 'Oh, shit,' and downed another glassful. Our Ukrainian guides overheard him and thought his curse was an English toast, and spent the rest of the night triumphantly shouting 'Oh, shit' as they threw back their vodkas.

Paracetemol tablets were selling for quite a few roubles the next morning and I sat down with a pot of black coffee and enjoyed a long chat with Richard. He had asked me how much I knew about the veteran Scots mountaineer and writer W. H. Murray as he was thinking about making a television documentary about him. I said

I had met him briefly a few times, but his books had been one of my main inspirations when I was a youngster. *Mountaineering in Scotland* and *Undiscovered Scotland*, were, as I recalled, rather old-fashioned and almost Gothic in style: more Frank Smythe than Chris Bonington, but they had a great emotional depth. Even when I first read them as a teenager I was already aware that there was much more to climbing mountains than successfully completing a rock climb or reaching a summit cairn. Those two books had touched me deeply and helped shape a lifelong journey of discovery, a search for the Holy Grail of the outdoors, the desire to 'connect' with wild land.

I had already glimpsed something of this awareness on an earlier visit to the Isle of Skye. As a relatively inexperienced youth I had sweated up the Great Stone Chute from Coire Lagan in the Cuillin. I reached the narrow stance between Sgurr Mhic Choinnich and Sgurr Alasdair and scrambled up to Alasdair's summit, trembling with the exertion and excitement. I had no idea Scottish mountains could be as precipitously rugged as this, and with the scree struggle and the steep scrambling behind me I felt I had undergone a rite of passage, an experience that had earned me a form of kinship with this remarkable mountain range. It was something more fundamental than ownership, more vibrant that a sense of achievement. I felt I had been accepted as part of the fabric of the mountain, part of that biotic community that is made up from rock and light and air ... I had connected with the mountain and in doing so transcended my own being.

Many years later, I made a television programme with the American outdoorsman Ray Jardine in which we hiked through the Three Sisters Wilderness in Oregon state, discussing various aspects of wild land and how we react to it. Sometime later, in a letter to me, Ray told me that he sensed the tensions I had been carrying on that backpacking trip: concerns and anxieties that go cheek-in-jowl with making a television programme. 'I was aware of a great eagle walking along behind me,' he told me, 'an eagle whose wings were tied and who so desperately wanted to cut loose and soar.'

Ray suggested why 'connection' with the land was so important.

'We might remember that despite our almost overwhelming technology, we are still flesh and bone. Our bodies are an integral part of Mother Earth. The air we breathe is her breath, rippling the grasses in the meadow. The water we drink is her life-blood, tumbling from the snowy heights. Every molecule in us is not our own, but a part of Mother Earth. We are borrowing those molecules from her, and will have to give them back when we leave. This is one problem with city life, where we tend to hide from all that. But in fact the more richly we connect with Mother Earth, the higher and farther we can walk our paths. With this in mind, each footstep blesses the earth and the journey itself becomes sacred. I think everyone experiences this.'

That may read as rather fanciful, a typical west-coast American response to experiencing the natural world, but I was attracted by Ray's concept of sacredness, reminding me of Bill Murray's descriptions of his relationship with mountains, which often appeared as hallowed experiences, as though a divine intervention had separated him from his former self to make of him something new, refreshed and recreated.

Without any doubt, Bill Murray's writings had made me look at mountains in a different light, as though there was something more to be gained from the experience, an intangible that was always just out of reach.

Richard and I chatted for some time about Murray's influence in the lives of so many Scottish mountaineers and some weeks later he telephoned to say that the BBC was interested in a film, but as part of a bigger six-part series documenting the last century of Scottish mountaineering. He then asked me if I would like to present the series. I had no hesitation in accepting, and so began a hectic few months of researching, recruiting climbers and television crew and filming the climbs, much of it in the depth of winter, from Ben Nevis to the Skye Cuillin. The resultant series, *The Edge – One Hundred Years of Scottish Mountaineering*, was a huge success with viewing figures of three million. The episode about Bill Murray was later awarded a Scottish BAFTA. More importantly, it was the beginning of a long and valued friendship and working relationship with

Richard and Margaret and their production company, Triple Echo Productions, later to change to Adventure Show Productions.

For me, the most memorable time in those hectic few months was when I spent a day with Bill Murray at his home at Lochwood on the shores of Loch Goil. Bill and his wife Anne couldn't have been more hospitable, even when we had to completely rearrange their small living room so we could erect lights and sort camera positions. The couple put up with our demands with good humour before we settled down and I interviewed Bill about the writing of what is probably his most successful book, *Mountaineering in Scotland*. This is an account of climbing in the Highlands in the years preceding World War II and the first draft was written in prisoner of war camps after he was captured in the Western Desert. Just as he had completed the first draft, Gestapo officials, who believed it might be some kind of coded message to Czech patriots, took it from him. He was interrogated at length and the manuscript was destroyed. Most of us would probably have given up at that point, the thought of starting all over again in such horrific circumstances being too much of a psychological barrier, but the tenacity that made Murray such a fine mountaineer turned what was a major setback into a positive benefit.

During our television interview, he described what happened next, 'This time I knew what I had to say so I was able to write faster and was actually able to improve greatly on the first version. I still kept the manuscript in my battledress tunic because we had numerous searches and it was a frightening time.

'Towards the end of the war we were all expecting the SS to come in and machine-gun the lot of us – we had heard they were doing that in Eastern Europe, but we had found ways of taking our minds off that thought and for me it was living in the mountains in my imagination. Although we were on a starvation diet of eight hundred calories a day – rotten turnips and potato peelings – one kept going mainly in the hope that the unexpected would happen and we would be released.'

Released they were, and Murray returned to the UK and his book was published by Dent of London. His editor wanted him to remove some of the content, which he felt was too 'spiritual' but Murray refused, insisting that such chapters were integral to the book, the circumstances of its writing and its subject matter. Many commentators have since suggested that it was this spirituality, the sacredness of Murray's relationship to wild nature and mountains in particular, that allowed many to gain a full measure of what mountains and wild land mean to us. It's an aspect of wildness that gave our aboriginal forefathers a meaning in life, a purpose, a belief system that supported them and gave them a reverence for the land. It's exactly this reverence for wild land that set William Hutchison Murray apart as a mountaineering writer and created an agenda for his later work as a landscape conservationist.

In the years leading to his death in 1996 I met Bill a number of times. He always struck me as mild-mannered, extremely polite and unassuming. To others, he seemed distant and preoccupied, a very private man. I knew that he had once considered entering the monastic life but after spending some time in a Benedictine monastery in Devon he decided that the life of a monk wasn't for him. Instead he would become a full-time writer. Indeed, it wasn't until I read *The Sunlit Summit*, an exceptionally good biography of Murray by Robin Lloyd-Jones, published a few years ago, that I began to fully realise the depth and nature of Murray's own spiritual search, a pursuit of meaning that was bound inextricably with his devotion to wild places.

The Sunlit Summit is a masterly biography; in terms of mountaineering books I would put it on an equal footing with Jim Perrin's wonderful biography of the mountaineer Menlove Edwards, and in the book I discovered much more about Murray's search for a spiritual life. It was in a prisoner of war camp that he met a young Indian Army officer called called Herbert Buck, who explained to him the concepts of something called Perennial Philosophy, which Wikipedia describes as 'a perspective within the philosophy of religion which views each of the world's religious traditions as sharing a single, universal truth on which foundation all religious knowledge and doctrine has grown'.

Perennial Philosophy was the subject of a successful book by Aldous

Huxley and had earlier been made popular by transcendentalists like Ralph Waldo Emerson and Henry David Thoreau in the US, but it would appear that Murray had little knowledge of the subject until he met Buck in Oflag VIII F at Mahrisch Trubau in Czechoslovakia. That meeting changed his life. Indeed, in a letter to his old friend and climbing companion, Douglas Scott, he said the prisoner of war years were 'the most profitable of my life'. He wasn't only referring to the writing of *Mountaineering in Scotland*, but also to his spiritual development.

In *The Sunlit Summit*, biographer Lloyd-Jones asserts, 'From the point of meeting Herbert Buck onwards, the quest to find self fulfilment through union with the Divine Essence, with Absolute Beauty and Truth, was the most central and important thing in his life. To try and understand him on any other terms than this is to misunderstand him.'

So, what was it that Murray discovered and what was this mystical philosophy that was to become the driving force in his life? I suppose many people today would equate Perennial Philosophy with New-Age thinking, and they probably wouldn't be far wrong. In populist terms, Murray was closer to George Harrison than Cliff Richard, choosing a pick-and-mix type of religion that embraced Hinduism and Buddhism, transcendental meditation, a hint of pantheism all mixed in with a good dose of traditional Presbyterianism. 'Denial of self' was an essential condition for reaching his spiritual 'sunlit summit'.

In many ways Bill Murray trod a similar path to John Muir, who once suggested his 'mountainanity and Christianity came from the same source', but Muir's religion was more directly related to Christian doctrine. His father had been a fundamentalist lay preacher and evangelist and Muir rarely travelled anywhere without his copy of the New Testament. Murray's spiritual studies tended to have more of an Eastern flavour, and led him into a life of service in terms of his conservation work and his enthusiasm for encouraging others.

Murray's own conservation ethic was an interesting one. He often commented that the hills were becoming too busy and what we required was a more measured and sustainable management of our mountain environment that not only recognises the needs and aspirations of the human communities who live there, but also the conservation of the landscape and wildlife that also live there. The fundamental question that many people were asking in the sixties and seventies was 'what are our mountains for?'

Not long before he died, Bill Murray answered that very question in a little booklet called *Scotland's Mountains: An Agenda for Sustainable Development*. This is what he wrote:

> 'Walking and mountaineering can certainly teach how vital wild land is to our physical and spiritual health. It teaches values, gives purpose and enjoyment. But wild land is not there simply to minister to our needs of recreation. Beware the exploiters who blindly assert that 'mountains exist for public enjoyment' and then proceed, for expedient motives or money, to destroy the very qualities that most make the mountains worth knowing – their natural beauty and quiet. Land and wildlife have their own being in their own right. Our recreation is an incidental gain, not an end in itself to be profitably pursued by exploiting land where that means degrading it. The human privilege is to take decisions for more than our own good; our reward, that it turns out to be best for us too.'

Bill Murray's spiritual thinking was one of reverence for and celebration of wild places, not in the normal anthropocentric view of man being dominant, or even as man having stewardship of the earth, but offering instead an ecocentric perspective that suggests the earth does not belong to man. Conversely, man belongs to the earth. Bill realised that wild places should not merely be regarded as an arena: neither for attempting to conquer nature, nor as a racetrack, nor as a playground in which people can try and sharpen their personal spirit of achievement, but as a place of worship. Through the spirit of wildness the achievements we gain are measured more in terms of fulfilment and depth-of-being rather than how many mountains we can climb over a long weekend. Mountains and wild landscapes helped Bill Murray to discover realms of his own life that he was previously unaware of, realms that enabled him to transcend the limits of his own human-centred thinking. He clearly had no desire to even attempt to separate the mountains from the mystic, to take the sacred out of wildness. He wanted to experience more, much more, than the cold relics of the earth's bare bones.

The Edge was a fantastic opportunity to make my mark as a presenter of flagship adventure programmes, but it turned out to be more than that. For several months I worked with some of the finest climbers and mountaineers in the country and shared some of the stories and experiences that had given Scottish mountaineering such a valuable legacy in world terms.

We had two major problems. Firstly, how on earth were we to choose the subjects for six programmes from the plethora of great mountaineers Scotland produced in the previous hundred years, and secondly, we only had four months to film and produce the six programmes. We started filming in January 1994 and had to deliver everything by Easter. It was an incredibly tight schedule but we were blessed with some phenomenal winter conditions and a film crew that was willing to work incredibly long hours in the most difficult conditions. On many occasions our camera operators and safety crew wouldn't get off the hill until well after dark, on some occasions as late as nine or ten in the evening, and then be up at the crack of dawn to start again. Without their commitment and professionalism, we wouldn't have produced anything.

This attitude contrasted greatly with stories I had heard from Tom Weir about film crews insisting they were back at their vehicles by five o'clock, and cameramen who demanded proper lunch breaks. In contrast, virtually everyone in our crew was a climber: camera operators, sound operators, runners and producers, and we were supported by a superb safety team made up of seven qualified mountain guides expertly led by international mountaineer Brian Hall. The combined experience and mountain awareness of the whole team was to prove invaluable.

Before we began filming, Richard and I spent a lot of time visiting and talking to climbers about the subject matter. Tom Weir was very helpful, as was Hamish MacInnes who, sadly, couldn't appear in any of the films as he was busy. Eventually we decided on a mixture of biographical and thematic films that we hoped would each represent a particular era in the development of mountaineering in Scotland between the 1890s and the 1990s.

We began with an examination of one of the finest climbing partnerships in the history of the sport, the unlikely pairing of Victorian scientist, Professor Norman Collie, and the Skye-based mountain guide, John Mackenzie. The two climbed together every time Collie visited Skye. He would contact Mackenzie at Sligachan, and the two would formulate their plans. The guide to client relationship quickly grew into a deep friendship and the two men, from such contrasting backgrounds and cultures, were bound together by a common love and appreciation of the Skye Cuillin. They were eventually buried side by side in the little graveyard near Sligachan on Skye.

Our original inspiration, W. H. Murray, was the subject of the second programme, representing the era up to the outbreak of World War II. We decided to film an account of his ascent of Tower Ridge on Ben Nevis, his last climb in Scotland before going off to war. During an amazing week in February, the crew filmed a superb re-enactment of this climb with three Scottish-based climbers acting the parts of Bill Murray and his two companions on that climb, Jimmy Bell and Douglas Laidlaw. Scottish mountaineer Graham Moss played the part of Murray, and mountain guides Alastair Cain and Mark Diggins played Jimmy and Douglas. Those three really earned their crust, tackling the snow- and ice-bound Tower Ridge dressed in the gear of the thirties: tweed jackets, hemp ropes and nailed boots. It was gripping stuff, even if the boots didn't grip very well.

On Bill Murray's return from the war, he didn't try and compete with the new generation of Scottish climbers, people like John Cunningham, Tom Patey, Jimmy Marshall, Robin Smith and Hamish MacInnes. According to Murray, these men 'had a speed and confidence we simply hadn't possessed'. Another era was about to begin and we concentrated largely on the contribution made by Edinburgh climber Jimmy Marshall and his relationship with the likes of the younger Robin Smith and Dougal Haston, both phenomenal mountaineers. Haston went on to become, along with Doug Scott, the first Briton to climb Everest. However, the American mountaineer Yvon Chouinard described Jimmy Marshall as being 'the real genius of the decade'. He was six years older than Smith and eight years older than Haston but Marshall was the inspiration behind the climbing success of a whole bunch of young Edinburgh climbers, collectively known as the Currie boys.

Though a relative unsung hero of Scottish and UK mountaineering, Jimmy Marshall has been inextricably linked to the development of cutting-edge climbing in Scotland during the fifties and sixties. In one legendary week on Ben Nevis in 1960, Jimmy Marshall and Robin Smith transformed the shape of Scottish winter mountaineering, advancing it a full ten years. On consecutive days, the two men climbed six first winter ascents, including the mini Alpine-route Orion Face Direct, while also making the second and much quicker ascent of Point Five Gully for good measure, in seven hours as opposed to more than 40 hours when previously climbed. We filmed Jimmy climbing with his old Glaswegian pal John McLean on Buachaille Etive Mor and, even at the age of 62, there was a precise ballet-like movement in his climbing, a vertical grace that was sheer joy to watch.

Robin Smith became one of Scotland's finest ever climbers but sadly died at the very young age of 23 in the Pamirs. After climbing Everest, Dougal Haston moved to Leysin in Switzerland where he died in an avalanche in 1977.

The fifties and sixties saw a huge explosion in interest in climbing and mountaineering in Scotland, with standards rising proportionally. While the Creag Dubh club in the west and Marshall et al. in the east were leading the way, many climbers were heading to the unexplored grounds of Scotland's far north-west. One of them was Dr Tom Patey from Aberdeen, one of the most charismatic Scottish mountaineers of the century. Few climbers have matched his long-lasting charisma, and when he died in an abseiling accident after climbing the Maiden, a quartzite sea stack off Whiten Head in Sutherland on 25th May 1970, it brought to an end a tremendous mountaineering career that had lasted twenty years. To the public at large he was known mostly through the Old Man of Hoy BBC television spectacular in 1967 (which had an audience of fifteen million), but inside the small mountaineering world he was a familiar and well-loved figure. From his very first ascent on Lochnagar's Douglas-Gibson Gully in 1950 to his very last climb, which led to his premature death at the age of 38, he was a major and significant player.

Our final programme was very much a look at modern developments, as they were then, and we followed the climbs of three young Scottish Mountaineers: Rab Anderson, Dave Cuthbertson and Dundonian Graeme Ettle. This was at a time when climbing was changing fast. Better equipment, different attitudes and higher fitness levels saw the likes of our three climbers search out and climb some of the most technically difficult routes in the country, but other forces were at work too. Indoor climbing walls were becoming fashionable and young climbers were training hard for sports climbs, bolted climbs and even climbing competitions. It seemed that traditional climbing in the Scottish sense was being overlooked.

In an interview at the time, 26-year-old Graeme Ettle said, 'There are any number of climbers of my age climbing hard on indoor walls or on bolted routes, but very few are active at the highest levels during the winter. In areas such as Beinn Eighe there are acres of climbable lines, all in the top grade, the equivalent of E3 routes and above in winter conditions. If more young climbers had as much commitment to winter climbing as they have to summer sport climbing the result would be tremendous, but it's not happening. Wall climbing takes place in such a controlled environment that it is very hard to imagine anyone breaking away from it. If I am on a route and fail, then I am involved in hours of hassle before I reach safety. If you fail on a wall, you simply drop off and go home. Where is the comparison?'

Today, twenty years after Graeme's comments, that specialisation he refers to has solidified. Rock climbers flood to the sports-climbing crags of the south while others, like Dave MacLeod, have brought the gymnastic skills of the climbing walls to outdoor crags on Dumbarton Rock, Ben Nevis and Strone Ulladale on the Isle of Harris. Six years ago, in another Richard Else-led outside documentary, viewers watched a live ascent of the great overhanging prow on this Hebridean rockface by MacLeod and fellow climber Tim Emmett. It was a fascinating and gutsy display of modern rock climbing at its very highest level.

While it's safe to say that much of the earliest exploration of the Scottish Highlands took place in the first half of the twentieth century, climbers are still discovering new crags and new potential lines, even on some of the popular crags. I recently bumped into Andy Nisbet, one of Scotland's climbing legends, who was very wary about telling me where he was heading. There is still a strong competitive element amongst those who seek out new crags and new lines and few Scottish climbers have as many first ascents to their name as Andy.

There have always been peaks and troughs in the development of climbing in Scotland and in all the peaks, and more importantly, all the troughs, there have still been climbers on the hills. Most will not be challenging the prevailing standards, nor creating new routes, but accepting the challenges the mountains pose for them as individuals. Most climbers, then and now, don't particularly worry whether the sport that we know as mountaineering is developing or stagnating. It's a personal game, and most of us take part in it, and love it, at that level. Twenty-odd years from the filming of *The Edge*, there are still those pushing the standards of mountaineering in Scotland, and while hundreds annually line up in queues to climb Everest, the mountains of Scotland still provide a technical challenge for the best climbers in the world.

The Edge was such a huge success the BBC immediately commissioned another series from Richard. He and I had discussed the possibility of taking some interesting people for a long walk, camping out overnight, and discussing with them their own life and, more importantly, what wild places meant to them. We called the series *Wilderness Walks* and a television reviewer in *The Times* described it as 'Parkinson in anoraks'. I couldn't have described it better myself.

We decided to choose guests who were not necessarily well known to the public-at-large, wanting to avoid the personality cult that television was being accused of helping to generate in the mid-nineties. We looked for individuals who were leading interesting lives or had an occupation that folk would find stimulating. What was essential as far as we were concerned was that our guests had a passion for wild places and could discuss that passion at some length.

Finding suitable guests wasn't as easy as you would imagine. We identified numerous folk who were leading fascinating lives but had little interest in wild places, although they described themselves as 'keen walkers'. Others simply weren't physically capable of spending several days climbing mountains, and then there were those who were fanatical about the outdoors but couldn't really talk about anything else. Interestingly, we were pointed in the direction of several well-known individuals who had presented 'outdoor programmes', either walking-type shows or wildlife shows. I think that was when I first became aware of the glaring differences between a television presenter who does outdoor programmes, and keen outdoor folk who present television shows. I fall into the latter category and so does the only regular television presenter we had on either of the series, Nick Crane, of the BBC's *Coast*. Both Nick and I are, first and foremost, outdoor enthusiasts who happen to occasionally front television programmes about the outdoors. I know of a number of folk who present television programmes about the outdoors but who have little interest in the subject. It's just another telly gig to them.

I had an interesting experience of this 'personality presenter' world when Hamish Barbour, Muriel Gray's hubby, asked me to become involved in a series he was making for BBC1. The series was to be called *Mountain* and the general idea was to celebrate the mountains of Scotland, England and Wales and the people who lived close to them and climbed them. My role was supposed to be advisory and I naturally assumed that Muriel would be presenting, so I was a little taken aback when Hamish admitted that the programmes were to be fronted by Griff Rhys Jones, the actor and comedian. I thought

1. Gina on the Pinchot Pass, John Muir Trail, Cailfornia.

2. With Donnie Munro, former lead singer with Runrig, on his
home territory of the Isle of Skye.

3. With writer and broadcaster Lesley Riddoch on the summit of Carrauntoohill, the highest mountain in Ireland.

4. With the legendary Hamish Brown in the High Atlas mountains of Morocco.

5. My dear friend Jim Perrin and me, enjoying a televised pilgrimage in Ireland for our Wilderness Walks series.

6. Ray and Jenny Jardine, lightweight backpacking gurus who taught me about 'connecting' with the landscape.

7. The Ordesa Gorge in the Pyrenees with writer and
broadcaster Nick Crane.

8. My good friend, film producer and Newtonmore neighbour,
Richard Else.

9. With Jimmie MacGregor at the unveiling of the Tom Weir statue.

10. A proud Pappa with Grace and Charlotte.

11. With Hannah and Gordon on Tsergo Ri, Langtang Himalaya, Nepal.

12. On the summit of Gokyo Ri, with Everest in the background.

13. Looking towards Seana Bhraigh from Eididh nan Clach Geala.

14. Lifelong pal Hamish Telfer and me arriving at Malin Head after cycling the length of Ireland.

15. Morning light in Rothiemurchus Forest, a magical place among many in Badenoch and Strathspey where I live.

16. With one of my musical heroes, the great fiddler Duncan Chisholm.

17. Gina, our sirdar Dorje with Meg and Richard Else
climbing above the holy lakes of Gosainkund in Nepal.

18. Becoming campervanman for television series,
Roads Less Travelled.

19. The McNeish clan, all together for a friend's wedding.

20. Packrafting on Loch Insh, near Kincraig.

21. Receiving the Oliver Brown Award from Grant Thoms,
editor of the Scots Independent newspaper.

22. With Sam Heughan at the My Peak Challenge Gala Dinner in 2017.

Griff was an odd choice but the series was to be broadcast on BBC1 and that popular channel appears to have a limited celebrity list of talking heads who appear on most things. Griff later admitted to me that he had never climbed a mountain in his life.

However, it wasn't my problem if things turned out bad and I could only advise as best as I could, but as I was travelling to the Lake District to give a talk to the Keswick Lecture Society my mobile rang. I was driving so Gina took the call for me.

'It's Hamish's television company and they want you to guide Griff Rhys Jones up Ben Hope for the first programme in the series,' she said.

'When?' I replied. More muffled conversation on the phone.

'Wednesday,' she said.

'Ah, tell them I can't,' I replied. 'I'm giving my talk in Keswick on Tuesday evening and there's no way I can get to Ben Hope (the most northerly of the Munros) by Wednesday morning.'

Gina relayed this message and I thought that was that but a few minutes later the phone rang again. This time I pulled into a layby and took the call myself.

'The BBC is very keen that you take Griff and the film crew up Ben Hope on Wednesday and Griff will interview you about Munros and Munro-bagging. What time will you finish your lecture in Keswick? We can then hire a helicopter to pick you up and take you to Tongue.'

I couldn't quite believe what I was hearing, but the first germs of excitement were beginning to take root, not at the thought of climbing Ben Hope with Griff Rhys Jones but at the prospect of a helicopter ride from Keswick to Tongue. I checked with Gina that she'd be happy to drive home on her own and agreed a time to be picked up. A few minutes later the phone rang again.

'Sorry, but we've just discovered the helicopter can't fly in the dark, but we've made alternative arrangements. If you can drive from Keswick to Loch Lomond after your talk you can catch a seaplane near Balloch and fly to the Kyle of Tongue. How about it?'

By this time I was almost convinced someone was taking the mickey, but I agreed anyway. They would get back to me later with directions about where and when to meet the seaplane. That evening, the night before I was due to give my talk, the company rang and told me there was a problem.

'Apparently there's a big snow storm coming in and the seaplane won't fly, so here's the new plan. If you drive home to Newtonmore immediately after your lecture in Keswick we'll arrange for you to be collected by someone in a 4x4 vehicle about one or two in the morning. It'll take about five or six hours to drive to Tongue so you can be with us for breakfast, and with someone else driving you'll be able to get a kip in the back of the vehicle.'

By this time I was convinced I was the one who was mad but, ever-keen not to let the side down, I left Keswick just after nine and made it to Newtonmore by about 1.30a.m. Gina just kept shaking her head, muttering words like mad, fool, idiot, prat . . .

No sooner had we arrived home than the 4x4 turned up and I began one of the wildest journeys I have ever experienced – a long, slow drive into the teeth of ferocious gales and snowstorms. I didn't get a wink of sleep but my driver was simply amazing and just kept ploughing through the drifts despite me nagging him to stop and take a break. He delivered me to the hotel in Tongue at 8 a.m., just as the crew were arriving, still sleepy-eyed, for breakfast.

'Where's Griff?' I asked, when everyone else had assembled.

'Oh, we have a slight problem with Griff,' the director explained. 'His agent has written into his contract that he will only stay in five-star hotels so he's at the best hotel we could find, the Altnaharra, a luxury huntin', fishin', shootin' hotel about seventeen miles to the south of Tongue.

'The problem is we can't contact him. The phone line is down and nobody can get a mobile signal.'

Meanwhile, Griff was having his own adventures. He had a hire car with him but when he saw all the newly fallen snow he asked the hotel staff if he could borrow the hotel's Land Rover. Grabbing his gear, he blasted off and, after three or four miles, drove it into a snowdrift. He was stuck, and he couldn't get a mobile phone signal.

A rescue party retrieved him once the bad weather abated and I had to spend another night in Tongue with the plan of climbing

Ben Hope next morning. Griff eventually turned up dressed like the Michelin Man. I lost count of how many layers he was wearing and told him there was no way he would climb Ben Hope dressed as though he was going to bivvy in the Arctic. To his credit, he took my advice and climbed the hill in impressive fashion, under pretty gloomy and miserable conditions of snow showers and low cloud.

The series was reasonably successful but Griff was obviously inexperienced and more than a tad uncomfortable in the role of mountaineer. The next I heard was that he was to present a series about sailing. I saw something of the first programme and he was in a Canadian canoe. By the way he was paddling he clearly wasn't a canoeist either. Ho-hum.

For *Wilderness Walks* Richard and I didn't want personalities but ordinary folk who would be passionate about their outdoors experiences and would inspire our viewers with their enthusiasm. I think, largely, we succeeded. Twenty years on I frequently hear from people who tell me it was a *Wilderness Walks* guest who inspired them to start climbing hills and mountains. Numerous folk have told me it was seeing Chris Brasher use trekking poles on telly that made them think of getting hold of a pair to save wear and tear on their knees and hips, or that Hamish Brown convinced them to visit Morocco, or that Ray and Jenny Jardine made them think seriously about how much weight they carried in their packs. For me these were all important issues and I was thrilled to present them to a BBC2 nationwide television audience.

Only one potential guest turned us down, and that was a real disappointment to me. For years I had been a huge fan of the travel writer, Dervla Murphy. She had travelled by bicycle to India, Iran, Afghanistan and Pakistan and when her daughter was born out of wedlock she claimed it was to spite the Irish church. I loved her independence, her sense of humour and her willingness to get herself into potentially dangerous situations and then suggest that the most dangerous thing she has ever experienced is accidentally tripping over one of her five dogs or three cats. I thought she would make a fabulous walking companion and guest on *Wilderness Walks*.

We managed to contact Dervla, who lives in Lismore in County

Waterford, but she didn't seem very keen. She told us that she hated television, didn't own one and didn't want to appear on one. Rebuffed but still determined, I asked my good pal Jim Perrin, who knew Dervla well, if he could perhaps try to persuade her. Jim agreed, so we all travelled to Waterford and Jim went off to court the indefatigable Dervla. The plan was that he would suggest we all meet at our hotel, we would wine and dine her and soften her up, and then pose the question again. Hopefully she would see we were not the smooth television types she so loathed and would agree. Initially, it all went well. Jim turned up at the hotel with Dervla in tow, and we booked a table for dinner. Richard ordered some pre-prandial drinks in the bar and Dervla had a pint or two of Guinness and a cigar as well as a considerable amount of wine with the meal. We retired to the bar and after more pints of Guinness I thought she had perhaps mellowed enough for me to broach the subject again. She listened patiently, smiled and blew a cloud of smoke from her cigar. She then leaned across the table and took me by both hands. 'Yer a lovely boy Cameron, and I'd love nothing more than to take a long walk with ya – but no fuckin' cameras.' That was that.

13

WILDERNESS WALKS

Let me tell you about some of the guests we invited to walk and talk with us on *Wilderness Walks*. Series one got out of the starting blocks with my old pal Chris Brasher who decided he wanted to take a long walk in the Cairngorms, so we devised a route from Aviemore to Braemar over Braeriach and Cairn Toul. Chris had recently helped form the Knoydart Foundation, one of Scotland's first community buy-outs and he was very keen on some of the work being carried out by the National Trust for Scotland in their Mar Lodge Estate in the Cairngorms. So, conservation issues formed much of our conversation, as did his amazing career as a journalist and television film maker, Olympic gold medallist, pacemaker in the first four-minute mile, a pioneer of British orienteering, running shoe and hiking boot manufacturer and racehorse owner. Chris Brasher was the original 'man o' many pairts'.

Despite all his huge achievements, I suspect Chris may be long remembered for his enthusiastic description of the Cairngorms as we stood on the summit of Braeriach, the third highest mountain in the UK. As we gazed across this magnificently high, rolling land-scape I asked him why he was so passionate about the Cairngorms? He waved his hands expansively towards the view, smiled and said, 'Just look at these hills, they're like the great billowing breasts of a beautiful woman.' It was a quote that did not go down well with a certain section of our audience, and certainly not with our next guest, journalist, broadcaster and women's libber, Lesley Riddoch.

Our executive producer at BBC Scotland, Ken MacQuarrie, was, quite correctly, keen that we had a number of female guests on the show. We were discussing the possibilities one day in Glasgow when Kenny suggested Lesley Riddoch. He was vaguely aware that she had a little bothy somewhere in upper Donside where she would take herself to from time to time and he thought she was quite an enthusiastic outdoor person, a hiker and keen cyclist.

I knew Lesley a little bit, having taken part in a couple of radio programmes with her. I was well aware of her enthusiasm for women's rights. I was also aware that she had a fierce intellect (she had been chair of the debating society at Oxford) and that she seldom took prisoners with those who disagreed with her. I confessed to Kenny that she sounded like a possibility but the fact was I was terrified of her. That was the wrong thing to say. 'Brilliant,' exclaimed our executive producer, 'she'll be absolutely ideal then'.

Lesley turned out to be a great guest. Brought up in Northern Ireland to Scots parents, Lesley was actually born in the English Midlands. The family moved back to Scotland when Lesley was in her teenage years. When we asked her where she would like to walk she had no hesitation in choosing a route in County Kerry in Ireland. The highlight of the walk was our ascent of Carrauntoohil, the highest peak in Ireland and a magnificent mountain of steep crags and sinuous, narrow ridges. Lesley and I enjoyed lengthy discussions about the merits of isolation and using mountains to get away from it all but she was surprised by my insistence that I could happily live as a hermit in the hills. 'That's utter nonsense,' she said. 'It would be the end of civilisation as we know it if everyone had that attitude. How would we procreate if everyone went off on their own?' It was a fair point.

My overiding memory of that expedition with Lesley came when she showed her soft side, and sadly we failed to catch it on camera. We were about to eat our lunch somewhere near the summit of Carrauntoohil when one of our runners, a local lad, pointed to his mother's farmhouse in the glen below us. It looked like an extremely isolated and lonely place but the young man suggested that if our helicopter pilot, who was with us to get some aerial shots, was willing to take us down he would get his mother to put the kettle on and we could have lunch in comfort. Lesley was highly enthusiastic about this idea and convinced us that a brew in a cosy farmhouse kitchen would be infinitely better than eating soggy sandwiches in the drizzly rain on top of the mountain. So, down we went, and one County Kerry farmer's wife had the surprise of a lifetime when a helicopter landed in her front garden.

Her son introduced us and she put the kettle on her peat fire. As we waited for it to boil Lesley asked her a thousand and one questions about life on an isolated Kerry farm. At one point the old lady admitted that, although she had spent her entire life in this house at the very foot of Ireland's tallest mountain, she had never actually stood on the summit. I knew what was going to happen – I just sensed it and I was right. Lesley grabbed me by the arm and virtually dragged me outside.

'Do you think we could fix a ride in the helicopter for her, up to the top of the mountain? She won't have to get out – just hover near the summit and let her see what it's like?'

I had a quiet word with Richard and we agreed to ask the pilot. He said he'd be delighted. Better than that, he had to fly to Shannon to fill up with fuel so he would be happy to take the auld lady with him, give her a real treat. Needless to say Lesley was over the moon. She ran back inside and asked the old lady if she's like to go up the hill in the helicopter. 'Oh, sweet Mary,' she said, 'T'would be a dream come true.' But she wouldn't go immediately.

She disappeared into her bedroom to change into her best outfit, complete with a handbag and a dash of Tweed perfume behind her ear. We paraded out to see her off and, as the helicopter wound up to take off our new-found friend just waved and waved in delight through the window. As the great bird rose into the air I turned around to say something to Lesley to see tears running down her face. She couldn't speak because of the emotion.

Another emotional encounter happened when I walked across the Island of Mull with former MP Chris Smith, now Lord Smith of Finsbury and Master of Pembroke College, Cambridge. Chris was the first, and indeed the only MP, to have climbed all the Munros, and it was he who encouraged the former leader of the Labour Party, John Smith, to take up hillwalking as a means of keeping fit.

Towards the end of our walk, on the summit of a hill called Creach Bheinn at the end of the Ardmeanach Peninsula, we looked down on the isle of Iona, where John Smith is buried beside some of the ancient kings of Scotland. Chris told me of his emotional devastation when John suddenly died of a massive coronary and why he believed that had he lived, he would have been one of the finest prime ministers the UK has ever had. Richard and I had previously agreed that at this point I should ask Chris, on camera, if he would like to finish our walk together on Iona, rather than on the summit of this windswept hill. He was delighted and told me he had never visited the grave. Such an opportunity would turn our walk into a pilgrimage.

We arranged that Chris would go to the grave, and I would meet him as he came out of the graveyard and ask him for his thoughts. Unfortunately, Chris was so overcome with grief and emotion that he could barely speak, but after a few moments he managed to get out a few words. It was a very highly charged emotional moment, and a rare thing to find a politician at a loss for words. It went down well with our audience.

For as long as I could remember I had been a fan of the folk-rock band Runrig. I loved their music, even though I couldn't understand the meaning behind the Gaelic songs, but as a band they probably did as much good for the Gaelic language as anyone. I'm not a Gaelic speaker myself but I've always been a supporter of attempts to keep the language alive and thriving. Indeed my two granddaughters, Charlotte and Grace, both attend a Gaelic-medium school in Inverness and are fluent speakers.

As we searched for potential guests for *Wilderness Walks*, Richard somehow discovered that Donnie Munro, who had just stood down as lead singer with Runrig after 23 years, was a former member of the Skye Mountain Rescue Team. It was a fairly logical assumption then that he was, or had been, a keen hillwalker or climber. Meg rang him up and had a long conversation with him and the outcome was that, yes, he was a keen walker and he would be delighted to take a long walk with us for television. I was over the moon and Donnie turned out to be a great guest, describing his love of Skye, his island of birth, his desire to promote the Gaelic language as much as possible and his new direction and passion in life: politics. He was just about to stand in parliamentary elections for his home constituency of Ross, Skye and Inverness West as a member of the Labour Party. In the event he didn't win, but managed to significantly make a dent in the majority of the sitting MP, the late and much missed Charlie Kennedy.

Donnie was keen to walk through Skye, from the Sligachan Hotel down Glen Sligachan and up to the summit of Marsco, a hill he had gazed on thousands of times and had even sung a song about, a song called 'Nightfall on Marsco'. Despite that, he had never actually climbed the hill. We would then hike over the bealach to Loch Coruisk and follow the coast to Camasunary where we would climb Donnie's favourite mountain, Bla Bheinn.

It was a great trip. Donnie and I exchanged countless songs and came to the firm conclusion that between us we knew the first lines of a thousand songs, but only the first lines.

For most of the walk we didn't see many people but as we wandered around in the vicinity of Coruisk we came across lots of folk who had come on a day trip on the ferry from Elgol. Because I was in my habitat, so to speak, many of these people recognised me and stopped to chat and ask for an autograph. Sadly, no one recognised Donnie, dressed as a backpacker. No one recognised him that is, until we had crossed the infamous Bad Step, a steep trending crack that runs across a vast boulder high above Loch Scavaig. As we scrambled down from the far end of the crack we met a trio of young, German backpackers and stopped to chat. I asked them where they were from and they said Hamburg. Donnie then asked if they knew such and such a music venue and they said they did; had he been there? 'I've played there,' said Donnie, his chest puffed out with pride. The three young lads looked at him, then looked more closely before bursting out in harmony, 'Ahhh, you are Runrig!' Donnie was delighted.

During that walk I realised just how much of Donnie's life had been shaped by the landscape of Skye and, in particular, the Cuillin. As well as being a fine singer, Donnie Munro is an artist, who trained at Gray's in Aberdeen before becoming an art teacher. He also has a profound love of the Gaelic language and culture – at the time of writing he is development director at Sabhal Mor Ostaig on the Sleat Peninsula, a Gaelic-medium college – and, of course, his love of singing and music. Indeed, Donnie told me that the vast majority of the music written by the Macdonald brothers in Runrig had been inspired by the landscapes of the Western Isles.

Encouraged by Donnie, I later looked more deeply into this notion of a mountain/culture connection and learned that the great Gaelic bard, Sorley MacLean, had been equally inspired by the landscape of the Cuillin. In a poem describing the homecoming of Gaels after the war, he refers to the Cuillin peaks as 'the mother breasts of the world, erect with the universe's concupiscence'. 'Here lies the very heart of Gaeldom,' he wrote, 'the white felicity of the high towered mountains,' beckoning the Gaels to their homeland. And it's rather interesting, that when the late John MacLeod of MacLeod put the Skye Cuillin on the open market for a cool £10 million many of the local Skye people made their own claim on the Cuillin, referring to it as a 'cultural' claim, as against the 'emotional' claim to ownership that many of we mountaineers felt. It's all about a sense of belonging.

If someone were to ask me where I most belonged I'd have little hesitation in saying the Cairngorms. These are the landscapes with which I have greatest familiarity, and having spent forty years living in their shadow I think the time I've spent immersed in the area has given me an experiential knowledge of the place that has been vitally important in forming and developing a sense of belonging. I sincerely believe that the wild lands that surround us help shape our culture, and the more we despoil, or even lose, aspects of that wild land the more we run the risk of shifting our society into a 'placelessness' where culture and history become unimportant and we, as a society, begin to lose our sense of identity.

My guess is that the vast majority of mountaineers, climbers, hillwalkers and backpackers who go to the mountains and wild places of Scotland very rarely even consider the word 'culture'. There may well be a subliminal understanding that there is a cultural aspect to their activity, or they may be aware that the likes of Wordsworth and Coleridge, or Henry David Thoreau and John Muir were stimulated in their literature by the landscapes they experienced, but for most hill-goers their most immediate interest is in the physical challenge: the titillation of the senses and sense of achievement. Or, as I've read one hillwalker suggest, it's just a good day out with the lads.

I have to admit that my own awareness of culture in the mountains was pretty limited until I took that walk with Donnie. When I say that awareness was pretty limited I mean that while I was aware of the cultural connections between our landscapes and art, music, literature and photography, I just hadn't considered those connections very deeply, and I guess that's the same for most folk.

I had the opportunity to discuss this whole question of culture in our mountains with a writer whose work I had appreciated for many years. Jim Perrin was born in Salford of an English father and Welsh mother. A top rock climber in the seventies and eighties, Jim went on to become one of the most respected landscape essayists in the country, a man with an acute understanding of the link between wild places and culture. I had read somewhere that human wisdom found its origin in the inspiration of natural landscapes and the wildlife that inhabited those places and, perhaps, the biggest challenge we face today is for individuals to reconcile their spirit with those eternal truths that offer an enhanced perspective of such landscapes. It's so easy, in a world that creaks and groans with technology, in a world that accepts the concrete jungle as the norm, to become divorced from the land. And when such a separation takes place a peculiar and disturbing mindset takes hold. We become more rational, unduly logical and endlessly analytical, at the expense of our instinctive and intuitive side. As those basic senses dissolve we lose something much more fundamental – the ability to dream and to wonder.

There are those, like the poet William Blake, who believe that imagination, and not reason, is the essential constituent of the intellect:

To see a World in a Grain of Sand
And a Heaven in a Wild Flower
Hold Infinity in the palm of your hand
And Eternity in an hour

Albert Einstein once wrote that whoever is devoid of the capacity to wonder, whoever remains unmoved, 'cannot contemplate or know the deep shudder of the soul in enchantment, might just as well be dead for he has already closed his eyes upon life'.

Jim Perrin travels extensively, but in particular through the mountains and hilly landscapes of his beloved Wales. He travels with his eyes wide open, and his ears, and his mind. I once asked him what the most important lesson was for a tyro travel writer and he told me it was acute observation – the ability to see beyond the obvious. Jim was sparing in his advice because, throughout his writings, it is patently obvious that he not only shares Einstein's 'deep shudder of the soul in enchantment' but that he can experience such sensations, and share them with others, because he not only opens his eyes and ears and mind but most crucially – his spirit.

Uniquely amongst British travel writers, he uses all his senses, (many of which have become dormant in most of us,) to tease out the resonances of the landscape, to tune in to those echoes and reverberations of bygone times and relate them to the present. There is often an element of mysticism in his writings, a sacredness that recognises the deep mysteries of the land's power to sustain us, both spiritually and in the flesh. It was no surprise then that Jim also chose to walk in Ireland for our *Wilderness Walks* series, a land that clings proudly to its spiritual and cultural heritage. We began our walk at the foot of a holy mountain that is considered by many Irish folk to be a very spiritual place.

Croagh Patrick is in County Mayo, and was apparently the place where St Patrick fasted for forty days and nights before casting out all the serpents in Ireland. I've climbed the hill three times (for the wonderful views across Clew Bay rather than for any religious purpose) and on each occasion I have met pilgrims either crawling up the badly eroded gravel track on their hands and knees, or tiptoeing uphill in their bare feet as a form of religious penance.

From the holy mountain of Ireland we traversed the neighbouring Sheeffry Hills before climbing one of the great hills of Ireland, Mweelrea. At the foot of this great hill lie the waters of the wild Atlantic with, close to the coast, the tiny island that was our final

216

destination, a rather special place where we would have our final camp. We were picked up on the mainland beach and taken to Inishturk Island, Inis Toirc in Irish, which translates as 'island of the wild boar'. This small, attractive island is located nine miles off the coast of County Mayo, between the islands of Clare and Inishbofin. Inishturk is only two miles long and one and a half miles wide but is rich in archaeological and historical sites and breathtaking scenery. But it was another, smaller island, that was our final destination, an island that lies close to Inishturk.

Caher Island is uninhabited but is an ancient pilgrimage site. It boasts an early Christian monastery with the remains of a chapel in an enclosure, and several carved slabs and a seventh-century Celtic cross. There are also remains of what are thought to be the hermitages of seventh-century monks. We were ferried across to Caher on an Irish currach, a boat with a wooden frame over which animal skins were once stretched, although nowadays currachs are covered with tarred canvas. It's believed this was the kind of vessel that Columcille, or Columba, used when he travelled from Ulster to Iona to begin his evangelical crusade into Scotland.

In the course of our walk, I suggested to Jim that if he had been a photographer or artist I would have asked him to produce a painting or an image that defined our journey together. As he was a writer, the challenge was to write a few paragraphs that summed up our pilgrimage through County Mayo. Later that evening, in the shadow of the Celtic cross, as day eased itself into dusk, Jim read out his literary offering. I was deeply moved by the words and absolutely delighted that he had opened his mind and had allowed his thoughts to spill out in such a way – his own spinning windmill of scenes and sounds and scents. It was a magical moment of television.

'We find the places we have always known, where being is to be more real; as here on Croagh Patrick's stony, worn and rearing track. I hear talk of those who labour barefoot to its crest. In them, immanence, who turn always to the west. Hills crowd ocean's space, sea frets can drown them. Outstretched, the Sheeffrys rise; red with cushioned sundew, pearled with mist. Spear-grass is carmine tipped; by winter's frosts rocks are gapped around. On bulky Mweelrea a widening sunlit world. I fancied the presbytery walls gone; an old priest, voice like flaking ash, whisky glass to hand, sat on the grass we walked across.

Looking on waves, all came back to me: his gift of mind, though his faith had gone; who talked of Yeats and Joyce as tiercel might, at dusk, chattering to its crag in some brief stilling of wind before it muffled down that hint of swift and cruel life. What brought me here to thread through the hills' pattern? Why tease at nature's embroidery, that maybe does not signify; just is, as source and spring? Why set to journey, when we seek our rest? Here at this world's end no answers; except sky-roofed church, texture, paradox. I learned a voice to express: but quartz, the spirit stone, still spoke it best.'

There were many other magical moments in both series of *Wilderness Walks* – when polar explorer Matty McNair, the first American to ski to both the North and South Poles, and I stood outside our tent in temperatures approaching –40°C as the northern skies were floodlit by the glows and throbbing intensity of the Aurora Borealis; when John Mackenzie, the Chief of the Clan Mackenzie and fanatical climber realised he didn't have any dry underpants after Richard Else had made us cross the deep river below An Teallach several times so Keith Partridge could get a rear shot and a close-up shot and a wide shot and another for good luck. At one stage the water was up past our waists.

Our last night with Nicholas Crane in the Pyrenees will remain in the memory for a long time for very different reasons. We had hiked up through the Breche de Roland from Gavarnie, the great natural notch in the ridgeline that separates France from Spain, and made our way along the fabulous Ordesa Gorge. On our final night in the mountains we stayed at a high mountain hut and, in celebration of what had been a great journey, began drinking cans of the local beer shortly after lunchtime. By dinnertime we had built the empty cans into an enormous mountain and then someone produced a bottle of cooking brandy from the kitchen. We were so wasted, cameraman Keith Partridge and I couldn't climb the stairs to the bunks and elected to sleep on the verandah where Richard narrowly missed us with his nocturnal pee. Keith was so drunk that he used an empty aluminium Sigg bottle as a pillow.

Next morning, we presented a sorry bunch as we began the climb back to the Breche and the long descent to Gavarnie. Mountain guide and safety officer John Whittle thought his tongue had become stuck to the roof of his mouth. Our hangovers were intense but amazingly, the mountain air and litres of fresh, icy mountain water cured us and we arrived safely back in Gavarnie ready to start over.

We filmed with writer David Craig in Knoydart, where I learned of the cruel events of the Knoydart Clearances. David, an Aberdonian by birth, was professor of creative writing at Lancaster University and is one of the most enthusiastic climbers I have ever known. He is also a poet, a characteristic which was immediately evident in his conversation as he exclaimed his delight at the west Highland surroundings – the salt flats at the head of Loch Hourn, the views of the 'back' of the Saddle and Sgurr na Sgine, and the sound of our first cuckoo of the year.

Our plan was a simple one: to take the shoreline footpath for six miles to Barrisdale where we would camp for the night before climbing Ladhar Bheinn, the most westerly of the mainland Munros. From there we would descend to the Mam Barrisdale, the high pass that crosses the spine of the land, and hopefully climb Luinne Bheinn and Meall Buidhe, before dropping down to Inverie to head for Doune on the west coast, where some old friends of mine, the Robinsons, were organising a ceilidh for us. That was a good incentive not to tarry too long on the hills, but this was to be more than just another wilderness walk. David Craig is also the author of a book called *On the Crofter's Trail,* a highly acclaimed account of the effects of the Highland Clearances, and I wanted to learn more about this awful period in Scotland's history. David's interest in things historical, and indeed in all things Scottish, stemmed from a childhood that was spent wandering around the castles of the north-east with his uncle, the noted historian and writer, Douglas Simpson.

David had learned that for a long dark period in Scotland's history many of her people had been forcibly evicted from their homes, the homes that had been their parents' and their grandparents' before them, by landowners, many of whom a few years earlier had been their clan chiefs: patriarchal figures in the community system which was the traditional way of life throughout the Highlands and Islands. In researching his book, he travelled through twenty-one islands in both Scotland and Canada, searching out the memories of the descendents of those forced to leave Scotland by the Clearances. This oral tradition was important to him, and I was keen to hear his observations on what he claimed was ethnic cleansing.

Just after the 1745 rebellion there were over one thousand young men, the clan's fighting force, working the land in Knoydart, paying what was known as 'warrior rent'. Townships were sizeable in places like Skiary and Barrisdale, Doune, Airor and Glenguserain, Sandaig and Inverie. Even inland, in Gleann an Dubh-Lochain and Glen Meadale there were farmlands growing grain and potatoes, and an etching from the last century shows forty to fifty trading ships at anchor in Barrisdale Bay.

The townships have gone. Today, Inverie is the only real modern settlement, with a pier, a cluster of whitewashed cottages, a pub and a guest house. Stretching west from those rugged mountains which form the romantic sounding Rough Bounds of Knoydart, the peninsula is sequestered from the rest of the mainland by long, winding, sea lochs. Common belief suggests that Loch Hourn and Loch Nevis are corruptions of the Gaelic words for Heaven and Hell, placing Knoydart in some sort of montane limbo.

Bill Murray, possibly Scotland's greatest ever mountaineering and landscape writer, once described Knoydart thus, 'These numerous glens and tracks, free from all motor traffic, give excellent walking through wild country. They breathe a peace that other areas lack, they have a remoteness without desolation, and a beauty without blemish.'

On the contrary, the late Seton Gordon, that marvellous old sennachie of the wild places had described it as 'a wild country of dark sea lochs and gloomy hills, often mist shrouded. Here the clans of the uruisgean, or spectres, must roam, here the each uisge [water horse] and the tarbh uisge, the water bulls, perhaps fight fierce battles. I do not think the daoine sith, the hill faeries are here. The country is too vast and forbidding for the little people.'

A beauty without blemish, or vast and forbidding? I've known Knoydart wear both guises. I've festered in the sun high on Luinne Bheinn and Ladhar Bheinn, soaking up the breathtaking beauty of the place, and I've struggled over the high Mam Barisdale in drifting snow, the surrounded hills swathed in cloaks of grey. Knoydart can certainly be a place of contrasts.

With the few buildings of Kinloch Hourn behind us and the pull of the west in front, we talked of the emptiness of the land, this man-made wilderness – not only in Knoydart, but throughout the entire Highlands and Islands.

'The emptiness is there,' David remarked. 'Strath Brora is empty, and Kildonan and Ousdale and Strath Halladale and Aberscross and Strath Naver above all. Until the Countess of Sutherland's gangs came with their writs and torches in 1814 and 1819 there were clachans all along Strath Naver: sixty-four townships housed 338 families. It is one of the oldest sites of civilisation in Britain – its population peak was probably reached in the Bronze Age – it could have a civilisation again. Instead, for 150 years, it has had Masters of Fox Hounds from the Home Counties who go up there to fish and shoot, owners of airlines, princes, the head of the Liverpool Cotton Exchange who made a fortune selling khaki for use in Passchendaele and Vimy, Lords-Lieutenant of various shires, and their friends, loitering heirs of city directors, whom we actually saw one day, their Range Rovers parked on the roadside above the salmon river, the males in Barbour jackets and caps with nipped peaks... as though a Country Life photographer was expected at any moment.'

His dislike for the gentry undisguised, he told me of his first encounters with landowners, as a youngster stravaiging the length of the western seaboard during long holidays. 'I'll always remember it,' he said, 'this walking Harris Tweed cocking a finger at me.' 'What are you doing on my land?' came the clipped tones. 'How can it be your land?' remarked the young Craig, 'nobody owns the land.' The landowner turned out to be no less than Sir Hereward Wake,

221

who instantly condemned David as being a communist, and 'drove off in a blue cloud of high dudgeon'.

A few miles on we dropped down towards Barrisdale Bay, past the roofless walls that were once the community church. It's a magnificent location. Across the bay, Ladhar Bheinn rears up in Alpine glory, its notched and toothed outline above Coire Dhorcaill rising to a single snow-corniced summit. Further down the loch, the blue outline of Skye's Sleat peninsula fills the horizon. In front of us, a narrow tidal promontory reached out to a small green islet where the gravestones of some of the evicted form a sad testimony to the harshness of man. We walked out to it, in the dimming light of evening, remembering those, like Gaeldom's *Deirdre of the Sorrows*, who had to leave a land they loved, their homeland, for an unknown future. David painted a poetic word picture of the ship easing its way out of the sea loch, the tear stained faces of the emigrants silently bidding farewell as the sound of the pipes echoed around the now empty hillsides. I wanted to cry.

Mere flakes of stone, some standing, some flat – no inscriptions recalling the names of the dead, no epitaphs telling of their hardships, only the distant crooning of eider ducks portraying any sense of pibroch lament, an evocative and ghostly sound. We talked of the evictors and the evicted, the sheep and the flockmasters from the south who quickly realised that it would pay them to hire ships to remove all those who stood in their way – and it was with a sense of guilt that we eventually concluded that what we have left is a land emptied of people, in which we can enjoy our passion, the enjoyment of wilderness, even if it is a man-made wilderness created at such a terrible cost. If you take the people away from a land, from places where generations have worked and toiled to earn a living from ground which is uncompromising in its difficulty, that land will, in no time at all, re-assert its hold. Bracken fronds will eagerly swallow up the lazy beds, old run rigs will fade into mere tracings and green and ochre lichens will creep over the ruckles of stone which once housed families and their cattle.

This could well have been a description of the kind of empty landscape I explored with Rebecca Ridgway, the first woman to kayak around Cape Horn, a sea passage that has struck fear into the hearts of seafarers for hundreds of years. Rebecca was brought up with adventure as a cornerstone of her very existence – she is the daughter of John and Marie Christine Ridgway, long-time adventurers who ran the John Ridgway School of Adventure at Ardmore in the far north-west of Scotland. Along with Chay Blyth, John had been the first person to row across the Atlantic and he and Marie Christine had gone on to enjoy a huge number of adventurous undertakings, often with young Rebecca in tow.

Becs was now independent and ran her own adventure school across the waters of Loch a' Chadh-Fi from Ardmore. Together we kayaked from Ardmore to Oldshoremore to walk the northern coast to Cape Wrath via the atmospheric Sandwood Bay. From the Cape, the most north-westerly point on the Scottish mainland, we crossed inland to climb the two Corbetts of Beinn Spionnaidh and Cranstackie before returning to Ardmore for a grand barbeque.

Curiously, we were soon to begin an exploration of a very similar emptied landscape in the company of my old friend Hamish Brown. Introduced to the North African country of Morocco by the writings of Gavin Maxwell and Tom Weir, Hamish had visited the mountains of Morocco dozens of times – they had become a second home. With Hamish, I walked and climbed in the High Atlas, accompanied by his long-time Moroccan friend El Aouad Ali from Taroudant, and learned of his infatuation with this wonderful country and the friendly Berber people who inhabit the pastures and villages of the narrow valleys.

I think Hamish must have passed on his enthusiasm for Morocco to me for I've visited the High Atlas several times since, climbing Toubkal, the highest mountain in North Africa, twice, and enjoying a sensational traverse of the range between Ighil M'Goun (4,017 metres/13,356 feet) and Toubkal (4,167 metres/13,671 feet), a magnificent two-week journey.

Our final *Wilderness Walk* took us to Oregon on the west coast of the USA. As a mountaineer and as someone with a deep love and attachment to the wild places of the world, I've learned that there are fundamental laws that govern how things work in the natural world. The crucial point is that these are laws that never change. The cycle of the seasons; the cycle of day and night; the pulse of the tides; the necessary ingredients for plant growth; our own need for the air we breath; the trueness of north. Perhaps one of the most important of these natural laws is the interconnectedness of things, the understanding that all of us – man, birds, animals, plants, whatever, are part and parcel of a great web of creation. Everything is inextricably linked together.

'When we try to pick out anything by itself, we find it hitched to everything else in the Universe,' proclaimed John Muir.

The poet Francis Thompson wrote, 'If thou picketh a wild flower, you disturb a star.'

So why is this interconnectedness important? I want to use it as an example to help us understand why nature's life laws, those laws that make the world go round, are the same life laws that work in human life and society, and I couldn't think of anyone better equipped to explain all this to a television audience than an adventurer who lived on the west coast of the US.

I had come across the writings of Ray Jardine a few years earlier when I became almost obsessed with the notion that nature is evenly balanced – we cannot disturb her equilibrium. We know the law of cause and effect is the unerring and inexorable law of nature, but we constantly fail to find our own equilibrium as nations and as individuals because we've never learned that the same laws work as inexorably in human life and in society as in nature. I was aware that Ray Jardine fully understood and demonstrated this principle. Through his writings, and in the way he lived his life, I learned that Ray had chosen to abandon a promising career in NASA as a specialist in computer-simulated space-flight mechanics to become a full-time adventurer, learning from the natural world the most effective way to live, with as little impact on the planet as possible.

It was a mountaineering expedition to South America that made Ray reconsider his career. For the next seven years he lived out of the back of an estate car in California's Yosemite Valley, climbing some of the hardest rock routes of the time. During this period, he developed the protection and anchoring camming device known as

Friends, a tool that revolutionised the sport, and discovered and climbed the world's first 5.13 route, the Phoenix, in 1977, six years before sticky rubber-soled climbing shoes appeared on the market. Not everyone liked Ray's inventive approach to rock climbing. Some claimed that Friends had ruined the sport, making it too easy to find protection in natural cracklines. After a period, Ray decided to move on to something else. He had a notion to sail around the world but had two major problems: he had never sailed and he didn't have a boat. So, he built one and learned to sail it. Simple. During this time, he met his lovely wife, Jenny, who was to share all his future adventures and they spent three years aboard their ketch, 'Suka' (acronym for Seeking Unknown Adventures), sailing round the world.

After their extended voyage, the pair decided they needed a long mountain walk, so in 1987 they walked from the Mexican border to the Canadian border, largely along what is known as the Pacific Crest Trail, a journey of some 2,500 miles, in four months and two weeks. Unhappy with the 'style' in which they had hiked the route (they felt they carried too much unnecessary gear and weight), they cut down considerably on their pack weight and did it again. In 1991, they walked the distance again but this time in three months and three weeks. Still they were not satisfied, so they decided to make their own super-lightweight gear. On their third attempt, this time from Canada to Mexico, they walked the route over three months and four days, and their average base pack weight (everything other than food and water) was eight pounds. That was about the same weight as the *empty* pack that I used at the time.

These long hikes, interspersed with all kinds of other adventures like sky-diving and hang-gliding, kayaking through the North-West Passage and designing ultra-lightweight hiking gear, produced a book, *The Pacific Crest Trail Hiker's Handbook*. That book was not just a guide to hiking one of the world's great trails, but a book of hiking philosophy and it was that way of thinking, the values that Ray emphasised, that encouraged me to contact him and ultimately, change my own thinking about how I behaved in the outdoors. I had first come across the notion of 'connecting with the wilderness' through the writings of Colin Fletcher, a Welsh-American back-packer whose books have also inspired Chris Townsend and many others.

This notion of connection is essentially about shrugging off our western anthropocentrism, casting aside the urban notion that man is dominant and that everything else in nature has been created for man's welfare, or pleasure. Paradoxically, connection often comes in a sudden revelation of man's *insignificance* when compared with the more lasting reality of mountains, forests and star-studded skies. A bear encounter can have a curiously humbling effect on us, and an Alpine electrical storm can portray a force and a power that is way beyond us. Ray Jardine defines connection more in terms of style, suggesting that our wilderness outings should be more than just physical walks along trails.

'More important is our presence in the wilds,' he later told me. 'How we carry ourselves, how softly we move upon the landscape, how aware we are of the patterns of life around us, and how we interact with them. This "earth philosophy" is a bridging of the gap between human and nature, a bringing together for a greater aware-ness and deeper understanding of the natural world around us in all its glory, of our relationship with that world, and of our own inner nature.'

Ray, Jenny and I discussed this phenomenon at some length as we spent a week backpacking through the Three Sisters Wilderness in the Jardines' home state of Oregon. As we hiked along the undu-lating trail I was aware of their well-being, their oneness with the landscape we passed through.

Ray suggests that the reason why 'connection' is so vitally impor-tant is that it's like a stepping stone in the middle of a wide creek we could never jump across.

'We might remember that, despite our almost overwhelming technology, we are still flesh and bone,' he says. 'Our bodies are an integral part of Mother Earth. The air we breathe is her breath, rippling the grasses in the meadow. The water we drink is her life-blood, tumbling from the snowy heights. Our flesh comes from the soft, rich earth, our bone from the sun-baked rocks. Every molecule in us is not our own, but a part of Mother Earth. We are borrowing that molecule from her, and will have to give it back when we leave. This is one problem with city life, where we tend to hide from all that. In fact, the more richly we connect with Mother Earth, the higher and farther we can walk our paths. With this in mind, each footstep blesses the earth and the journey itself becomes sacred. I think everyone experiences this.'

I loved this concept of sacredness for when connection does occur, it is often a hallowed experience, as though a divine intervention has separated us from our former self into something new, refreshed and re-created – a born-again experience. The lessons I learned from the Jardines have enriched my relationship with wild places. I don't rush around any more, collecting summits or trying to reach the top before everyone else. These days I'm not even that interested in going all the way to the summit. It's simply being there that matters, appreciating the landscape, the plants, the whorls and delicate patterns of lichens on the rocks, the wind in my face, the call of a bird or cry of an animal. Essentially, it's about being part of the fabric of the mountain, and knowing that mankind is a crucial part of this great interconnected web of creation we call planet earth.

Making the two series of *Wilderness Walks* turned out to be a great experience but for me it was much more than that. It was a collection of experiences and interactions with a fascinating range of individuals that taught me so much about wild land and our place in it, a variety of lessons that I would put to good use later, when I found myself appealing to politicians for the protection of such places.

14

WILDERNESS AND WALKS

After the success of our two series of *Wilderness Walks* we were flat-out researching and interviewing guests for a third when a bombshell hit us. Mark Thompson, the controller of BBC2 was promoted internally (he eventually went on to become the director general of the BBC) and was replaced by a new controller who informed us that the kind of outdoor programmes we made were not high on her list of priorities. She wrote to Richard to tell him that our *Wilderness Walks 3* proposal had been effectively dumped. She did say she intended spending more resources on 'gardening programmes'.

This could have been the end of the line for Richard and Meg, but they are made of sterner stuff. Richard had sacrificed a good career with the BBC to follow his first love, making outdoor adventure programmes, and his record was second to none. He was the man who pursuaded the reclusive Alfred Wainwright onto our television screens. His climbing series, *Wild Climbs*, won eleven international awards. *The Edge – One Hundred Years of Scottish Mountaineering*, was described in one newspaper review as 'the perfect documentary' and went on to win a Scottish BAFTA. It was later described by the then culture minister, Chris Smith, as one of the ten most important programmes made for television. Our long-distance walking shows, *Wilderness Walks*, had massive viewing figures, but despite all that success the new controller of BBC2 wasn't interested.

Fortunately, Richard had a parallel academic career as a Professorial Fellow at St Chad's College at Durham University, so he temporarily returned to academia while Meg kept Triple Echo Productions afloat with some radio work, including a ground-breaking environmental series. An investigation into nuclear power won a Clarion Award, recognising best practice in communicating the importance of corporate social responsibility, sustainable development, social inclusion and ethical debate.

Luckily, a BBC Scotland editor by the name of David Harron appeared on the scene. David was television editor of sport and wanted to expand the corporation's sports coverage into something more extreme than football and golf. His family came from Lochinver in Sutherland and he had a deep affinity with the hills and wild places of Scotland. He asked Richard and Meg to tender for a new occasional programme, provisionally titled *The Adventure Show*, which would cover extreme marathons, triathlons, cycling and mountain biking events, with other items covering more traditional activities like hillwalking, backpacking, paddling and climbing. To Richard and Meg's delight, their company Triple Echo won the contract, and one of BBC Scotland's sports reporters, Dougie Vipond (who is also the drummer in the rock band Deacon Blue) was asked to front it.

As the show developed, Richard had some discussions with David Harron about breaking up the main event of each programme with additional features, perhaps a technical feature or an item on technique, gear or specialist diet. Somewhere along the line Richard asked me to make a short five-minute film of a local walk in Glen Banchor, just behind Newtonmore, and talk a little about what I get from a short walk like that. We went out on a pleasant summer day and I was filmed by one of the *Adventure Show* camera operators, a young chap called Ian Burton. Meg then edited the piece and Richard showed it to David Harron with the idea that I might present a little series of hill walks for the programme. We called them *Wild Walks*.

David loved the film and immediately commissioned Richard. After a couple of years, BBC Scotland asked if they could broadcast these 6–7 minute *Wild Walks* at those odd times when they had a few minutes to fill, so every so often you'll find me popping up just before the news or after *River City*, extolling the virtues of the Cobbler or Lochnagar or some other worthy hill. The films may have been short, but they certainly raised my public profile. For the first time, people were stopping me in the street, asking if I was the guy who had climbed the Buachaille on telly last night. It was all good fun. I greatly enjoyed making the hillwalking shorts and when they appeared to be successful we thought up the idea of creating an annual hour-long 'Christmas Special'. The shows were filmed during the spring, summer and early autumn months and we initially hit upon the idea of creating a long backpacking trip through a particularly beautiful part of Scotland. The very first one, almost in a nod of appreciation to David Harron, was a hundred-mile-long route between Lochinver and Tongue. We called it the Sutherland Trail and began filming on that wonderfully iconic mountain of Assynt, Suilven.

Thomas Pennant, on his eighteenth-century tour of the Highlands, called it the Sugar Loaf, a rather prosaic and uninspiring description of what is one of the most popular small mountains in Scotland. Sula Bheinn, the Pillar Mountain, doesn't reach the 3,000-feet elevation that would make it a Munro – it doesn't even make the 2,500-feet height that would give it Corbett status but, despite its lack of height above sea level, it's a remarkable mountain in every respect. It's got bulk, it's got character, it's steep sided and impressive and its Torridonian sandstone tiers make it look twice the height it actually is. From the sea, and from Lochinver, Suilven appears as a great barrel-shaped monolith. From Elphin in the east it takes on a Matterhorn-type leanness. In between these two aspects, the mountain forms a steep-sided and serrated ridge, some 1.2 miles in length. The highest point, Caisteal Liath, the grey castle, lies at the north-west end of this ridge. There are two other summits: Meall Meadhonach (the round middle hill), the central point of this ridge, is 723 metres/2,372 feet, while Meall Beag (the round little hill), lies at the south-eastern end.

It was probably because of its iconic status that we chose Suilven as the starting point of this journey through Sutherland. There's something about this hill's shape and character that has given it an almost legendary status and it stands out alongside some of the most impressively shaped mountains in Scotland. Go to the beach at Achnahaird and take a look at the litany of mountains that rise from the horizon. Ben More Coigach, Stac Pollaidh, Cul Mor and Cul Beag, Canisp and Quinag, and there, in the middle of them, catching the eye as few other mountains do, is Suilven

Rising from the lochan-splattered moorlands of Inverpollaidh and Assynt, Suilven stands in isolated splendour, as do its neighbours, and that's one of the factors that makes this region of north-west Scotland so visually stunning, and the subject matter of a television show. I've heard so many hill-goers, over the years, swear that the landscape north of Ullapool is God's own country, and there is nowhere else quite like it in the whole of Europe. When rain curtains sweep across the knolls and tumbled moors of Inverpollaidh, and the dark clouds are pierced by shafts of brilliant light, then Suilven wears her wilderness gown with poise and subtlety, only revealing her shapely form through a haze that's turned incandescent by the lowering light.

We began the Sutherland Trail in Lochinver, once Richard managed to prise me out of the wonderful Lochinver Larder (whose wonderful pies have a worldwide reputation). Slowly we eased ourselves into this rough and tumbled landscape where the Lewisian gneiss, the ancient bones of the land, pierce the thin-soiled skin. Not far beyond Lochinver the tarmac stops, and where the black stump finishes, a bulldozed track runs past Glencanisp Lodge, now run by the Assynt Foundation, past the bothy at Suileag and on to Loch Gainimh, whose waters reflect the tiered battlements of Suilven itself.

If you've timed your walk well you'll pitch your tent before taking an evening climb up the eroded path to the Bealach Mor just east of Suilven's main summit. When you reach the cairn take in the view: west to the sea and Tir nan Og, the fabled land of the ever young, and east to the route you'll be following over the next few days, a route that revels in its northness, where the quality of the light is matched only by the sweetness of the air, a district that is far removed from the soubriquet that is often bestowed on Sutherland: the Empty Lands.

This old county, the South Land of the Vikings, is far from empty, despite an appearance that suggests there is almost as much water here as land. In the course of our televised journey I spoke to Assynt crofters – who talked through the tears of the Clearances and how their grandparents had been left with infertile strips of land along the coast after being removed from the more prosperous hinterland; geologists – who spoke with pride of the exploits of Peach and Horne, the doughty pair of mountaineering explorers who proved the existence of the Moine Thrust; cavers – who had discovered the 6,000-year-old remains of bears in the labyrinth of caves below the hills of Inchnadamph; prawn fishermen – who supplied the Spanish and Italian markets with freshly caught west coast langoustine; sea kayakers – who boasted of the wonderful waters and atmospheric island campsites of the north-west coast; fly fishermen – who showed me some of the most idyllic hill lochs imaginable and almost turned me away from the hills to become an angler; and shepherds – whose local sheep market at Lairg is still the biggest in the world. Believe me, while I may misquote the author Lillian Beckwith, the hills may be lonely, but there is plenty going on in the rest of Sutherland.

Before we began filming, Gina and I took a week and recced the route, leaving Lochinver to head east across some of the most iconic landscapes in the country. This recce was to prove useful and that became the form for future programmes. I'd walk the route first, often with Gina but sometimes on my own, and check out what was on offer: the best GV's (general views), camping spots, possible interviewees and making sure the route itself was walkable!

Meg and Richard would then take over and research the route, finding and checking if potential interviewees could actually chat happily and enthusiastically about their subject, and organising transport and accommodation for the camera operator and film crew. My role as presenter was, in many ways, the easy part of what was always a team performance.

The recce for the Sutherland Trail took us through south Assynt, a district synonymous with recent land reform legislation, over the shoulder of Canisp to follow the river through fields of yellow broom to Inchnadamph with its limestone caves and old stalkers' paths that ease the contours and follow well-trodden yet sly lines up, through and over the hills to the Eas a'Chuil Aulin that overlooks the secretive waters of Loch Glencoul. This is the highest waterfall, at 180 metres/600 feet, in the UK and it drains a vast wind-scoured and frosted wilderness of rocky crags, hummocks and hollows, each bowl caressing its own green-tinted lochan, which, in turn, gives birth to its own bubbling cascading stream, all harnessed by the steepening gradients into the roaring, raging cataract that drops with frightening abruptness over the black, glistening crags of the Leitir Dubh into the waters of the loch below.

We followed the eroded tourist track back to the main road at Loch na Gainmhich and then descended further down the longest stretch of road on the entire route: four miles down the grassy verge, drawn by the prospect of a night in Kylesku, a tiny hamlet clustered round a pier that boasts one of the best hotels in the Highlands. No camping for us tonight. We fed on freshly made haggis and freshly caught langoustine, drank locally brewed beer and French wine and slept in a comfortable bedroom that overlooked Loch Glencoul and Glendhu – the waters of Kylesku of the Celtic song – lulled to sleep by the sounds of the surf and gently wakened in the morning by the cry of gulls. It was wonderful and Gina and I, as we often do, couldn't help but recall our early days in the hills together when we couldn't afford a decent tent never mind a luxury breakfast in a very atmospheric hotel.

Next morning, fortified by scrambled eggs and smoked salmon, we crossed the slender Kylesku bridge and left the dancing waters behind. Our route now lay north and east, crossing the divide between Scotland's western seaboard, a land of hill, glen and deep-biting fiords and into the mountainous hinterland. It would be three or four days until we reached the sea again at the Kyle of Tongue.

The hill track across the Reay Estate between Kylestrome and Achfary climbs steadily away from Loch Glendhu beside a rosary of hill lochs that stretch away to the east towards the curiously named Meallan Liath Coire Mhic Dhugaill, the 'rounded hill of the son of Dugall's corrie'. What story lies behind that name, and what stories lie behind the ruckle of stone that is marked as a single shieling on the Bealach nam Fiann before the track drops into the Achfary forest?

Beyond Achfary the road runs west for a short distance before the route crosses the river, passes Loch Stack and the locked bothy at Lone and climbs up to the cusp in the hills between the three Corbetts of Foinaven, Arkle and Meall Horn. We climbed Foinaven for the television programme following a midge-ridden camp beside Lochan na Faoileige. It is, undoubtedly, one of the best hills in the area, the veritable Queen of Sutherland.

We camped at Lone and next day took the path to Gobernuisgach Lodge and into the historic Strath More below Ben Hope. The weather was dull and gloomy and Gina tried to brighten things up by telling me of the meal she was planning for the next night in the Tongue Hotel: French onion soup, warm, freshly baked bread, scallops, fillet of venison and chocolate eclairs with fresh cream. All washed down with a good bottle of Shiraz. I brought her back to earth with the menu for tonight's dinner: pasta and cheese!

According to the map, we had to follow a big bend in the track to climb to the main road which we'd then follow to tramp through Strath More but, on an instinct, we decided to leave the main track and follow a little footpath beside the river. If fishermen used this river a lot there would be a path-of-sorts alongside it, and there was, for over a mile to a distinct and sudden dog-leg in the river just below the imposing ruins of the Dun Dornaigil broch, one of the best surviving examples of a circular defensive tower of the Iron Age.

From the ruins, the fast-flowing river leads the eye along the broad strath to where steep cliffs tumble down from Ben Hope. Indeed, there isn't much of Scotland left beyond Ben Hope. By the time Gina and I reached the start of the Moine Path, at the south end of Loch Hope, I was in the bad books. The long haul on the unforgiving tarmac had taken it out of her and, to add insult to injury, the only car that we had met on the road had actually stopped and offered us a lift. Gina was about to accept when I said no, rather too forcibly I suspect. She stomped off, to quote my old pal David Craig, in a cloud of high dudgeon.

The next morning, we packed in drizzly, dour conditions, and set out on the Moine Path to Kinloch and the Kyle of Tongue. The rough trail was sketchy in places and I hoped against hope that it wouldn't vanish altogether for we were crossing a bare and rather bleak stretch of moorland which, I'm sure, would have been alive with wildlife on good days with grand views south to the bulwark end of Ben Hope. Low mist and cloud obscured any distant detail. We were walking in a shroud of hodden grey, a wet vacuum of mist and, in its silent swirl, it was all too easy to imagine the people of the land climbing up here with their carts, grunting with the effort of digging the black, oily peat from the ground, loading it and carrying it back to their turf-roofed black houses. I wonder if the increasing cost of fuel will encourage the Highlander of today back onto the peat roads and peat banks of their forefathers.

The rain persisted as we tramped across the moorlands, unsure of whether the path would be clear all the way to the road at Kinloch. It may have been wet and misty but it wasn't cold, and we hiked on, uncomfortably hot in our cocoon of Gore-Tex waterproofs. It's often said that in hillwalking terms there is no such thing as bad weather, only bad clothing, and there is much truth in that.

It took us about three hours to walk the six or so miles of the Moine Path, three hours in which we saw very little other than the green flow of the moor around us. This whole area, the peninsula of land between Loch Hope and the Kyle of Tongue, is known as A'Mhoine, the moss, or the peat. It's a lochan-splattered wilderness, home to golden plover and dunlin, wheatear and skylark, hen harrier and peregrine. Red deer herds roam here, drifting between the lochans, but today we saw very little of either wildlife or scenery.

We eventually came out of the cloud to be greeted by a forlorn and grey Kyle of Tongue. The multi-topped Ben Loyal flirted with us through the mists, appearing and disappearing in the cloud. Past Kinloch Lodge we took to the minor road for the final few miles and the beginning of the track that would take us to Ben Loyal. Or perhaps not...

The end of any long walk is a bitter-sweet experience, the sadness at the conclusion of what is, in most cases, a great experience being offset by the simple pleasures of a hot shower and those little luxuries of life that are so often taken for granted.

Sometimes, just sometimes, the thought of those little luxuries can overwhelm us, especially when we are wet and a little cold and that hot shower and a meal are only minutes away. In such circumstances it's tempting to cut the trip short and high-tail it back to that other life we belong to, the existence that enjoys comfortable beds, central heating, three course meals and bottles of ice-cold Chardonnay.

Gina and I crossed the Moine Path from Gleann Mor in fairly miserable conditions. Low cloud had obscured any possibility of the promised views of Ben Hope's northern crags, underfoot conditions were wet and often boggy and heavy showers had forced us into full waterproofs. On reaching the tarmac at Kinloch near the foot of the Kyle of Tongue we knew we had three or four miles of tarmac bashing, albeit it on a quiet minor road, to the road end for Ribigill Farm and the route to Ben Loyal. We also knew that this would be the testing point of our willpower. From there it would only be a couple of miles to journey's end at Tongue, and a comfortable hotel room with hot showers. I suggested to Gina we bash on to the Tongue Hotel and leave Ben Loyal for another day. Her broad smile confirmed agreement. All trace of guilt vanished. A couple of hours later we had booked in, enjoyed a shower and headed for the bar.

The making of the Sutherland Trail came at a difficult personal time for me. My mother was dying. She had been diagnosed with a malignant melanoma and all summer I had watched her deteriorate. When she finally lapsed into a coma I was, fortunately, in Glasgow. The hospital managed to get hold of Gina on the phone and she rang my son Gordon, who lives in Glasgow. He and his partner Hannah immediately went to the Southern General Hospital and I arrived later. My two sisters, Helen and Heather, and brother-in-law Raymond arrived and Gina drove south from Newtonmore. We were gathered around her bed when she passed away, something that would have pleased her greatly.

Moments after her passing I looked out from the hospital window to see a wonderfully majestic sunset. The whole of the western sky was in various shades of red, gold and orange and in my grief I felt curiously soothed. It was almost like an omen, a sign that she had moved on to something better.

While we were relieved that she would have no more suffering, and was finally at peace, I battled with various demons for months afterwards, particularly a sense of guilt that I hadn't spent enough time with her, that I might have done more to ease her suffering in her final days. She loathed being in hospital and the ward was very run-down with little privacy for someone who was at death's door. I've been a lifelong supporter of the National Health Service but there were some days I wished I could afford to transfer her to a private hospital where she may have been more comfortable, or at least may have spent her final days in slightly more pleasant surroundings.

Since then, the Southern General Hospital has been substantially renovated but I look back on those difficult days with the conviction that if we were all willing to pay a penny or two more in our income tax we might be able to afford a National Health Service that is more suited to the twenty-first century, a health service we could be proud of again. As things stand, this fine institution, once the envy of the world, is chronically underfunded.

The next year we decided to take a long walk through the Isle of Skye for our Christmas show. A friend, the photographer David Paterson, had written a book a few years previously, outlining a long hike through this wonderful island, but our routes differed in a number of ways, largely because we had to film it for television. We called it the Skye Trail and our final route was a stunner.

We began filming on a chilly yet sun-drenched evening in May. We sat above the grue-ing, gurgling waters of the Minch at the very northern tip of the Isle of Skye at Rubha Hunish. Beyond the shoreline lay the small islands of Fladda-chuain and Eilean Trodday and beyond those rocky outposts, lying in dim outline against the horizon, lay Scalpay and the hills of Harris. Our route lay to the south, and would link two of the most impressive landscapes in Scotland: the Trotternish ridge and the Cuillin.

I knew Skye reasonably well. Numerous sorties to the Cuillin had become pilgrimages over the years. Where else in the UK can one pay homage to the Norse/Celtic mountain gods? And I had tramped the length of the Trotternish ridge some thirty years before, but only in recent years had I begun peeking around the corners of these two landscapes, peering over the horizons of the pinnacled ridges to see what lay beyond. I had become intrigued by my new discoveries, enthralled by the history and the wildlife and the geology and the Celtic heritage of this island that, once upon a time, in the Mesolithic period, would have been a very desirable location to live: a wooded place of richness, with a Mediterranean climate, seas full of fish and forests full of animals. But volcanic activity and the scourings and gougings of glaciers had changed the face of the land. Just as the two major landscapes of Skye were linked geologically, the time had come, we decided, to link them together in a long walk.

Everyone knows about the Skye Cuillin. The savage grandeur of these Alpine-looking mountains is world famous and Munro-baggers know that they will be the most technical hills they will have to climb. But immediately to the south of Rubha Hunish lay a rolling escarpment of basalt, the 'best high-level promenade in Scotland' as it was described by Sheriff Alexander Nicolson in the nineteenth century. These are the hills of Trotternish, green hills that look to the tumbled landscapes of mainland Scotland. We spent our first night at Rubha Hunish, at the tip of the ridge's northern finger, a wild and remote camp on a grassy headland, with the expanse of the sea on three sides. After supper, before we crept into our tents for the night, we took a short stroll to the rocky headland and gazed out to sea for a time. We had been told this was a prime spot for watching minke whales. Within minutes of settling down, someone yelled 'Yar she blows', or words to that effect, and sure enough, about a hundred metres offshore, slicing though the agitated sea surface, we saw the arched shape and fin of one of these incredible sea mammals.

It may not have been watching humpback whales off Vancouver Island or kayaking with orcas off the coast of Alaska, but watching these minke whales had a curious effect on us. We all walked back to our tents in a state of mild euphoria, that condition of heightened awareness we reach when we are fortunate enough to encounter animals that are truly wild. Here we were, a hard-bitten, seen-it-all television crew, four grown men experienced in the ways and sights of the outdoors, yet we were as thrilled as children, as excited as puppies.

Not for the first time, I lay in my tent and pondered this curious reaction to seeing nature in the raw. It seems that we are so removed nowadays from the sights and sounds of nature that any close encounter with wildlife gets us really excited. In watching a whale arching into its dive, or wondering at the majestic flight of an eagle, it would appear that we become aware of the simple magic of the moment, an instinctive celebration of natural order and harmony. Ancient Celtic spirituality was based on a deep connection with the natural world, and the Celts had an intellectual curiosity about all the creatures they shared their lives with. Perhaps our sighting of the minke whale stirred some ancient memory of Manannan mac Llyr, the sea god, the northern equivalent of the Greek deity Poseidon.

The Celts believed in an Otherworld, a realm of the imagination where your mind could expand and flow, circle and explore. This realm of the mind could be entered by anyone who found the portal to this world of dreams, and the Celtic people continuously watched for signs that an entrance to the Otherworld was at hand. One of these portals was through the eyes of a wild animal, an animal that would look at you and invite you to follow it ...

One of these curious 'Celtic connections' occurred later in the walk, after I had climbed Bla Bheinn. I wandered round the head of Loch Slapin, agitating a flock of oystercatchers who didn't mind showing their annoyance with some high-pitched shrieking, and stopped in the shade of a few trees near the village of Torrin. Lying on a bed of Durness limestone, which accounts for the surrounding greenery, I recalled there had been a community here at Torrin for over 2,000 years and our Celtic ancestors would have treasured the fertility of the place. The word 'druid' comes from the Celtic words for oak tree (*duir*) and knowledge (*wid*). The oak has a special significance: it was thought to be a portal to sacred knowledge. Druids also tended to meet in woodland groves and often slept on beds made from rowan (which was sacred to the triple goddess Brigid, and used as a protection against enchantment) to try and induce prophetic visions. Hazel was used in much the same way.

Druids were a hereditary class of priests and magicians who characterised early Indo-European societies. They were the Celtic equivalent of the Indian Brahmins or the Iranian Magi and, like them, specialised in the practices of magic, sacrifice and augury. They were the wise men, the councillors of the Celtic world.

The wood of various trees each had a function in the Celtic world, sometimes practical, sometimes symbolic. For example, the sap from the birch was used to treat rheumatism and was even thought to promote fertility. The yew, even today found in churchyards throughout the country, was associated with death and rebirth. The first three letters of the Celtic alphabet were associated with trees: *Beith* (birch), *Luid* (rowan) and *Nuin* (ash) and when a tribe cleared a tract of land they always left a tree in the middle. The symbolic power of the tree was very important. It was here, below the spreading branches, that their chiefs would be inaugurated.

The special relationship the Celts had with trees was recognised by Alexander Carmichael in his *Carmina Gadelica*, a collection of prayers, incantations, runes and blessings, collected from the Gaelic-speaking regions of Scotland between 1855 and 1910.

'Choose the willow of the streams
Choose the hazel of the rocks
Choose the alder of the marshes
Choose the birch of the waterfalls
Choose the ash of the shade
Choose the yew of resilience
Choose the elm of the brae
Choose the oak of the sun'

Amidst the general starkness and rock and water-dominated landscape of Skye, I discovered this area around Torrin to be something of an oasis. I chose an ash, the ash of the shade, and sat below it, allowing its essence to seep into my own being, expanding my own mind to the skyward reach of the uppermost branches. Did I gain any divine revelation? Was I aware of my spirit being refreshed and revitalised? Well, not exactly, I was still a little bit footsore but it was great to sit in the shade for a while, at least until the midges drove me on. The good old midges have a habit of bringing you back to earth with a bump.

Earlier in the year, Gina and I had enjoyed a most amazing reconnaissance trip to Skye, backpacking from Duntulm in the north of Trotternish to Elgol, the coastal hamlet that offers some of the most magnificent views across the sea waters of Loch Scavaig towards the Cuillin. Our plan, like the best, was simple. In astonishingly fine weather we walked from Duntulm down the length of the Trotternish ridge to Portree, visiting the two volcanic wonders of Trotternish, the Quiraing and the Storr, en route. From Portree we wandered down a quiet and tranquil road past Braes, scene of the last battle in Britain, before following a coastal path along the west shore of Loch Sligachan to the famous hotel of the same name (some claim it as the cradle of Scottish mountaineering). From there the footpath down Glen Sligachan took us below the skirts of both Red and Black Cuillin to the high pass over to Scotland's finest loch, Coruisk, before a skirmish with the infamous Bad Step and the scenic coastal path to Camasunary and Elgol.

With the television crew, producer and photographer Richard Else, cameraman Dominic Scott and safety officers Paul Tattershall and John Lyall, I repeated the route again, but this time we continued past Camasunary, over Bla Bheinn to Torrin and the old crofters' trail to the cleared villages of Suisnish and Boreraig. Beyond Boreraig the line of an old narrow-gauge railway took us past the old marble mines of Beinn Shuardail all the way to Broadford on the coast.

Our Sutherland Trail the previous year had been 'adopted' by the communities it passes through, communities who might benefit from the increased trade such a route brings. We hoped the Skye Trail might have the same effect. It's no less than the Isle of Skye, and the route itself, deserves.

Someone once observed that the wind is a constant companion on the Outer Hebrides. We had just travelled north through Vatersay where that small island is in real danger of being torn in half as the winds have drastically flattened and reduced the protective sand dunes. As we took the road out of Castlebay we suspected the gale would prevent us reaching the summit of Barra's highest hill, Sheabhal.

I had just embarked on a long bike and hike through the Outer Hebrides from Vatersay, the most southerly inhabited island of the Outer Hebrides, to the Butt of Lewis. We were filming the journey for our next BBC Scotland Christmas programme and Ben, our cameraman, was concerned that he wouldn't be able to hold his camera steady in the strong winds. Rather optimistically I had promised him it would be fine.

I should have known better. Five years earlier Gina and I had arrived on Barra with a distinct sense of foreboding. The ferry crossing from Oban had been spectacular but, as we crossed the Minch, dark storm clouds were gathering. Our intention had been to walk the length of the Outer Hebrides, starting with the little range of hills that forms Barra's spine. That turned out to be the best day of the trip, a journey we eventually abandoned because of the amount of road walking involved and some horrendously wet and windy weather. Like anywhere else, the Hebrides are rarely attractive in the dark, dour conditions we encountered but even a glimpse of sunshine can transform the Western Isles into the most glorious kaleidoscope of colours and rich landscape textures. I'd experienced enough of that magic to make me want to return.

This time, I wanted to link my hillwalking with some historical sites and, at the same time, learn something of the way of life of the modern Hebridean. I intended riding a mountain bike between the mountain areas, so keeping the amount of road walking to a minimum. Always happy to expect the unexpected in the Outer Hebrides, I had just enjoyed the finest curry I have tasted outside of India. Who would have expected that in a tiny restaurant in downtown Castlebay? The only problem was that I now had to climb the highest hill on Barra and attempt to cope with two kinds of wind!

With the afternoon sun promising more than it delivered we trudged up the main road to where it crosses the south-east ridge of Sheabhal (383 metres/1,256 feet). This ridge offered the simplest route to the summit, and we climbed past a statue of the Madonna and Child, a reminder that these southern islands of the Hebrides managed to escape the Reformation.

Beyond the statue we could barely stand upright in the south-east wind, so we tried to tuck ourselves behind the ridge and approach the summit from the south-west. This certainly helped avoid the worst of the gales and gave us a bit of a breather, and it was good to take a break and gaze down on the village, its wide bay and the castle that dominates it.

I remember hearing the Corries sing the song 'Kishmul's Galley' years ago and the ramblings of various folk singers always led me to believe that Kishmul was some kind of Hebridean pirate. The song, collected by Marjory Kennedy-Fraser, refers not to a person, but this castle in Castle Bay of Barra.

> 'Bravely against wind and tide
> They have brought us to 'neath Kisimul's walls
> Kisimul castle of ancient glory'

Kisimul Castle was the ancient seat of the MacNeils of Barra, and the song refers to the galley, or birlinn, from which the clan dominated these Hebridean seas. Indeed, such was MacNeil's authority that one story suggests that every night, when the clan chief had finished dinner, his piper would go on to the battlements of Kisimul Castle and proclaim a message to the world, 'The MacNeil has eaten. The other potentates of the earth may now dine.' I like that.

We reached the summit of the hill in just over an hour from the road and could just discern the tail-end of the Hebridean chain drifting off to the south: Vatersay, Sandray, Pabbay, Mingulay and Berneray, names that songs are made of.

We also got a good impression of Barra with its rolling hills and the broad sweep of the Borve glen leading to the west coast's gleaming beaches and machairs. After following the broad ridge north, we descended to the main pass that cuts through these hills from west to east: the boggy Beul a' Bealaich. Another climb took us to the next summit, Grianan, where a broad ridge runs past the chambered cairn of Dun Bharpa, one of the finest archaeological sites on the island. From there it was downhill to the ferry at Aird Mhor. Eriskay, of the love lilt, my favourite of all the Hebrides, was beckoning ...

Eriskay is famous for two things: it was here that Charles Edward Stuart landed at the beginning of his campaign to win the Scottish crown back for his father and it was near here that the SS Politician went down, along with its cargo of whisky. The book, and film of the book, *Whisky Galore*, put Eriskay on the map forever.

We were keen to learn something about the island from someone who had been born and bred here and who better than the oldest man on the island, the former parish priest Father Calum MacLellan? We sat in the sun and blethered about the changing face of the islands, and Eriskay in particular. Father Calum reckoned the causeway to South Uist had changed Eriskay irrevocably. In the old days he said, once the last ferry had tied up for the night you knew you wouldn't get any visitors. Thanks to the causeway, he could now expect people to arrive at the church door at any time of day or night. Father Calum also gave us an insight into his own childhood on the island, and elsewhere. 'I first left the island as a young boy and travelled to Glasgow. The first thing I saw there shocked me to the core . It was a woman, and she was wearing trousers! Even worse, she was smoking a cigarette!'

From Eriskay I crossed the causeway to South Uist where I wanted to climb the big hills of Beinn Mhor and Hecla but they were hidden in grey clouds and the weather forecast was for rain and gale-force winds. Instead the film crew took my bike and I set out to hike the length of the superb Machair Way, a new twenty-mile route that runs up the west coast through the delightful machairs of South Uist. It was invigorating to walk north with the stormy seas to my left and the south-westerly wind blowing me all the way to Rubha Thornais. Another causeway took me over to Benbecula where I took to the bike once more, making my way across the island to North Uist and an appointment with local artist and filmmaker Andy Mackinnon.

Andy and the respected artist Chris Drury had made a two-day trans-Uist journey by Canadian canoe across the island, from the south-west coast to Lochmaddy in the north-east, a journey that made extensive use of the Uists' lochan-splattered landscape. The result of that very physical experience is an extensive show in Lochmaddy's Taigh Chearsabhagh art centre, where Andy is the curator. The show includes the installation of an amazing suspended canoe that has been woven from heather, willow and salmon skins, a kind of open vessel for ideas, sensations representing the material landscape. He wanted to show me the route of his canoe trip and where better to view it from than the summit of a hill. Having missed the opportunity to climb Beinn Mhor and Hecla I was keen to get up high, even though our chosen hill, Eaval, was a mere 347 metres.

Andy lives under the shadow of this hill, which he describes as the 'Fuji of the Hebrides' and, as we walked towards the hill beside the mirror-like surface of Loch Euphort, he reminded me that this is an inhabited and named landscape going back to Neolithic times. As such, naming it and the language used, embeds it within the culture of the area. It's an area that is often described as wilderness but of course it isn't. Every loch, island and landscape feature has a name, and another exhibit at the Taigh Chearsabhagh proves that. Using digital technology Andy and Chris Drury recreated an image of the landscape as a lacework of words in Gaelic, Norse and English, naming all the lochs, islands and hills seen from the summit of Eaval.

Although fairly diminutive, Eaval has a character that's out of all proportion to its height. Viewed from the east the hill appears as a giant wave about to break over the watery landscape of North Uist. A nice scrambling route took us directly to the summit and the surprising panorama that ranges from the hills of Harris, over lochan-splattered acres of North Uist and across Grimsay and Benbecula to the big hills of South Uist and beyond them to Eriskay and Barra. Behind us, the hills of Skye and Wester Ross were perfectly clear. It was one of the best hill days I'd had for years, and I was already looking forward to the remote hills of North Harris.

More cycling took me to Berneray where I caught the ferry to

Leverburgh on Harris. Some of the best cycling of the trip then took me past the magnificent shell beaches of Sgarasta and Luskentyre to the start of another long walking trail: the 26-mile long Frith-Rathad na Hearadh, or the Harris Walkway. I'd had the pleasure of officially opening this route back in 2003 and I was looking forward to its variety, the climb over the spine of the island by an old coffin route to the east coast where the land is so rocky that people used to have to carry their dead to the more fertile soils of the west coast for burial. A combination of quiet roads and old tracks took me through the area known as the Bays up to Tarbert and the start of what was once described as the finest footpath in Britain – the trail to Rhenigidale.

A number of years ago I met the postman who walked three miles each way along a narrow footpath to deliver the mail to this remote village. He told me of his delight when the Western Isles Council put in a proper tarmac road in the early nineties, finally connecting the last remote village in Britain to the road network. Kenny Mackay, a former councillor for Tarbert and North Harris, said the road was a lifeline for the village, a lifeline that would ensure Rhenigidale's survival. No longer is Rhenigidale known only for its 'wilderness hostel'.

In 1962 Herbert Gatliff, a wealthy benefactor and a founder member of the Youth Hostels Association, bought an old house in Rhenigidale and opened it as a hostel, the first of the five Gatliff Trust hostels that still exist in the Western Isles. You could only reach it by narrow footpath or boat and the facilities were basic. Despite that, almost a hundred people stayed there in the first year, and many more were to follow.

Walking on the islands always offers a lovely interplay of hills and coast, with expansive sea views beyond the cliffs and crags, and today was no exception. As I crossed the high pass between Trolamul and Beinn Tarsuinn the Shiant Islands appeared below like great shark fins rising from the waters of the Minch. The path descended to the head of Loch Trolamalaig in a series of a dozen tight hairpin bends. A wooden bridge crosses the stream at the head of the loch before the path climbs again, out of the narrow glen and above the sea loch to the cleared village of Gary-altoteger. The buildings are set in a shallow hollow on the hillside looking down on the fiord-like Loch Trolamalaig.

I was tempted to linger for a while but a violent rain shower caught me unexpectedly. Sadly, it was the first of a few showers that, within the hour, was to turn to a persistent drizzle. I briefly visited Rhenigidale, well aware that I had a three-mile tarmac trudge up the glen to Loch Maraig and my next hill climb, to An Clisham, at 799 metres/2,621 feet, the highest hill in the Outer Hebrides. It's best viewed from the south, looking up into the impressively rocky Coire Dubh and its three summits of Mulla bho Dheas, Mulla bho Tuath and An Clisham itself. The last time I climbed this hill I wandered up its south ridge from the old whaling station at Bunavoneadar, on the Hushinish road. The advantage of starting from this point is that you can traverse the three tops in a fine horseshoe route, descending via the broad Tarsaval ridge. I was still keen to traverse the three tops that rise above Coire Dubh but I wouldn't be coming back down to the starting point again. My intention was to hike north from the summit of Mulla bho Dheas, into the wilds of North Harris. I wanted to camp for the night near Kinlochresort and meet the film crew, with my bike, somewhere on the B8011 road. From there I'd be on the bike all the way to the Standing Stones at Callanish and up the west coast of Lewis to the northern tip of the island, the Butt of Lewis.

In many ways that solo wander through North Harris was the highlight of my trip. It's an exceptionally wild and unspoiled region that fully deserves to be our third national park. The estate is now owned by the local community and the North Harris Trust has lost no time in making it clear to the Scottish government that they would like to see national park status for their area. I hope they succeed, although it might take a few years because of current economic uncertainties, but that would be no bad thing.

I don't think anyone would want to see the people of Harris rush headlong into setting up a national park as there are already many lessons to be learned from our other two parks. I'll leave the last word to the Western Isles MSP, Alasdair Allan, 'The people of

Harris have sent out a very clear signal that they want new life and prosperity for one of Scotland's most fragile island communities.'

Words from a 19th century song sum up what many of us feel about the Western Isles:

'From the lone shieling of the misty island,
Mountains divide us, and the waste of seas,
Yet still the blood is strong, the heart is highland,
And we in dreams behold the Hebrides.'

15

TRAILS FOR TELEVISION

I had got into the habit of describing these long walks for television as pilgrimages, but I found myself asking what exactly is a pilgrimage? It's been described as a journey or search for moral or spiritual significance and is often to a location of importance to the person making the pilgrimage. Such a location might be a shrine, as in the case of the well-known pilgrims' trail to Santiago de Compostella and the church of St James, or the Muslim Hajj to Mecca.

With these notions in mind we decided to construct a Pilgrims' Trail in Scotland for our annual Christmas television programme. I wasn't quite sure where to begin but Richard and Meg came up with a cracker of a route, a journey that partly fulfilled the 'spiritual significance' aspect of pilgrimage and partly fulfilled my own definition of a pilgrimage as a 'journey of discovery'.

The route began, not surprisingly, on the Isle of Iona, a centre of Irish monasticism for four hundred years and the island from which St Columba, or Columcille, set forth to bring Christianity to the Picts of Alba. This starting point really appealed to me as I've long been fascinated by our Celtic heritage and was keen to learn more of the ancient Scotland that Columba determined to evangelise, but I had another purpose in mind.

I wanted to take the opportunity to challenge my own perceptions about 'wild land', at a time when so many people are suggesting that Scotland is being 'industrialised' beyond repair, and that the finest of our wild land areas are being despoiled by renewable energy projects. Is industry in the Highlands a modern phenomenon and how genuinely 'wild' is our wild land? I hoped a 250-mile walk across Scotland, from the Argyll coast to the North Sea might offer me a deeper understanding of the issues.

A pilgrimage should end at a location of some importance and relevance to the entire route. When my producers suggested Portmahomack as a destination I looked at them curiously. Portmahomack? I wasn't even very sure where that was. A quick check on the map showed it to be on the Tarbat Peninsula, a sharp finger of land that juts into the Moray Firth between the Dornoch Firth and the Cromarty Firth. The village stands about three miles south of the lighthouse at Tarbat Ness, and finds of elaborate early Christian carved stones dating to the eighth to ninth centuries (including one with an inscription), in and around the churchyard, had long suggested that Portmahomack could be the site of an important early centre of religion.

Since the mid-nineties archaeologists have been making exciting finds in and around the grounds of the old Portmahomack Parish Church and are now convinced that the present building stands on the site of the only Pictish monastic settlement ever found in Scotland. The leader of the archaeological team, Professor Martin Carver of York University, told me that the site is 'Scotland's best kept secret' and is possibly as important as Iona, but more of that later.

Our pilgrimage route was designed as much to offer an exceptional walk as anything else, and we followed what turned out to be a highly original coast-to-coast route. From Iona I visited another coastal island, Inch Kenneth, by currach, the type of skin-covered rowing boat that Columcille and his contemporaries used. In those distant days of the sixth century the Celtic monks would have made full use of the sea as a highway, which was probably easier than negotiating the heavily wooded landward areas of mainland Alba, where wolves and wild boar freely roamed.

Our route then took me across the Island of Mull to Fishnish Bay on the Sound of Mull where I caught the ferry to Lochaline. But before that I was keen to deviate from the Pilgrim's Trail just a little, to take in the only Munro in Scotland that necessitates the use of a ferry to reach it.

In 1991 Ben More of Mull was my final Munro the first time round and I was keen to revisit, largely because in four ascents of the hill

I'd never had a view from the summit. This time I was lucky and, after a wild and windswept ascent, the weather gods relented and the sun burst through the cloud as I climbed the final snowy steps to the summit cairn. It was a good omen for the rest of the pilgrimage!

From Lochaline we travelled north, past the silica sand mine that has been exporting to the rest of the world since 1940. The extremely fine sand is used in the manufacture of optical quality glass and later in the day I passed some more mines, this time long-abandoned.

The old Lurga lead mines are found in Gleann Dubh, a few miles north of Lochaline. Mining took place here as early as 1730 and the open-cast works and drystone buildings are still evident. The site consists of the remains of the lead mines, opened around 1730, derelict by 1749, re-opened around 1803 and finally abandoned by 1850. Later, beyond Strontian, I came across more mine workings. Lead was mined here in the eighteenth century and it was here that the mineral 'strontianite' was discovered. From this the element strontium was isolated, and named after the Gaelic village name, Sron an t-Sithein, the 'nose of the faery hill'. Who says industry in the Highlands is a new and unwelcome phenomenon?

From Strontian I crossed the hills to Loch Shiel and followed the track along its eastern shore to Glenfinnan, a place forever associated with Charles Edward Stuart. It was here he began his campaign to regain the crown for his father, the place where he met with some of the clans who were to fight with him, a campaign that ended in bitter defeat on Culloden Moor. It was the aftermath of the defeat that interested me though, as Charles took to the heather for months on end, avoiding the government forces that were hunting him, until he could board a ship that would take him back to France. His journey, to the Western Isles and back, was a long and convoluted expedition that made my walk look tame in comparison. Our paths were to cross several times in the coming days.

From Glenfinnan I was joined by an old pal, naturalist Kenny Taylor, and we climbed a rough track over the high bealach of Gleann Cuirnean between Sgurr Thuilm and Streap before I dropped down to the head of Loch Arkaig on the very edge of Knoydart. From here another high pass took me into Glen Kingie, where the route turned east towards the Glengarry Forest before heading north again over the Mam na Seilg into Glen Loyne and Kintail.

I followed, in part, an old drovers' road into the pass but the original route dropped down to the shore of Loch Loyne where it abruptly vanished. This is pretty much all that remains of the old 'Road to the Isles', and this section once ran between the Cluanie Inn and Tomdoun. This drovers' road originally forded two rivers, which were dammed and flooded in 1957 to form lochs Cluanie and Loyne. The present A87 was constructed around the edge. This old track to Loch Loyne is still in pretty good condition but where it crossed what is now the extended Loch Loyne, thanks to hydro work, there were once two bridges and a small wooded island. These were submerged below the waterline and only become visible when the loch is at an unusually low level.

Over the next week or so we were to be faced with more and more evidence of Scotland's widespread hydro-electric industry as we crossed from Glen Affric, via the Munro of Toll Creagach, to the big dam at the head of Loch Mullardoch. Here I met up with fiddler Duncan Chisholm who has released a trio of albums named after three of the glens we had visited: Affric, Cannich and Strathfarrar – the *Strathglass Trilogy*. What we didn't know until we met with Duncan was that his father had worked on the Mullardoch dam, part of the Affric–Beauly hydro-electric power scheme.

'My father was born in Glen Cannich at Cosac Lodge which ended up submerged in water when Mullardoch was dammed in 1951,' he told me. 'Loch Lungard and Loch Mullardoch became one loch then when their height was raised by about 100 feet, leaving a very dark and very dangerous stretch of water. In fact, my great grandmother who had spent all of her life in either Glen Affric or Glen Cannich was so appalled by what had happened to her home she just couldn't bear to visit Mullardoch again after 1951. She died in 1967, having never returned.'

Beyond Glen Cannich I walked through a very remote landscape between the head of Glen Strathfarrar (the only Strath in Scotland that's also a glen ...) and Loch Monar. A wild camp, and a camp-fire on the stony shoreline of Monar, was highly atmospheric and memorable. Next day I crossed more high ground into the head of lovely Strathconon from where the River Conon and a series of forestry paths and tracks took me to the Blackwater River and the heavily forested Rogie Falls and more hydro-electric schemes. The Blackwater River rises high on the slopes of Beinn Dearg, some thirty miles away and runs into Loch Vaich to contribute to the huge Glascarnoch hydro scheme. A series of tunnels carries the waters from Loch Vaich to Loch Glascarnoch and then down to Mossford Power Station on Loch Luichart. The Blackwater River itself flows out of Loch Garve and eventually meets up with the River Conon just south-east of Contin.

Soon Ben Wyvis became the third Munro of the pilgrimage, and our first real view of any wind farm activity. The Loch Luichart scheme is pretty massive, and badly sited in my opinion, and I sincerely hoped that the nearby Glen Morie proposal was never given planning approval. I dropped down to the shores of lovely Loch Glass from Wyvis and then crossed a high ridge to the shores of Loch Morie, an area that was new to me and which surprised me by its feeling of remoteness and its natural beauty. It would be a disaster to spoil it with a large wind farm.

From Glen Morie, various byways took me to lovely Strath Rusdale and Strath Rory, all new to me, before some quiet roads led me east towards the Tarbat Peninsula and Portmahomack where I met up with Martin Carver.

Martin believes the remains by the church of St Colman are of one of the earliest Christian sites uncovered in Britain. It is the first Pictish monastery to be excavated, resulting in a window, opened on an unprecedented scale, on early monasticism, inspired by the Columban mission to Scotland in the late sixth century AD. The settlement has been dated from the sixth century and it's believed the monastery was eventually destroyed during a Viking attack, possibly in the ninth century.

Amongst other finds have been more than two hundred fragments of Pictish stone sculptures, including the 'Calf Stone', which shows a bull and cow licking their calf.

Between 1994 and 2007 the Church of St Colman and a one-hectare sample of the area within the enclosure that surrounds the church were fully excavated. What the archaeologists discovered was astounding. Their findings led them to believe that in the eighth and ninth centuries Portmahomack could have been the largest manufacturing centre in Europe, making illuminated books and church vessels like tin bowls and candle holders for the rapidly expanding number of monasteries that were being built. When I asked Martin Carver if it's possible that Columba visited here he thought it quite likely, possibly after visiting Inverness to try and convert the pagan King Bridei in AD 565, although the founder of the actual Portmahomack monastery was more likely to be St Colman, who had succeeded Aidan and Finan as Bishop of Lindisfarne.

The Tarbat Discovery Centre now displays many of the artefacts uncovered during the excavations and it's well worth a visit. As I wandered along the final three miles to the lighthouse at Tarbat Ness I pondered on all the trails and tracks I had followed from Iona, and the types of people who had trod them before me: saints, monks, soldiers, Jacobites, princes and cattle drovers, and in more recent times the miners, hydro and forestry workers, crofters and farmers and the hikers and backpackers of today.

Although few of these tracks and trails wound through truly wild land I had little doubt in my mind that the mountains we had crossed certainly did fall into that landscape category, although all of them had evident footpaths running to the summits. But wild land or not, and despite the industrial heritage to be found all across my route, the Scottish Highlands still have the ability to make you feel small and insignificant, that you are the only person in a vast and uncompromising landscape, reminding me again of its precious qualities for renewal and hope and of its immense natural beauty, qualities that I'm sure even Columcille would have been more than proud of.

It's not often the opportunity arises to visit five different islands in the course of a long-distance walk, but that's what our next route for television offered.

This was the seventh of our annual Christmas television walks through Scotland, and since we've previously walked from one end of the country to another, across the breadth of the country twice and completed other routes on Skye, in Sutherland and the Outer Hebrides, we had to scratch our heads a bit to come up with something new for this year.

Thanks to Richard and Meg we came up with a brand-new route of about 260 miles that begins on the most southerly point in Scotland, visits five islands and ends at one of the most popular towns in the western Highlands. We decided to call it the Western Way.

Richard and Meg had taken a well-deserved holiday in Galloway, and were so taken with the walking opportunities down there, and the number of new walking trails that have appeared in recent years, they suggested that we should use the glorious Mull of Galloway for a starting point.

Several evenings of poring over maps and sipping red wine eventually gave us our route, a wonderful journey that took me into some familiar areas and best of all, into some areas I didn't know at all.

Essentially we wanted to follow an area of coastline that would also give us the opportunity to climb a few hills, explore some old tales and historic links and give us the opportunity to discover something new about this marvellous country of ours. I think we achieved all these things.

Our route took us from the Mull of Galloway, from where we followed new footpaths to Portpatrick. We then picked up the start of the Southern Upland Way and followed it to Stranraer where the Loch Ryan Coastal Path took us to Glen App and the beginning of the excellent Ayrshire Coastal Path. Before heading north we took a bit of a diversion to climb the highest hill in the southern uplands, the Merrick, in the Galloway Forest Park.

After an incredibly windy day on the tops, we re-routed to the coast and at Girvan I managed to achieve something that's been on my bucket list for a long time: a visit to the bird sanctuary of the Ailsa Craig, one of the real highlights of the journey. The sight, and smell, of all those gannets took my breath away and I was amazed to learn that early last century day-trips to the Craig were so popular that the wives of the men who worked in the quarry, collecting granite to make curling stones, had a tearoom to entertain tourists.

Nothing like that today. Indeed, the place has an abandoned feel to it...

Fellow *Scots Magazine* columnist Keith Fergus joined us for a section of the walk along the Ayrshire Coast and gave us an excellent description of the full Ayrshire route. And he should know – he wrote the guidebook!

We left Keith at Irvine and I wandered through the landscapes and the beaches of my youth. In those far off days the hills of Arran seemed as remote as the Himalaya. Curiously, there is a connection today...

Arran is always a delight and an ascent of Goat Fell coincided with some good weather, which made the summit views even more spectacular than usual. We followed that with a visit to our second island, just off the coast of Arran at Lamlash.

Just off the shores of Lamlash Bay lies a smaller island, home to a community that has embraced a somewhat different, older, culture. A tiny ferry had whisked me across the bay to Holy Island, just off Arran's south-east coast, where a line of glistening white chortens and fluttering multi-coloured prayer flags led up the grassy slopes to the whitewashed Centre for World Peace and Health.

Holy Island is run as a centre for wisdom and learning within the Karma Kagyu tradition of Tibetan Buddhism and is open to people of all faiths and none, but that's not why it's called Holy Island. The place has a spiritual heritage that stretches back to the sixth century. Its earliest recorded name is Inis Shroin, or island of the water spirit, but when the Celtic missionary who became known as St Molaise lived on the island at the end of the sixth century, the place was named after him. During the early part of the nineteenth century the island gradually became known as Holy Island.

After Holy Island our route became slightly convoluted. A ferry from Lochranza to Claonaig led to a walk over the Kintyre peninsula to the ferry port of Kennacraig where another ferry carried me down West Loch Tarbert and across the Sound of Jura to Islay and an appointment to explore the ancient seat of the MacDonalds of the Isles at Finlaggan. For me, this was one of the highlights of the whole journey.

With Dr David Caldwell, a former keeper of archaeology at the National Museum of Scotland, we explored the island's remains of what was once a hugely important place in the history of the Highlands and Islands. Here, in the thirteenth and fourteenth centuries, was the administrative centre of the Lordship of the Isles.

The MacDonalds, Lords of the Isles, were descended from Somerled, a twelfth-century prince, and these lords, the chiefs of Clan Donald, chose Finlaggan as their home and the centre of their lordship. The Lords of the Isles ruled the islands and part of the west coast of Scotland, from Kintyre to Lewis, virtually independent of royal control. The heir to a strong Gaelic and Norse tradition, the Lord of the Isles (Righ Innse Gall) was one of the most powerful figures in the country with the small islands in Loch Finlaggan a centre of symbolic and administrative importance. The lordship came to an end in 1493 when the 4th (and final) Lord of the Isles, John MacDonald II had his titles stripped from him by King James III.

David Calder was a wonderful guide and with my head full of medieval tales I reluctantly left Islay and crossed the narrow stretch of water to Jura where I was keen to refamiliarise myself with the wonderful Paps of Jura. The quartzite domes of the three hills are split by low cols and surrounded by low-lying moorland, much of which is extremely boggy. The name Jura is taken from the Norse words that mean deer island and the terrain is much more suited to those fleet-footed beasts than it is to man. These are not easy hills by any means, and their traverse, including an add-on, Cora Bheinn, necessitates about 1,650 metres/5,400 feet of climbing in about ten miles. A big day by any standard with many long slopes of greyish-white scree to negotiate ...

Sadly the weather did not co-operate with our plans. Rain, wind and low cloud put paid to another traverse so instead I returned to Kennacraig and set out on the second half on my long walk – along the excellent Cowal Way from Portavadie to Tighnabruaich and the lovely Kyles of Bute, along Glendaruel to Glenbranter, Lochgoilhead and the big hills of the Arrochar Alps.

I felt I was amongst old friends again as I crossed the high bealach between Lochgoilhead and Ardgartan, before cutting through the hills to Inveruglas on Loch Lomondside. Yet another ferry took me to Inversnaid and a visit to the lovely falls where the Jesuit priest, Gerard Manley Hopkins, wrote his homage to wild places . . .

> *'What would the world be, once bereft Of wet and of wildness?*
> *Let them be left, O let them be left, wildness and wet;*
> *Long live the weeds and the wilderness yet.'*

Inversnaid was the beginning of a long stretch on the hugely popular West Highland Way – north to Crianlarich and an old and much-loved haunt, the Crianlarich Station Tearoom, before heading for Tyndrum and Bridge of Orchy. I hadn't seen so many people since I left the Ayrshire coast . . .

Over the hill from Bridge of Orchy I stopped for a while at the lovely Inveroran Hotel an old drovers' halt where Dorothy and William Wordsworth once stayed and Dorothy, who was a bit of a professional whinger, complained about the food. The present owner of the hotel agreed with me that Dorothy would have been a nightmare if TripAdvisor had been around in the nineteenth century . . .

From Inveroran it was into the wilds of the Blackmount Deer Forest for a couple of days. In the shadow of the towering Stob Ghabhar, Stob Coir'an Albannaich and Beinn nan Aighenan I followed Glen Kinglass round a big dog-leg, past Glen Kinglass Lodge to lovely Loch Etive, rejoicing in the autumn colours and the roar of stags. From Ardmaddy, a broad track took me down Etiveside past the old bloomeries at Bonawe before making my way to Taynuilt and the Royal Road to Oban.

This route was much celebrated between the ninth and eleventh centuries as the funeral procession route of Scotland's dead kings. They were carried down the length of Glen Lonan to Oban, en route to Mull and Columba's holy island of Iona, their final resting place. As if to celebrate the antiquity of the place I passed an ancient standing stone, the Clach Diarmid, which some believe marks the final resting place of Diarmid, one of the great heroes of Celtic mythology. Diarmid was one of the Fianna warriors but had the audacity to elope with Grainne, who was betrothed to the Fianna leader, the mighty Fionn MacCumhaill. It's said that Diarmid eventually died on a wild boar hunt when the boar's tusk pierced him on the ankle, his only weak spot.

My finish point was the bustling town of Oban. Always a delight to visit, it was good to stop and put the feet up in a nice hotel and reflect on what had been an outstanding long-distance walk. It was also an opportunity to look forward and already we had planned that Oban might be the starting point for a new adventure in 2015.

> '*Two roads diverged in a wood, and I — I took the one less traveled by,*
>   *And that has made all the difference.*'

These lines from Robert Frost's poem, 'The Road Not Taken', came to mind as we discussed a possible theme for our next BBC2 Christmas outdoor programme. For the past seven years the theme had been simple. I took a long walk somewhere in Scotland. I'd walked the length of Scotland, walked across Scotland twice from coast to coast, hiked and biked the length of the Hebrides and created other long-distance walking routes including the Sutherland Trail and the Skye Trail, but this year we wanted to freshen things up a bit.

For the past few years I'd been enjoying a lot of cycling, particularly cycle touring, or bikepacking as it tends to be called these days. I'd also been enjoying a fair bit of packrafting. Packrafts are tough inflatable boats that weigh a mere five pounds and pack up small enough to be carried in a rucksack. These lightweight yet tough craft originated in Alaska where adventurers use them to cross icy bays and negotiate wilderness rivers. The model I use is an Alpacka Yukon Yak, a multipurpose boat that is ideal for wilderness travel and wild river running. It can be inflated very quickly using a nylon inflate bag and packs down to the size of a two-person backpacking tent. It carries me, and my backpacking kit, with considerable ease. It can even carry my bike.

By using the bike and packraft as well as my normal hiking gear we thought we could diversify a little from my usual long-distance walk, so we filmed a campervan journey, with everything carried in the van. I've been a campervan man for more years than I can remember, and am now on my tenth incarnation of the 'mobile bothy', a vehicle that not only provides my transport and accommodation but also carries all the gear I need for a variety of adventures.

Robert Frost's idea of following less travelled roads appealed to us and so, maps scattered around, we worked out a sinuous and convoluted route that would allow me to climb hills, cycle trails and packraft to interesting places, as well as meet up with fascinating people, most of whom have chosen to live in lonely and isolated places and are completely at ease in doing so. We ended up with a rather complex journey between Oban and Ullapool, making full use of ferries and minor roads, a journey that perfectly fitted the doctrine of 'roads less travelled'.

A road trip like this is essentially about exploration, about peeping over the next horizon, and I confess to an almost infantile habit of following minor routes on OS maps just to see what lies at the end of them. I get an acute sense of excitement when these minor, and often single track roads can be linked by ferries, and even more of a sense of anticipation when the tarmac runs out to be replaced by tracks and trails. Beyond the black stump of the road-end was where I could leave the campervan and continue on foot, by bike or by packraft.

After a lot of debate, we started on the island of Luing, rather than Oban. I knew a little about the island's turbulent past and its more recent slate quarrying industry but I wanted to discover more and the brand-new information centre seemed like a good place to start. Local nurse Fiona Cruikshanks showed me around and took me on a great coastal walk to tell me about the slate quarrying heritage of the islands. I also wanted to enjoy a bit of walking on the lower hills of Luing and Seil and experience the stunning views to Mull, Scarba, the Garvellachs and the many other small islands that surround the slate islands.

From Oban I ferry-hopped to Lismore, an island I'd never visited before. It was a revelation and I loved it. Perfect summer weather helped me understand the origin of the island's name – from the Gaelic word for garden. This big garden is relatively low-lying and very fertile. It was also a major centre of Celtic Christianity. With a sixth-century monastery associated with St Moluag it later became the seat of the medieval Bishop of Argyll. The place is littered with ruined structures including an extremely impressive broch and two thirteenth-century castles.

Another lovely walk round the coast of Port Appin illustrated the complex geology of the area before I got on my bike and enjoyed a section of Sustrans Scotland's new Route 78, the Caledonia Way. The route runs all the way from Campbeltown to Inverness but I reckon the finest section runs from Oban to Ballachulish, much of it on newly constructed cycle paths.

This section takes in the scene of the murder of the Red Fox, the historical event that inspired Robert Louis Stevenson's novel *Kidnapped*, and since I had never actually visited the memorial stone where the murder of Colin Campbell took place, I took the opportunity of learning a little bit more about the event.

I couldn't pass Ballachulish without visiting my old friend Dave 'Cubby' Cuthbertson, mountain climber turned mountain photographer. As with many of us, years of trundling up and down hills has had a hard physical impact on Dave's joints so he has taken up photographing mountains rather than climbing them. On our wander up Beinn a' Chrulaiste in Glen Coe we discussed the irony of now having to climb the hills with a heavy pack full of camera gear and a tripod, when climbing gear is now probably more lightweight and easier on the joints.

From Lochaber I headed out west to Acharacle and a visit to the ceilidh king Fergie MacDonald, who not only gave us a tune or two on his button accordion but told us about a great walk in the locality that we later filmed.

Continuing on roads less travelled we stopped at Arisaig to meet sea kayak instructor Lizzie Benwell who accompanied me in her kayak as I packrafted out to the Arisaig Skerries with seals popping up in the sea all around us, a truly magical experience.

Another ferry carried the campervan and me from Mallaig over the sea to Skye, to Armadale. While most of the other passengers turned right and headed for the glory of the Cuillin, or the wonderful volcanic landscapes of Trotternish, or perhaps even the shops of Portree, I turned in the opposite direction and headed for the most southerly point on An t-Eilean Sgitheanach, the 'Sound of Sleat'.

Here, at Aird, I met up with a young jewellery designer called Heather McDermott who gets her inspiration from the seashore. She spends hours, she told me, beach-combing for ideas and I was fascinated by the link between old fishing nets, stacked creels and fankled ropes and beautiful necklaces and bracelets, or the simplicity between colourful floats that had been washed up by the sea and lovely earrings, small buoy earrings in Skye-inspired colours of gorse yellow, sky blue, sea green or dreich grey.

Heather lives with her folks at Aird and she touched on a theme that I was to hear time and again on my travels: the difficulty young local folk have in buying a house, even in remote locations like this one. The second-home market has killed the opportunity for local youngsters to stay and work in their own locality, an issue that I hope the current land reform debate can do something to address.

From Aird I parked the campervan and took to the bike again, with everything I required for a night's camping strapped to it, and negotiated a hilly and bumpy track down to the Point of Sleat itself, where crashing surf and the sound of gulls accompanied my slumbers at a wild and beautiful camp above the shore.

While I love the campervan, even its four tin walls can occasionally feel confined and now and then some deep-rooted impulse urges me to break free and connect with the natural world. The best way to do that is to sleep close to the earth itself. A tent, with the door open to the sights and scents of the night, offers the opportunity to feed that particular rat.

Free from filming for a short while, I made my escape and enjoyed a spectacular night beside Loch Slapin in the shadow of Bla Bheinn. In the morning the night mists took a while to blow clear but as they did I sat outside the camper, brew in hand and watched the mountain spectacle unfold. You don't always have to be on a mountain top to enjoy the mountain drama.

I returned to the mainland via the Kylerhea to Glenelg ferry, the only man-operated turntable ferry left in the world. As the Skye Bridge has robbed the island of a wee bit of its romance, this ferry makes a terrific alternative, and, as it's a community enterprise, supports the local economy.

Once over the spectacular Mam Ratagan, I caught up with an old pal, Willie Fraser, the property manager of the National Trust for Scotland's Kintail Estate. In the past I've gone sea kayaking with Willie but this time we walked and talked all the way up to the Bealach na Sgairne, one of Willie's favourite spots in Kintail, just below the big corries of Beinn Fhada. For the television camera it gave me a great opportunity to blether in depth to someone who is a keen mountaineer and an enthusiastic and appreciative deer stalker. The two disciplines don't always sit well together and it was great to hear Willie's wise and experienced perspective on both subjects.

One of the great joys of making television programmes like these is that I get the opportunity to visit some of Scotland's most treasured landscapes and share them with folk who, inevitably, have fresh and insightful viewpoints. My next two guests didn't let me down. Nevis Hulme is a geography teacher in Gairloch who has taught himself the Gaelic language so he could discover and record as many place names on the Melvaig peninsula as he could. At a time when there has been considerable criticism about the value of Gaelic, it was refreshing to hear why Nevis thought it was vital that we cherish the language and remember the old stories behind the place names.

This was a theme I continued in Torridon with former MP Chris Smith. I've known Chris for a long number of years and it was great to walk from his home at Inveralligin to Craig Cottage, a former youth hostel, which he once wardened. It's been quite a career journey for Chris, from schoolboy days in Edinburgh to a youth hostel warden in the Western Highlands to ministerial positions in a Labour government. He was just about to take on a new role, as Master of Pembroke College, Cambridge, his alma mater.

I finished my long, convoluted road trip in Ullapool, but before I climbed the Braes of Ullapool to look down on the old Norse settlement of Ulli's Steading I wanted a final walk. This time I was accompanied by the UK's Adventurer of the Year 2015, Will Copestake.

Will was born and bred in Ullapool and has a strong taste for adventure. He took me to a magnificent gorge near Corrieshalloch where he roamed, swam and canoed as a teenager, and it was clear from the conversation that he's never lost his love of this part of Wester Ross despite all his foreign travels. I left him as he was about to prepare for a long trip to Patagonia where he was going to spend the winter teaching sea kayaking. Was I a little bit envious? Well, perhaps a bit... but how can you be envious of anyone's travels when you've just experienced a journey like my *Roads Less Travelled*?

For sheer beauty and diversity of landscape and wildlife, it's almost impossible to compare the Western Highlands with anywhere on earth. I really hoped our television programmes exhibited these qualities and perhaps encouraged others to come and visit them, either on foot, on bike or on the water.

16

THE SCOTTISH NATIONAL TRAIL

I long nurtured a desire to walk from one end of Scotland to the other. A brand-new hiking trail had just been set up in Nepal, one that ran the entire length of the Himalaya, so was it not reasonable to assume that here in Scotland we could create a trail that ran from the Scottish Borders to Cape Wrath, the very north-west tip of the Scottish mainland: a genuine National Trail?

We already had some wonderful long-distance routes – marketed collectively as the Great Trails – so I wondered how possible it would be to link up some of those existing routes to create one long end-to-end route. I pulled out the maps, laid them out on the floor and managed to work out a rough route that linked sections of the St Cuthbert's Way, Southern Upland Way, West Highland Way, Rob Roy Way and Cape Wrath Trail, all tied together by rural footpaths, minor roads and canal towpaths.

The notion of a new trail running the length of the country wasn't a new one. I remembered discussing its potential years before with Hamish Brown. Indeed, he walked his own version of the route during his *Groat's End Walk*, a UK-length walk from John O'Groats to Land's End, in the late seventies. Another of his books, *Pennines to the Highlands*, offered a route between Byrness in Northumberland to Milngavie and the start of the West Highland Way and was very useful in my own route planning through the part of Scotland that I was least familiar with.

Now, it's all very well looking at a route like this on a map, but what would it be like on the ground? Did those little dotted lines still exist as footpaths, or would I discover that I had to link the already established trails with miles of tarmac bashing or footpaths that had become so badly overgrown that I'd need a machete to chop my way through?

One of the stipulations of the Land Reform (Scotland) Act of 2003 was that local councils should create 'core path networks' around towns and villages and, while I was aware of some excellent work in various parts of the country, I had no idea how many paths had been created, for example, in the Borders or around Glasgow. The only way to find out was to walk the route.

At this point I had a vague notion that we might be able to film me walking the route as one of our *Adventure Show* Christmas specials and, if it could be satisfactorily linked together, it might be worthy of a book. Richard and I had a good blether about it and put the idea to David Harron, our executive producer at the BBC. David liked the idea so it was time for me to go and have a look. I was really pushing the boat out with this walk for the plan was to recce it and then come back and do it all over again, but with a film crew.

It would be the longest and most ambitious of all our television walks and can be broken down into four sections: the southern section between Kirk Yetholm and Edinburgh; a route between Edinburgh and Milngavie following the Union and Forth and Clyde canals; a section between Milngavie and Kingussie in the Highlands; and the final haul between Badenoch and Cape Wrath. Total distance was in the region of 470 miles and I gave it the working title of the Scottish National Trail.

This title was partially inspired by the timing of the walk. It came about several years prior to the 2014 independence referendum, a time when many of us were evaluating just what this country means to us. Was Scotland comfortable enough in its own abilities and potential to leave the union of the UK and go it alone in the world? Could Scotland, minus her traditional industries like steel-making, mining and shipbuilding, survive on the newer industries like gourmet food, tourism and the nascent industry of renewable energy? And, of course, whisky.

In the context of my long walk I hoped to get a feel for the answers to some of those questions but, more than that, I wanted to experience the diversity of landscapes and horizons that Scotland had to offer. I was well aware of that diversity, the stark differences of our mountain landscapes in particular. I had always found it remarkable that we could boast of landscapes like the Cairngorms and the Cullin, so different in shape and atmosphere and yet so close together geographically. Or Torridon and the Angus Glens, or the idiosynctratic shapes of hills like Suilven and Stac Pollaidh lying cheek by jowl with the other hills of Assynt. I wanted to soak myself in this rugged beauty, I wanted to walk the byways of the land, seek out the quieter places and familiarise myself with an aspect of the nation that rarely makes it into political manifestos.

Most crucially, in the course of a 470-mile walk, I was eager to observe things at closer quarters than I could do by just driving through it. Travelling by foot not only allows you closer proximity to the land and the people who live on it, but also takes you into the kind of landscapes that most people, including policy-making politicians, are unfamiliar with. Walking offers the opportunity to study the small print of a landscape, those things you would miss from a car or even a bicycle.

When planning a long-distance route like this, particularly when laying down footsteps you hope others will follow, it's important you have a start and finish point that can be reached by public transport. I left Newtonmore and took the train to Edinburgh where I picked up a bus to Kelso. With just time to grab a bite to eat in that lovely Borders town I caught a local bus to my starting point at Kirk Yetholm.

If that name sounds familiar it's probably because it's the northern terminus of the highly popular 220-mile Pennine Way, the long-distance trail that follows the spine of England from Edale in the Peak District to the Scottish Borders. It's a lovely spot and represents one half of the twin communities of Kirk and Town Yetholm. Straddling the Bowmont River, which runs deep into the heart of the Cheviots, Yetholm lies about a mile from the border. Appropriately, the name Yetholm means a 'gateway', a portal to either Scotland or England depending on which way you are travelling. As such, the village has often been used by refugees fleeing from one country to the other, particularly gypsies. One story suggests that during a battle in France in the seventeenth century, a British officer was rescued by a soldier with Romany origins. The officer, a Captain Bennet, apparently held land in the Yetholm area and in gratitude to the soldier who had saved his life he made this, plus some cottages, available to him and his descendants. In the late nineteenth century Scotland's last gypsy king and queen, Charles and Esther Faa Blythe, were crowned here at Kirk Yetholm. The coronation carriage was drawn by six donkeys, and you can still see the little house, the Gypsy Palace, where the king and queen lived.

Kirk Yetholm is also on the route of the St Cuthbert's Way, a 62-mile walk that follows in the footsteps of Cuthbert, a seventh-century priest who became Prior of the Celtic monastery at Melrose. The route runs from Melrose Abbey to Lindisfarne in Northumberland and since I was heading for Melrose it seemed a little daft not to follow in the well-trodden footsteps of the good saint. On a more prosaic note, I felt some relief at being able to follow a signposted route for the first couple of days. Normally my backpacking trips are in the Highlands, where you can virtu-ally walk where you please and camp where you please. Here in the south I knew that I'd be walking on agricultural land, around fields, on country lanes and along minor roads. I was also a little unsure about wild camping in such an agricultural environment and I was concerned about finding water to drink that wasn't spoiled by sheep or agricultural run-off. Although the Land Reform (Scotland) Act suggests you can camp wild for one or more nights it does say you should be out of sight of houses and roads. That might not be easy in landscapes such as these, although I also had the option of finding a small inn or bed and breakfast to stay at. Camping isn't the only form of accommodation on a route like this, but it certainly is the most convenient.

Well filled after a traditional Scottish breakfast and a comfort-able night in the Border Hotel I wandered out from Kirk Yetholm along the riverside path to where the road splits – one route runs to Cocklawfoot, where I'd enjoyed some great hillwalking in the past, while my northbound route followed the minor road for a mile or so before turning onto an old farm track that climbed to an obvious ridge. A dry stone wall followed the ridge to the summit of Wideopen Hill, an appropriately named top with well spread views of the surrounding countryside. It's about 1,270 feet in height, with extensive views across to the Cheviots, the lovely rounded hills of the English Border.

Anxious to get miles under my boots I dropped down towards the village of Morebattle to the sound of skylarks, the first I'd heard this year. Still lower, oystercatchers dutifully patrolled their patch, screeching in annoyance at my disturbance, and the woods were full of spring birdsong which compensated a little for the three to four miles of tarmac bashing that lay before me. Climbing up the road into the village was hot work and I craved caffeine.

Beyond Morebattle I tramped along the roads towards the gaunt remains of the fifteenth-century Cessford Castle and down to the two rows of terraced houses that constitutes Cessford village. A dirt track made its way between the two terraces towards Cessford Moor and I followed it with some relief, now walking on reasonable tracks, and not tarmac. From the top of the hill I began to follow a series of field verges, with some very pleasant walking along the edges of woods and vast, prairie-like fields. Where had all the wooded copses gone, the hedgerows and the bush-filled ditches? Sacrificed for the better returns of modern intensive farming?

More field edges and woodland tracks carried me north towards the banks of the River Teviot where I crossed the river over a long suspension bridge into the lovely ornamented grounds of Monteviot House. This is the seat of the earls of Ancrum and earlier earls of Lothian and dates from 1740. The gardens were designed in the sixties by Percy Cane and are well worth a visit. The weather, which had been fine for much of the day, had dulled considerably with a pallid hint of grey over everything, but now the early evening sun had broken through the cloud and cast a shine on everything. The daffodils were in full bloom, and patches of snowdrops and blue-bells still looked vibrant and fresh. A path through the gardens and some lovely mixed woodland took me onto open moorland: the old Roman route called Dere Street, which originally ran between York and Edinburgh. Originally known as Agricola's Road, it didn't stretch the imagination too much to think that St Cuthbert used it himself.

Dere Street follows a long, low ridge, with huge prairie fields on one side and on the other, just beyond some sheep pastures, the busy A68. By a touch of good fortune, I noticed the sinking sun glint on some very small puddles in a field and when I investigated I realised it was a spring, a small seep that quickly evolved into a tiny stream. There was a patch of flat ground close by, beside a drystone wall, a good spot to spend the night, my first camp on the Scottish National Trail.

Settling to the sounds of the countryside was nothing short of idyllic. A dog fox barked in the near distance, perhaps a little unsettled at my presence. Owls called from the nearby woods and oystercatchers and peewits kept their calls going until dark. At one point I heard rustling beside me and when I looked out I disturbed a roe deer that took off in fright, around a tree and over the wall behind me. It's beautiful, graceful movement as it arched over the wall took my breath away . . .

Things were different in the morning. It had rained heavily in the small hours and I woke to a damp and misty dawn with rain still splattering on the tent. Once on the move things didn't feel so bad and I enjoyed the easy walking along Dere Street towards the village of Maxton on the River Tweed, the birthplace of the medieval scholar, John Duns Scotus. Lovely riverside paths took me to St Boswells and Newtown St Boswells, then, after a good lunch in an excellent cafe-cum-bookshop, I made my way up to Bowden and the start of the climb over the Eildons towards Melrose.

The three conical mounds of the Eildons are the remains of a volcanic lava flow that, millions of years ago, intruded into the underground sandstone. Eons of weathering by wind, rain and ice has since exposed the mass into the three distinct lumps we know today, the 'Trimontium of the Romans'. If prosaic geological description leaves you a little cold, then consider this: legend claims the Eildons were formed not by volcanic activity but by the supernatural powers of Michael Scott the Wizard, who was ordered by the devil to split a single 'Eildon' mountain into three separate hills. Some time later, Thomas the Rhymer, a thirteenth-century bard and seer, claims to have been spirited away by the queen of the fairies, and spent seven years in Elfland, below the Eildon Hills. Less fanciful, but still fascinating, is the fact that the Eildon's North Hill was once the site of an ancient city, the home of the ancient Selgovae tribe. Archaeologists suggest there could have been over three hundred hut circles here about 2,000 years ago. Later, the Romans used the site as a fort and signal station.

Next morning, after a very comfortable night in a Melrose hotel, it was windy and wet and I was facing a long day of walking. The well-signposted route of the St Cuthbert's Way finished at Melrose Abbey and now I'd be following the route of the Southern Upland Way through Galashiels, over the hill to Yair and then up through the forests to the high point of the whole route, the Minch Moor. My plan was to camp high on the historic ridge and descend to Traquair the next day but gale-force winds cast some doubt on my plans. I had to hope the wind would ease off in the course of the day.

More riverside walking on the banks of the Tweed took me to Galashiels where I glimpsed, through a large plate glass window, rows of people working at their desks. I think it might have been a call centre. The large window must have been a distraction to the workers. Several waved to me and I waved back, smug in the knowledge that despite the rain and wind I wasn't shackled to a desk. Once again I felt the familiar surge of relief at the decision I made all those years ago, the bold decision to do my own thing and try to carve a living out of my love of the outdoors. The thought was curiously uplifting as I left the urban environment of Galashiels to climb over Hog Hill to Fairnilee House, from where it was only a few minutes down to the tumultuous Tweed and the little car park and shelter at Yair. It was a good spot to get out of the rain and grab some lunch before the climb up through the forest to the Three Brethren and the start of the Minch Moor.

The tall cairns known as the Three Brethren decorate the summit of Yair Hill, which is on the route of Selkirk's Common Riding, an annual event that sees a cavalcade of horse riders go round the bounds, or the marches, of Selkirk Burgh. The Brethren are three tall cairns, one of each standing within the districts of Selkirk Burgh, Yair and Bowhill. By now, the wind had dropped from gale

271

force to slightly mischievous and from time to time the sun broke through the racing clouds. It was great to be up high for a while and I was in good spirit as I headed west along the broad path to the Broomy Law (any relationship to Glasgow's riverside Broomielaw I wonder?), down into a fine little wooded glen and then uphill again towards the summit of Brown Knowe, where, at 525 metres/1,725 feet, a cairn marks the high point of the route.

Just beyond Brown Knowe, the Minch Moor road drops down the ridge between Hangingshaw Burn and Gruntly Burn, past some woods lower down and then into other woods above Yarrowford. It's a route of considerable antiquity. Edward I came this way to conquer Scotland in 1296 and, after the Battle of Philiphaugh, James Graham, the Marquis of Montrose, crossed the route to Traquair House where he hoped to find shelter. More recently, in 1931, a party of Scottish Youth Hostel Association officials crossed the Minch Moor to Broadmeadows to open Scotland's very first youth hostel.

I camped in the forest and, thankfully, the winds blew themselves out overnight. Wakened to a sunny, but cool, morning, it didn't take me long to drop down to Traquair where I was expecting a long road walk to Peebles. I was dreading it; indeed I was concerned about any road walking because at that time I had been suffering problems with my feet, pains along the outside edges and in the arches whenever I walked on hard surfaces like tarmac. It was a problem that was to get worse as the years went on but for the moment I could get by on a diet of ibuprofen and paracetemol.

As I set out along the road to Peebles I noticed a little sign marked 'Tweed Trails' on a gate. It was the start of a lovely forest walk that climbed above the road and paralleled it almost all the way into Cardrona. But that wasn't all, another Tweed Trails sign pointed me across to the north bank of the river where a good footpath ran along the riverbank all the way into Peebles. I felt as though I had won the lottery.

As part of the Land Reform (Scotland) Act, when Scotland was given access laws that have become the envy of the world, councils were asked to develop core path networks around villages and towns. Tweed Trails is one such network and I was to make full use of it over the next couple of days. Just beyond the campsite at Rosetta on the north side of Peebles a TT signpost pointed out a route over Hamilton Hill and down to Upper Kidston. Beyond the farm, another trail climbed to the bealach between White Meldon and South Hill Head and down to Meldon Burn. I followed the road north for a short distance before following a track through the forest to the farm at Stewarton. From here more TT signs led me past Courhope and down to Flemington Burn, a lovely spot at the foot of a long grassy nose called Green Knowe. Larks were rejoicing in the sun that had just broken through the clouds, and I rejoiced with them as I wandered up the footpath above Fingland Burn and over the hill to Romanno Bridge.

A footpath, which appeared obvious on the map but failed to materialise in reality, should have followed the Lyne Water to West Linton, but despite searching, I couldn't find it. Instead I followed a minor road into the delightful village where, with aching feet, I booked in for the night at the Gordon Arms. I had a big day before me next day and I reckoned I needed a good sleep and a full Scottish breakfast in the morning.

My plan was to climb over the long line of the Pentlands via the Bore Stane from Carlops to Balerno, which meant I'd have to follow the A702 for about three miles into Carlops. Road walking is bad enough but walking alongside a busy road like the A702 is sheer hell on earth, so once I had eaten in the hotel, I had a little scout about in search of an alternative route, and I found one. After a stiff climb from West Linton, a path continued north towards the Cairn Muir and the Cauldstane Slap but, well before I reached the Muir, I noticed a minor road running off to the right. This eventually metamorphosed into a track that followed the line of a Roman road past Linton Muir and Hartside all the way into Carlops. From there, another track ran uphill past Fairliehope to the North Esk Reservoir, where a footpath continued north-east, past Cock Rig and the Bore Stane and down the other side to the farm at Listonshiels. From there a series of minor roads took me into Balerno and the start of the Water of Leith walkway that was to take me all the way into the very heart of auld Edinburgh toon.

Flowing for twenty-four miles from its source in the Pentland Hills, the Water of Leith winds its way through Balerno, Currie, Juniper Green, Colinton, Slateford, Roseburn and Dean Village into the heart of Edinburgh, before continuing on its way through Stockbridge, Canonmills and Bonnington to the Firth of Forth at Leith. The Water of Leith Conservation Trust works to conserve and enhance the river and its banks and does a fantastic job. The footpaths alongside the river made a superb ending to the first section of my long walk, a fitting finale to the initial stage of a long journey that was to take me all the way to Cape Wrath, the most north-western point on the Scottish mainland.

You can't title a walking route as the Scottish National Trail and not include our capital city. After the long walk north from Kirk Yetholm it was good to settle down in an Edinburgh hotel for the night and enjoy a bit of comfort, a shower and an Indian curry. I felt I could indulge myself a bit for the next day's walking since it didn't look too difficult. The Water of Leith footpath made a delightful climax to the first section of the trail, from Kirk Yetholm to Edinburgh, and a great start to the next section, from Edinburgh to Aviemore. Next day I was heading for Kilsyth on the Forth and Clyde Canal.

The footpath meets the Union Canal at Slateford, close to the Water of Leith Information Centre. From here I escaped the hustle and bustle of the city and followed the canal towpaths all the way to Falkirk. Here, the marvellous Falkirk Wheel, a huge boat-lifting device, connects the Union Canal with the Forth and Clyde Canal and allows boats to travel between Glasgow and Edinburgh. From Falkirk, more towpaths took me to Kilsyth, where I spent the night, and then on to Kirkintilloch and Cadder, near Balmore. From there it was a short stroll to Milngavie and the start of the West Highland Way, Scotland's first official long-distance trail that runs north for ninety-six miles to Fort William.

Sharing the first dozen or so miles with the West Highland Way, the Scottish National Trail follows footpaths, tracks, lanes and an old railway line as far as Drymen before diving into the sprawling Garadhban Forest on the route of the Rob Roy Way, which is then followed to Pitlochry.

For the next 120-odd miles, forest tracks, rights of way, footpaths and drovers' roads took me on a rough and straggling north-easterly line through forests, along lonely glens, over high passes and across the ridges that form the grain of the Central Highlands. Here, the gables of a thousand ruins bore testament to former communities who worked relentlessly on the land. There are remains of Roman camps and standing stones and here and there vitrified forts reflect even older times.

Ancient tribes once inhabited these districts between what we now call the Grampians and the River Forth in the south. They didn't speak Gaelic, or Pict, not even Irish, but a form of 'British' that had a relationship to today's Welsh, Cornish or Breton. Known as Verturiones, these ancient people were heavily influenced by the Irish who increasingly occupied the lands, particularly during the Roman occupation. In time, the northern area became known as Ath Fhodhla, or New Ireland, nowadays known as Atholl, and further south Strath Eireann, or Ireland's strath, eventually became known as Strathearn. Loch Earn is derived from the same source.

Another Irish link is to be found in upper Glen Artney, just north of Callander. Where Gleann a' Chroin rolls down from the great corries of Stuc a' Chroin and Ben Vorlich and meets Glen Artney, a house called Arivurichardich still stands, an old building fully exposed to the winds and the rains that sweep the length of the glen. According to the writings of Seton Gordon, the name of the house is a corruption of Airigh Mhuircheartaich, or Moriarty's Shieling, another suggestion of an Irish link in the place-name chain of this vast district.

There are Roman links too. As I followed the old railway into the town of Callander I passed a field that appeared to be curiously corrugated. This is the site of an old Roman camp, a temporary camp, as the might of the Roman legions never quite managed to quell the Scots to the north of the Antonine Wall. There are also Roman links with Glen Almond.

From the Loch Ard Forest I followed good tracks to Aberfoyle but initially I took the line of an aqueduct that carries water from Loch Katrine in the Trossachs to the city of Glasgow. Work on the aqueduct was started in 1855 in typical Victorian fashion – no expense spared, and the watercourse is lined with stone beehive-shaped water cisterns with black iron basketweave railings over the top. Industrial heritage at its finest.

Less than thirty miles from the city centre of Glasgow, the village of Aberfoyle sits slap bang on the very edge of the Highlands. Indeed, the village sits on the geological fault line that runs across Scotland from the south end of Loch Lomond to Stonehaven on the north-east coast. All before it is lowland. To its north lie the Highlands, rich in promise, generous in splendour.

The clans who inhabited these northern regions were, until comparatively recent times, as Sir Walter Scott so succinctly put it, 'much addicted to predatory excursions upon their Lowland neighbours'. As such, Aberfoyle has a turbulent history! Graham's *Sketches ... of ... Scenery ... of Perthshire*, published in 1806, explains, 'Tis well known, that in the highlands, it was in former times accounted not only lawful, but honourable, among hostile tribes, to commit depredations on one another; and these habits of the age were perhaps strengthened in this district by the circum-stances which have been mentioned. It bordered on a country, the inhabitants of which, while they were richer, were less warlike than they, and widely differenced by language and manners.' Fear not, you won't notice that wide a difference today.

The next few miles, over the Highland edge itself and along the Menteith Hills to the foot of Loch Venachar, certainly emphasised the geographic difference between those districts to the north and to the south of this geological faultline. The southern views take in some of the flattest land in all Scotland: Flanders Moss, leading eastwards and then opening out towards the distant blue rise of the Ochils, and across to the lowland swell of the Campsie Fells and the Kilpatricks. To the north, a jumble of high hills and mountains dominate, a raised and tumbled land, as different as chalk from cheese.

Despite its popularity with those who want to visit the Highlands, Callander itself is very much a lowland town. It consists of a long, broad main street from which narrower streets and lanes run south towards the River Teith, which forms its southern boundary. The first bridge across the river was built in 1764 and was replaced by the present bridge in 1907.

The poet John Keats passed through Callander in 1818, describing it as 'vexatiously full of visitors'. It can still be a bit like that, especially on holiday weekends. The person to blame is Sir Walter Scott, whose novels and writings on the nearby Trossachs, particularly the long romantic poem *The Lady of the Lake*, caught the imagination of the nineteenth-century public. They flocked to Callander and to Aberfoyle to experience something of the atmosphere of 'the Children of the Mist', Rob Roy MacGregor and *The Celtic Twilight*.

Behind the town the beautifully wooded Callander Craigs rise to a height of 335 metres/1,100 feet. Views over Callander towards the distant Gargunnock and Fintry hills were nothing compared to the view that opened as I reached the summit cairn. Sitting in the sun for a good twenty minutes, I gazed west along the length of silvery Loch Venachar, its head seemingly choked by the high hills of the Trossachs. To the right I could see into the very bosom of Ben Ledi, into its great wild north-east corrie, while to the east my gaze carried me along the broad strath to Stirling, the Ochils and beyond to the dim outline of the Pentlands near Edinburgh, which I had crossed only a few days previously.

Beyond the summit cairn, built in 1887 to commemorate Queen Victoria's Silver Jubilee, a footpath descended through young birch woods and groves of Scots pine and offered good views over heather moorland, open land that stretches into the long dog-leg of Glen Artney. A public road runs as far as the farm at Braeleny and from there a track took me into country that becomes increasingly open and bare. Nodding its head to the peaks of Beinn Each, Stuc a' Chroin and Ben Vorlich, the glen eventually bends away to the north-east before dropping down to its beautiful, wooded lower stretch where the Water of Ruchill cascades down a deep channel towards the village of Comrie.

It was wet and windy when I arrived but I was thankful it was nothing worse – small earthquakes are a common occurrence hereabouts. The village is apparently situated close to several geological fault lines. Consequently, the world's first seismometers were set up here in the nineteenth century and you can see models of them at a house called The Ross, to the west of the village.

The road up lovely Glen Lednock led eventually to Invergeldie at the foot of Ben Chonzie where, beyond the farm, a rough track rose to a bare windswept bealach that looked down on the head of Glen Almond. Beyond its head, Gleann a' Chilleine runs down to Ardtalnaig on Loch Tay but, in the opposite direction, a track runs for some six miles down the length of Glen Almond, whose hillsides are largely given over to the farming of sheep and the shooting of grouse. Here and there lie the tell-tale signs of former settlements, not least the memorial cairn built on the site of the Stuck Chapel, the church that once served the population of this part of the glen. Today the solitude is tangible, almost overwhelming when the mists hang low over the tops and winds sigh down the long miles of the glen.

Beyond Auchnafree, the narrow-sided pass of Glen Lochan links Glen Almond with Glen Quaich where I followed a hill track that climbs above the waters of Loch Freuchie and makes its way over a high, partially forested plateau. I turned right at a small lochan and made my way down the length of Urlar Burn to the wonderful Birks of Aberfeldy and the wooded glen of Moness Burn, celebrated in verse by no less a worthy than Robert Burns, who visited the area in August 1787.

From Aberfeldy, a combination of rough paths and a quiet road followed the northern banks of the River Tay to Edradynate where a minor road climbed high above the meandering river, past the farms of Blackhill and Lurgan. Another hill track climbs over the Farragons from here, past Loch Derculich and the rugged eastern slopes of Farragon Hill before turning north-east to pass close to the summit of Beinn Eagagach at well over 609 metres/2,000 feet. The long and winding descent to Loch Tummel gave welcome views of the Atholl hills, where Glen Tilt slices its way north in an uncompromising line towards the Cairngorms and the final splendour of the marvellous Lairig Ghru.

Once across the Tummel (there is a bridge further downriver

towards Faskally), a quiet road runs up Glen Fincastle where I found another hill path that took me over a low ridge and down to Blair Atholl. This was my last chance to stock up on provisions before the final forty miles or so up the length of Glen Tilt and through the Lairig Ghru to Coylumbridge and Aviemore.

There is a growing awareness, as you tramp the empty miles of Glen Tilt, of a gradual constriction as the valley narrows to a cleft, a defile, before broadening out again to a windswept and desolate beauty. The ruins of the old Bynack shieling remain here, a soft spot in the harshness of these high moors, a good place for a camp before the few miles to White Bridge and the threshold of the Lairig Ghru.

This was the route I chose for my initial exploratory trek up the length of the Scottish National Trail but, after some consultation with the rescue lads, we decided not to take the route over the 822-metre/2,700-foot high Lairig Ghru. Snow can often lie in the Lairig until well into June so we decided to divert the route just before White Bridge into Glen Geldie, over the watershed into Glen Feshie and on to Kingussie where I made full use of a new track that runs below the Monadh Liath hills to Newtonmore. The Cairngorms Outdoor Access Trust has been building and improving footpaths and trails on both sides of the Cairngorms and the walk between Kingussie and Newtonmore is typical of many of the new routes that are being created.

This lovely walking route climbs beyond the Kingussie golf course to the remains of the Glen Gynack township before following a newly built path along the south shores of lovely Loch Gynack to the ruckles of stone and boulders that's all that's left of the old village of Auchtuchle. At first glance there's little left, but when you leave the path and start looking around it doesn't take long to discern the rectangular shapes of buildings, of low walls covered in heather and grass. The village is situated on a terrace on the west slopes of Creag Bheag and comprises a group of at least twelve buildings, a kiln barn, two enclosures, some rigs, some lazy-beds and a head-dyke. As I poked around, the Feshie hills stood clear across the strath of the Spey, their sensuous curves and rounded shapes emphasised by the blue shadows of their corries.

The riverside path in Glen Banchor took me through to Laggan where I had to endure a few miles of road walking and sore feet, albeit on a very quiet road, past General Wade's old barracks to Garva Bridge and on to Melgarve bothy. From here the Corrieyairack Pass makes its way through the Monadh Liath to Fort Augustus. Historical accounts generally paint the Corrieyairack in shades of grimness. Montrose's Covenanting army avoided it; Bonnie Prince Charlies's troops didn't like it; Mrs Grant of Laggan, in her 1781 *Letters from the Mountains* said it was 'impassable in winter'; the governor of Fort Augustus, in 1798, suggested it was 'wild desolation beyond anything he could describe', and a short time later the Honourable Mrs Sarah Murray claimed the whole road was 'rough, dangerous and dreadful, even for a horse'.

Despite the criticisms, General George Wade and his squad of soldiers-cum-navvies did a pretty good job on the road, which runs past Corrie Yairack and over the shoulder of Corrieyairack Hill. It's only fairly recently that this, still officially a 'road', was closed to vehicular traffic although, to be fair, only rugged four-wheel drive vehicles could successfully negotiate the ruts and rough cobbles. It's certainly not a road I'd want to drive on. Having said that, as a walking route it may not be the most inspiring route in the Highlands either. The line of goose-stepping electricity pylons that accompany the old road certainly spoils any claims of natural beauty, but the route does give easy access to the whole of the Corrieyairack, Aberchalder and Braeroy deer forests.

From Fort Augustus the towpath of the Caledonian Canal took me west to Glengarry where I began a long, tough trek through some of the most majestic, remote and stunningly beautiful landscape you could imagine. There are no 'official' long-distance footpaths through these northern hills so I gave myself several rough guidelines: the route should follow a south to north line as close as possible; it should allow passage through the most scenic areas; it should try and avoid tarmac and paved roads or paths but instead follow existing footpaths and stalkers' tracks as much as possible and it should avoid crossing mountain ranges and major rivers except where necessary.

The Cape Wrath Trail is a stunner, without doubt the finest long-distance walking route in the land. Beyond Glengarry the mountains rise higher and steeper until you find yourself wandering amongst some of the finest landscapes imaginable. I thoroughly enjoyed the wild and lonely Glen Loyne between Glengarry and Glen Shiel, and soaked up the atmosphere of the deep Fionngleann and Glen Lichd as the path tumbles down between the great mountain walls of Kintail.

One of Kintail's finest features is the tumultuous Falls of Glomach, not quite the highest waterfall in Scotland but certainly the most impressive, especially after a bout of heavy rain. The top lies about a mile beyond the Bealach na Sroine, above Morvich on Loch Duich. As I wandered towards it I took note of the sprawling strath of Gleann Gaorsaic and its various streams and burns that feed the main river, water courses that drain the slopes of big mountains like Beinn Fhada and the magnificently sculpted Sgurr nan Ceathreamhnan. All that water is harnessed into a narrow stream and directed into a narrow, rocky cleft where it plunges for some 120 metres/400 feet, twice the height of Niagara, into a deep, black chasm.

You can normally see the spray and hear the thunder long before you see the waterfall itself. Needless to say, great care should be taken on the normally wet path that skirts the top of the falls.

Below lies Glen Elchaig where you walk in some of the loneliest landscape in Scotland – the wild miles between Bendronaig and Bearnais in the Attadale deer forest. Beyond Bearnais bothy another footpath runs over a high (600 metres/1,968 feet) pass below Sgurr na Feartaig from where it wriggles down towards the Achnashellach Forest and a footbridge over the River Carron to the A890 road at Achnashellach station.

Presiding over the Achnashellach Forest like some prehistoric watchtower, the 907 metre/2,976 feet Fuar Tholl, or cold hole, is one of the most impressive hills in the land. Its three tops are guarded by steep cliffs of Torridonian sandstone, soaring skyward from the lower pine-clad levels of Coire Lair.

The track that climbs out of Achnashellach and into Coire Lair is a delight. You can cross the railway, with care, and you'll be pleased to know that Network Rail hasn't seen fit to ban pedestrians from crossing the railway line here as they've done in dozens of other crossings throughout the nation. From here the forestry track climbs through the woods before dropping down to the old stalkers' path that follows the deep gorge of the River Lair. What a fabulous section of walking this is, with pine trees sheltering the path that climbs over sandstone slabs, crinkled and creased with streaks of quartzite glinting and sparkling in the sun.

As I surmounted the lip of Coire Lair I paused for a while to take in the scale. Two Munros are the normal attention-grabbers here: Sgorr Ruadh and the long, curving ridge of Beinn Liath Mhor. The classic Coire Lair Horseshoe walk gathers both of them in, the two Munros linked by a high pass, and stronger walkers often add the Corbett of Fuar Tholl, almost as an afterthought, although it's the finest mountain of the three.

Now in Torridon, the ancient geology of the region would dominate the scenery for the next couple of days. As I gazed on Beinn Eighe, near Kinlochewe, I couldn't help but contemplate the geology of the hill. This isn't so much a single mountain as a mini chain of them, a complex range whose terraced cliffs are cut at frequent intervals by long, vertical gullies that drop down into great fan-shaped stone chutes. If the visual impact of this hill doesn't take your breath away, its enduring quality certainly will. Beinn Eighe has been a National Nature Reserve for just over fifty years, a mere flicker of time in the life of a mountain, but at least it offers us a tangible time span to grapple with. It's rather more difficult to wrestle with the comparatively abstract notion that the sandstone of our Torridon mountains was originally laid down about a thousand million years ago on a platform of Lewisian gneiss that could well be two and a half thousand million years old!

Beyond Kinlochewe, the only resupply point on this section of the route, I entered a region known as the Letterewe Wilderness, between Loch Maree and Little Loch Broom.

The north shores of Loch Maree are rich in oak wood and associated undergrowth and the glens are full of wild flowers: orchids, bog asphodel, lousewort and milkwort. Higher up, the quartzite and Torridonian sandstone ridges, crags and tops offer all the challenge Snyder could ask for and I certainly experienced some of that archetypal power beyond the Heights of Kinlochewe, treading pretty wearily over the Bealach Gorm and down to Loch an Nid, a lonely stretch of water that lies in a deep cleft between Creag Rainich and the great corrie-bitten wall between Mullach Coire Mhic Fhearchair and Beinn a' Chlaidheimh.

A high-level path, cairned for much of its way, runs between Corrie Hallie, below An Teallach, and the A835 Ullapool road. On the north side of the road a private forestry track runs up through the Lael Forest into the lower part of Gleann na Squaib, a pleasant place with some spectacular waterfalls and good pools for bathing when the weather is warm enough. Higher up the glen, the stalkers' path zig-zags up the steeper inclines towards the Munros of Meall nan Ceapraichean, Beinn Dearg and Cona' Mheall but my route to Cape Wrath took a more northerly direction, up and over the wilds of Glen Douchary, along the shores of Loch an Daimh to Duag Bridge at the foot of lonely Strath Mulzie, and along the River Einig to Amat and Oykel Bridge.

Oykel Bridge lies on the River Oykel, twelve miles west of Lairg. An inn was built here in 1831 to serve travellers on the road to Assynt and today it serves as a traditional angling establishment. It's a wee bit 'huntin'fishin'shooting' but hey, long distance backpackers can't afford to be choosy!

From the rather benign and low-lying country of Glen Oykel the scenery changed dramatically beyond Loch Ailsh as I entered the Benmore Forest and skirted the wild and imposing eastern slopes of Ben More Assynt.

Geologically, this whole area is predominantly made up of gneiss on top of which sandstone mountains have been weathered by frost and wind to create some of the magnificent smaller mountain peaks that dominate the landscape further west: Stac Pollaidh, Ben Mor Coigach, Cul Mor, Cul Beag, Suilven and Quinag.

While the Munros, Ben More Assynt and its close neighbour Conival perhaps lack the mountain architecture of some of these smaller hills, they rise from a desolate and water-scarred landscape. Their shy and retiring nature is protected by the rough, naked miles of their approach. There is a prehistoric rawness in their appeal, but their geology is also more complex. The gneiss bedrock rises to a greater height than on the western hills and on Ben More Assynt it almost reaches the summit. Add the crystalline Moine schists that are also found here, the white quartzite blocks and the limestone glen below and you begin to understand why one guidebook described the area as an 'internationally acclaimed geological showpiece'.

This rather long section could be broken, if necessary, by following the infant River Oykel to its headwaters in the great corrie below Ben More Assynt and Conival, and climbing through the high bealach south of Conival where a rough path will take you down to Gleann Dubh and the hotel at Inchnadamph. From there a footpath over the brow of Glas Bheinn leads to Loch na Gainmhich from where you'll have to follow the road north to Kylesku.

The route from Benmore Lodge is tough and remote and really only for those willing to embrace all aspects of a wilderness experience: pathless stretches, river crossings, rough terrain and solitude.

Approaching Kylesku from Loch na Gainmhich, the first glimpse of Quinag can be intimidating. On dour days of scudding cloud she can look distinctly menacing, the main backbone of the mountain shy and retiring, hidden by the perspective of the land behind steep, barrel-shaped buttresses of terraced rock. In the fiery light of a winter sunset she can look fierce and distinctly threatening.

Beyond Kylesku and its modern bridge I crossed a spine of land into the Reay Forest, an area I always think of as the land of the great northern diver. The bird's melancholy call seems to embody the spirit of these northern parts. The great Highland writer Seton Gordon once described the wild and compelling cry as one that might come from 'one of the uruisgean or gruagachan which in tradition and folk-lore people those sea-girt isles'. It's an eerie sound in the half-light of a late summer evening, especially if you're camped by some remote hill loch.

The trail continues now below the great cliff-bands of Arkle and out to the road at Rhiconich from where seven miles of tarmac bashing took me past Kinlochbervie (the Fisherman's Mission is a great place for a fry-up) and past straggling croftships to Blairmore and the track to magical Sandwood Bay.

Here lies one of Scotland's finest beaches and the feeling of remoteness is powerful. At the south-west end of the bay a 91-metre/300-feet high sea stack, Am Buachaille, rises from its sandstone plinth. Behind the beach and sequestered from it by the sand dunes lies a freshwater loch, Sandwood Loch with, sitting on the grassy hillside above, the ruins of Sandwood Cottage. The area is owned by the John Muir Trust.

On the face of it, Sandwood Bay is little different from countless other bays which dot the storm-lashed western seaboard of Scotland, but there is a spirit abroad here, a spirit of place which is curiously atmospheric and compelling. Some claim it is the principal hauling-up place in Scotland for mermaids. A black-bearded sailor supposedly haunts the shores. Seton Gordon tells of walking here in the 1920's and of how astonished he was at the number of shipwrecks that littered the shore. He believed these were old vessels, lost on this coast before the building of the Cape Wrath lighthouse. He also posed the question of whether or not there could be Viking longboats buried in the sands. Indeed, was it the Vikings who named this place Sand-Vatn or Sand Water?

It was also the Vikings who named Cape Wrath, as a 'turning place' before sailing down the western seaboard of Scotland. Rough footpaths link Sandwood Bay with Cape Wrath whose lighthouse was designed in 1828 by Robert Stevenson, grandfather of Robert Louis Stevenson. It's a rather nice link because RLS was a great traveller and adventurer who once said, 'For my part, I travel not to go anywhere, but to go. I travel for travel's sake. The great affair is to move.' I suspect he would have liked the idea of a Scottish National Trail, running through the length of this wonderful country of ours. I let his words go with me as I headed off to catch the postbus to the Kyle of Durness where the ferry would carry me across the waters to near Durness. From there a bus would take me to Inverness and I could catch a train home to Newtonmore.

Some time later I asked Alex Salmond, then Scotland's first

minister, if he would be kind enough to officially open the route for us. Alex's walking is enjoyed mostly on the golf course but he agreed, and this was his reason for agreeing, 'My mother was the most influential person in my life and she had been president of the Linlithgow Ramblers. She had climbed over seventy Munros and she had all your books, Cameron. Sadly, she died of a heart attack during a walk in the Cairngorms, so I like to think that wherever she is, she might look down on me that day when I open your walk and say, thank God you're doing something useful, Alex.'

This route was devised predominantly as two television programmes so I was delighted when my friends Paul and Helen Webster offered to compile a step-by-step description of the book for their excellent website. You'll find all the details at www.walkh-ighlands.co.uk/scottish-national-trail.shtml.

17

Boots and Bikes

I decided to resign from the editorship of the *Great Outdoors* when I reached the age of sixty. Although more and more people of my age, and indeed older, still happily climb mountains in their retirement years I felt that the magazine should be taken forward by a younger person. Emily Rodway, a very talented journalist and magazine editor, had been my depute since John Manning left for his Yorkshire idyll some years earlier, and I was confident that she would take the magazine on to great things, despite the very difficult market conditions after the 2008 economic crash.

I decided to give up trek leading at the same time. Very few people want to spend a lot of money on their dream trek of a life-time only to discover their trek leader was an old greybeard who should have retired years before. But there was another reason. My final trek was the one from Dana to Petra in Jordan that I described earlier, a wonderful journey through an amazingly hospitable country, but memories of that trek were considerably darkened when an an obscure volcano in Iceland erupted just before we were due to fly home. The massive eruption caused particles of ash to gather in the stratosphere, disrupting air flights throughout the world. Our flight home from Jordan was cancelled and we had to sit in our hotel day after day, running up extra bills and checking with BBC Worldwide as often as possible to see which planes were flying and what travel arrangements were being put in place for stranded passengers.

The amount of help I could expect from KE Adventure Travel was limited as they had trekkers stuck in countries from the Himalaya to South America. As the group's trek leader and the company's representative I had to make the best of a very difficult situation, a

287

state of affairs far removed from the normal day-to-day issues that arise when leading an overseas trek.

Needless to say, we eventually made it home but only after a long and convoluted journey that took us from Jordan to Spain then France and eventually a freight ferry across the Channel back to Blighty.

It was a hellish travel experience and was a huge factor in my decision to give up trek leading. I was getting too old for all the hassle and responsibilities involved in looking after others and I think it was a good decision, especially in view of what was to befall me health-wise in the months to come.

As a final farewell to the magazine, Gina and I had agreed to take part in the *TGO* Challenge, a coast-to-coast backpacking event that the magazine had organised annually since 1980. This is a hugely popular event, well organised but uncompetitive, with three hundred enthusiasts leaving from a dozen starting points on the west coast to hike east on a route of their own choice, either high-level or through the glens, usually camping along the way, to finish somewhere near Montrose on the east coast. The Challenge had become a massively social event with challengers meeting in pubs, hotels and bothies along the way. Individuals met and friendships blossomed. There had even been marriages and at least one wedding has been held midway through an event, with all the guests turning up at the church in sweaty base layers and hiking boots.

Whilst I have always been a huge supporter and, as the *TGO* magazine editor, always attended the final get-together and dinner in Montrose, the event was never personally my cup of tea. I took a lot of criticism from certain individuals for not taking part, even though I edited the sponsoring magazine, but my personal feelings were simple. If I wanted to walk across Scotland I probably wouldn't want to choose a time when three hundred other people were also doing it. I'm not a social beast and would rather avoid the busy bothies and campsites and all the chat about what is the lightest plastic spoon on the market or which underpants best soak up sweat. While there was nothing to stop me choosing a route that avoided the excesses of the Challenge's social scene, I didn't see much point in entering so I could get a badge and a certificate. That said, Gina had participated several times and being much more sociable than I, absolutely loved it. She thought it would be fitting for me, after twenty years of editing the magazine and being associated with the event, to swallow my prejudices and take part. 'Leave the magazine on a high,' she said, 'even if just to prove to your critics that you can still do it.'

I guessed it could be seen as my official farewell to the magazine so I went for it, along with Gina and my brother-in-law Raymond Bainbridge. Raymond had taken up Munro-bagging several years earlier and had become an accomplished and very fit hill-goer. Gina and I were delighted to have him along and we enjoyed his company. We chose to start in Knoydart and finish just north of Montrose but from day one I suffered problems with my feet. Years earlier I had noticed that towards the end of a long walk something was pressing into the ball of my foot, just behind the toes, as though a stone had lodged between the lugs of my Vibram soles. I changed boots, tried different kinds of footwear but the pain and discomfort persisted. If I stopped for a few minutes the discomfort went away so I persevered and blamed advancing years.

I had almost become used to it but had suffered problems earlier in the year on the route between Dana and Petra, which I put down to poorly designed boots, but one day on the Challenge, on the Corrieyairack Pass between Fort Augustus and Laggan, I had to stop several times because my feet had virtually cramped up. I also suffered chronic pain along the outside soles of my feet, as though my boots were too tight. I limped to the end of the walk but made an appointment to see my doctor when I got home. Dr David Pinney is a hillwalker himself so has always been very sensitive to my various needs, but on this occasion he suggested the problems were possibly down to 'years of pounding up and down mountains wearing a heavy pack'. However, he did make an appointment for me to see a consultant at Raigmore Hospital in Inverness. Some weeks later I saw the consultant and he arranged to have my feet X-rayed. By that time I had seen another doctor, a specialist in sports injuries recommended by David, and an NHS podiatrist, and they seemed to think I may have been suffering from a nerve problem called a Morton's Neuroma.

I fully expected the X-rays to show signs of this Neuroma but they didn't. My consultant looked grave when he called me in and showed me the results.

'There's no sign of a Morton's Neuroma, and no real sign of any osteoathritis that might be causing the pain, other than on the joint of your big toe, but look at this. Do you see that white line that runs down your lower leg into your feet? That's an artery, and it's blocked. Do you smoke? Are you diabetic?'

I was immediately referred to a vascular surgeon who made arrangements for me to have a full body scan. When the results arrived, he called me in to his consulting room where he had the scans up on a computer screen. He looked a little confused.

'Look at these,' he said. 'This is a scan from your neck to your waist and all your arteries are completely clear and functioning normally. Now this one is from your waist to your knees and as you can see the arteries are again nice and clear. But look at this one, from your knees to your feet. The main artery on both legs is completely blocked, and I've no idea why that should be the case.'

We then went through a long process of questions and answers about my lifestyle and he was particularly interested in the fact that my father had died from ischaemic heart disease at a relatively early age. But I wasn't a smoker, I kept fit, I didn't have any problems with cholesterol levels, I had a pretty normal diet, I wasn't diabetic. There was no apparent reason why these arteries were bunged up with plaque. I asked him what the prognosis was and he shrugged his shoulders. The blocked arteries could be the reason I was suffering from sore feet, but there again it could have been something else. All he could suggest was that I try and keep active and come back and see him in a year's time. For the time being he put the blocked arteries down to genetic factors. 'We all carry around some genetic baggage,' he told me, 'this appears to be yours.'

As you can imagine, I was pretty shocked. I immediately went home and did something we should never do under such circumstances. I switched on my computer, went online and googled peripheral vascular disease. What I read shocked me even more.

Page after page suggested the most probable outcome of my condition was eventual gangrene and amputation.

I went back to see David Pinney and he tested me for diabetes. The tests were negative and he gently suggested I was overreacting to what I had read on the internet. Despite his encouragement I fell into a real depression and, as the months slipped by, managed to convince myself that walking in the hills would soon be out of the question. If I only had a few more years to enjoy physical activity I should find something active that didn't make my feet painful all the time so I decided to take up cycling. I bought a road bike and began to enjoy the freedom of the open roads. Because there was no pounding involved, my feet didn't hurt in the slightest and I soon found myself cycling longer and longer distances, and loving it. I bought panniers and enjoyed the cycling version of backpacking: loading up my mountain bike with backpacking gear and cycling off on a variety of forest tracks and bulldozed tracks into lonely and beautiful glens. I badly missed the hills but at least I could ride along the glens and look at them and by using a mountain bike I could still get in amongst them.

The next summer, despite the pain in my feet, I limped my way from Kirk Yetholm in the Borders to Cape Wrath and then went back with the *Adventure Show* film crew to film sections for our annual Christmas television programmes. It was painful, but with the help of bottles of ibuprofen and paracetemol it was do-able. I had long and serious conversations with Richard and Meg, urging them to look for another hillwalking presenter because I didn't think I'd be able to do much more. They were incredibly understanding but I'm not sure just how aware they were of the mental turmoil I was going through. Not only was I grieving because I thought my hill-going days were over but I wondered when the day would arrive when I'd lose my lower legs.

A year later I went back to see the vascular surgeon. He admitted that when I first went to see him he had no idea of who I was or what I did. His nurse had told him I was a 'well-known mountaineer' so he had since checked my website and noticed that I had recently walked the length of Scotland.

'Compared with my usual clients who are suffering from peripheral vascular disease you are way off the radar,' he told me. 'Go home and get on with your life and don't come back unless things become drastic.'

I took a lot of encouragement from that and since then I've suffered no ill effects from the vascular problem. Other than my feet getting a bit cold in winter I've virtually forgotten about it, but the pains in my feet have persisted. I continued to walk as much as I could but cycling became my new focus. I got together with Hamish Telfer, the long-suffering pal of my youth, whom I had sporadically kept in touch with over fifty years, and discovered he had recently taken up cycling too. 'Let's do a trip together,' I suggested. 'What about Land's End to John O'Groats?' There was silence on the phone before a quiet voice said, 'Mmm, okay.'

That was it, and over the next three years we enjoyed an annual trip together on our bikes. We called it our Cycling Triple Crown: Land's End to John O'Groats, the length of France from the English Channel (La Manche) to Montpellier and an end-to-end tour of Ireland.

We weren't so much MAMILs (middle-aged men in lycra) as OFILs (old farts in lycra) and we had a lot of fun. There were distinct parallels with *Last of the Summer Wine*, particularly so on the last trip of our Triple Crown. We've agreed that our Irish end-to-end cycle trip, from Mizen Head in the south to Malin Head in the north, was the best of the three. Land's End to John O'Groats was a bit of a learning curve for us both, the first long bike trip we had attempted at just short of a thousand miles and the ride between La Manche and the Med through France was, in some ways, too easy. I don't think either of us would want to spend days biking along canal towpaths again – too similar, too flat, too boring. Although the wine in the evening was very pleasant.

The ride through Ireland was very different from the other two. For a start, the quality of the scenery we rode through was sustained all the way as we roughly followed the route of the Wild Atlantic Way. The landscapes were fabulous – everything from great coastal scenery – Mizen Head, Cliffs of Moher, Aran Islands, Malin Head, to some lovely mountainous country – Caha Mountains, Moll's Gap and Killarney National Park, the Reeks, James Joyce Country – to the green, rolling, agricultural land where the fields are still separated by hedgerows vibrant with wild flowers, particularly my own favourite, the blood red fuchsia, which seems to grow alongside every minor road, intermingled with thorn bushes.

What is it about the Irish that makes them so friendly, and inquisitive, and such wonderful conversationalists? I lost count, on our first couple of days, of the number of people who simply approached us, asked what we were up to, and entertained us with tales and stories and anecdotes. I'm not the most sociable of people but I simply loved this aspect of Ireland. More than anything else it was incredibly welcoming and warm hearted, and where else would you see a sign at the side of the road that said 'All-day breakfasts, served from twelve noon'?

In total we cycled just over six hundred miles, but 192 of those were getting to Mizen Head from Cork (a wonderful two days of cycling along the south coast – highly recommended) and reaching Larne from Malin Head (via County Antrim's Causeway Coast, another wonderful bike ride, particularly the stretch from Ballycastle to Cushendall). We took two weeks for the entire trip so we weren't exactly pushing it, but you wouldn't want to push it in Ireland. It's a place for slowing down, enjoying the scenery, blethering to people, listening to the music and soaking up the Celtic atmosphere of a land that will always be, for me at least, cloaked in romance and legend. And the highlights? I'm no great lover of cycling up hills but I loved the ride over Moll's Gap in County Kerry where we had our first view of Carrauntoohil, Ireland's highest mountain, and our visit to the Aran Islands, one of the most curious landscapes I've wandered through: simple yet complex, wild yet lived-in, romantic yet rough. Craggy Island it may be, but it certainly doesn't feel desolate or dour.

As outdoor ploys go I'm rarely short of ideas and plans and now that I had left the time-consuming embrace of the magazine I thought I would have loads of free time to bike, hike and generally do all those things I wanted to do while I was still physically able.

Life is rarely that simple but one bit of self-indulgence I have been able to enjoy is my love of traditional folk music.

When I lived in Kincraig I helped run the Badenoch Folk Club, which met once a month in the Glen Hotel in Newtonmore. The idea of starting a folk club came from a bunch of us who met regularly for informal music sessions: piper Hamish Moore, who at that time was a vet in Kingussie and who went on to a glittering musical career with bands like Jock Tamson's Bairns before becoming a respected maker of lowland pipes; Ross Noble, who was then the curator of the Highland Folk Museum and a wonderful storyteller; David Taylor, another piper who tutored a young musician called Martyn Bennett who, in turn, went on to become one of the most influential musicians in Scotland, and Martyn's mum, Margaret Bennett, folk historian and Gaelic singer with the purest voice of any singer I know.

When we met in Margaret's house in Kingussie she always insisted in getting young Martyn out of bed to give us a tune or two. The wee soul would appear in his pyjamas and play his pipe tunes and little did we think we were listening to a youngster who would one day influence a whole generation with his wonderful music. Sadly, Martyn died in his early thirties and Scotland lost a musical genius. His album, *Grit*, a fusion of traditional songs and tunes with a modern treatment featured as the opening concert at Celtic Connections a few years ago under the leadership of his good friend Greg Lawson. It was a magical experience for everyone who was there and I've no doubt that Martyn Bennett, along with the late Gordon Duncan, was massively influential in breaking down the boundaries of traditional piping, inspiring a whole new generation of traditional music performers.

Our regular monthly sessions in the Glen Hotel featured some wonderful folk singers and musicians: Dougie MacLean, Danny Kyle, Rod Paterson, Mirk from Caithness, big Adam McNaughtan, writer of the jeely piece song, Willie Lindsay and Stuart Campbell of Findask and a host of others. We also organised some special one-off concerts with the likes of the Battlefield Band and Boys of the Lough and several weekend folk festivals although we couldn't always agree on what guests to book. For our very first festival someone suggested we invite a couple of young lads from Edinburgh whom I had never heard of. They were called Phil and Johnny Cunningham and they played in a band called Silly Wizard.

'What do these guys play?' I asked.

'Johnny plays the fiddle and his younger brother Phil plays the accordion,' said the others.

'An accordion? Come on guys this is no' *Take the Floor*!'

In those days the accordion was the instrument of Scottish country bands and very rarely appeared in folk clubs. Even Phil Cunningham himself admits that it's not very sexy. However, despite being chairman of the folk club I lost the vote, Phil and Johnny duly came to Newtonmore and, I admit, completely knocked us out with their music and their humour. They were a huge hit with our local audience, so much so that a couple of years later, when we were organising another event, we thought we should bring them back to Badenoch. I phoned Phil, who at that time was living at the Crask of Aigas near Beauly, to book him, but he said Johnny had moved to America where he was playing in a band. 'However,' said Phil, 'I've teamed up with another fiddler you may know. His name is Aly Bain. We're doing our very first tour soon. If you like we'll come to Newtonmore after that.'

As it happened, we had booked Newtonmore village hall on a Friday night at the very end of Phil and Aly's tour, so to this day I'm rather proud that our wee village hall hosted Phil Cunningham and Aly Bain on their first ever tour of Scotland. How cool is that?

I've loved traditional music ever since I was a teenager when I went to see Archie Fisher perform at a folk club in Aberdeen. From that day I was hooked. I was also a great fan of The Corries and went along to as many of their big sell-out concerts as I could. The Corries were responsible for enthusing a whole generation of folkies in the late sixties and seventies. Sadly, Roy Williamson died in 1990 but just a few years ago I had the opportunity of meeting Ronnie Browne when I was invited to a book launch by a pal of mine, Andy Hall from Stonehaven.

Andy had this wonderful idea for a book with the title of *A Sense of Belonging to Scotland.* He asked a bunch of 'celebrities' what his or her favourite Scottish view was, then he went and photographed it. The images appeared in the book alongside a biography of the celeb and why they had chosen their particular view. A number of the celebrities were at the launch in Edinburgh including Jimmie Macgregor, Eileen McCallum, ex-footballer Gordon Smith, Ian Rankin, Dorothy Paul, Fred MacAulay, Dougie MacLean, Barbara Dickson, Kirsty Wark, Kaye Adams and the one and only Ronnie Browne of The Corries.

As is normal at functions like this you tend to wander around with a glass of wine in your hand introducing yourself to those you don't know. I introduced myself to Ronnie, one of my all-time folk music heroes, and asked him what he was up to these days. I was a wee bit taken aback by his loud and vociferous answer.

'Fuck all!' he roared. 'Absolutely fuck all, I've retired and I'm loving it.'

I was convinced that while most of the faces in the room were recognisable to me, most of these celebrities would have absolutely no idea who I was, so I wandered round introducing myself as 'I'm Cameron McNeish and I climb mountains.' That seemed to work until I introduced myself in this fashion to Ian Rankin. Po-faced he shook my hand and said, 'I'm Ian Rankin, I don't.' I couldn't help laughing, it was pure Rebus.

Gina and I go to as many folk festivals as we can and usually spend at least a week every January at the wonderful Celtic Connections in Glasgow, probably the biggest of its kind in the world. The event lights up the dour and dark days of January and is, for us, almost a harbinger of spring. After Celtic Connections we know it's time to begin planning our summer trip in the campervan. Two or three years ago, with the prospect of becoming old age pensioners looming close, Gina and I thought we'd do something to mark the occasion. For the first time in our married life, all forty-three years of it, we decided to take an extended break and head off in our campervan without any fixed plan for an objective or final destination. We'd been using campervans virtually all of our married life, especially when Gordon and Gregor were growing up, and in the past few years had 'progressed' from an old Renault Trafic home conversion to a brand-new Hyundai campervan.

This is smaller, drives like a car and can be parked like a car. The 2.5 turbo diesel engine means it's no slouch on motorways and inside it has all the comfort we need, including a porta-potty, a fridge, a grill and oven and a pop-up roof. It's definitely not a motorhome, it's a campervan, and there's a huge difference between the two.

I would describe a campervan as a tent on wheels. You have to be something of a minimalist in terms of what you carry and the experience is very much more akin to camping than that of living in a large motorhome where you can virtually have all the comforts of home, including a telly, a microwave cooker and a shower.

The iconic campervan is of course the VW Transporter, which recently celebrated over sixty years in production. We've had a few VWs in our time but the iconic status tends to go hand in hand with cost. VWs are not cheap and our Hyundai offers all the benefits of a VW-sized campervan but at a much lower price. In addition, the Wellhouse conversion is quite superb, boasting marvellous craftmanship that is lacking in many of the ad-hoc conversions that you see in VWs today.

We've taken campervans to Europe before, but usually only as far as the Alps. More recently we have travelled further afield, mixing a bit of old and new, visiting places we'd never been before as well as some old favourites – Bruges, the Julian Alps of Slovenia, the Alps and in particular Chamonix and Zermatt (twenty-five years to the day since I climbed the Matterhorn) with some new destinations like Germany, Austria (the Tyrol), Croatia and the Italian Lakes. It all sounds like a pensioner's grand tour of Europe but we hike as often as we can, swim in lakes, ride our bikes and enjoy countless barbies and lots of wine. More than anything we just want to be campervanman and woman for a few weeks of the year. We just love the lifestyle. Choosing where to stop for the night, eating outside in the sun or having a barbeque with a bottle of wine before a relaxed evening of reading or simply doing nothing.

Next morning it can be an early start or a more relaxed approach depending on how far we want to travel that day. Often we won't travel at all but simply go for a walk, ride a bike or just become tourists for the day and take photographs. I know it sounds as though I've abandoned wild camping in a tent but I can assure you I haven't. That's enjoyed mostly with a bike these days, and I still enjoy a few days' backpacking in the mountains, but the campervan allows me to journey on roads less travelled, roads that take me to special out-of-the-way places where I can walk, bike or packraft. It's just another way of exploring the wild places of our land, and further afield. You just have to accept older age as a concept and adapt to it as much as possible, and using a campervan has allowed me to do that.

These were options I didn't think I would be blessed with when I began having problems with my feet and when the various internet medical geeks hinted that I might face a very uncertain future but, after seeking help from several consultants, GPs, sports physiotherapists, doctors and podiatrists, I was recommended a sports podiatrist who consulted just over fifty miles away in Inverness.

On our first appointment, Lindsay McKerrow of the McKerrow Practice, who looks after the feet of both of the Highlands' professional football teams, got me to take my shoes and socks off and jump on his couch. He pressed and pulled my toes and instep and within a couple of minutes announced that I was suffering from two conditions and that he could fix them both. I couldn't quite believe my ears. I had been suffering this pain for well over a decade and had consulted all kinds of specialists and here was someone telling me categorically that I was suffering from hallux rigidus, a big toe joint stiffened by osteoathritis, and plantar fasciitis, and that my feet were certainly not beyond repair.

I'd been aware of the toe problem and had an annual cortisone injection to help alleviate the pain and had disregarded the idea of plantar fasciitis, not having recognised the symptoms listed on the various internet sites I had visited. Lindsay rolled his eyes as if to say 'bloody internet,' and suggested that, since I'd had this problem for a long time, it had become pretty chronic, and it might take up to two years for my feet to get back to normal.

The plantar fascia is the flat band of tissue (ligament) that connects your heel bone to your toes. It supports the arch of your foot. If you strain your plantar fascia, it gets weak, swollen and irritated. Then your heel or the bottom of your foot hurts when you stand or walk. Lindsay reckoned I had strained mine by over-pronating (my feet rolling inwards too much when I walked) over a long period of time. He asked me to describe, on a count of one to ten, how painful my feet were at their worst. From time to time I couldn't bear to stand upright at all so I suggested a ten. He then made some temporary orthotic insoles and told me to wear them all the time, taking a careful note of the pain threshold, between one and ten, when I walked in the hills.

I wore them the very next day when I took a stroll up a wee hill called Carn Glas-choire near Grantown on Spey. At worst the pain reached a number four. Since then my feet have improved enormously and I wear orthotics in all my footwear. About six weeks after my first consultation with Lindsay, Gina and I went off in the campervan to the Picos de Europa of northern Spain where I enjoyed some of the first relatively pain-free walking I'd had for years.

The moral of the story is simple: if you have an injury that threatens your jaunts to the hills seek expert advice as soon as possible and, if there's no improvement, continue seeking help until you find someone who can fix the problem. I believed my feet were completely knackered and I really thought my hill days were over. The day I climbed Carn Glas-choire was wet, cloudy and cold and there was no view to speak of but it was like coming home. It was like rediscovering the hills all over again and there was an immense delight in knowing I still had many great hill days ahead of me.

18

ANY PLACE WILD

I still cycle as often as I can and I bought a fat bike to tackle the snowy trails of winter. The big studded tyres grip like a limpet and along with the long rear-end of the frame prevent backslip on snowy ascents. The tyres work just as well in muddy conditions but the real joy of this fat bike is that it will roll over very rough ground with ease and even a certain amount of comfort. Those big fat tyres soak up the bumps and act as a very effective suspension system and, to my surprise, you get a real feel for the ground you're rolling over, much more than with a suspension system.

Although I can climb the hills again and grab as many days on the mountains of Scotland as I can, cycling continues to be a mainstay of my activities. With our Irish trip, Hamish Telfer and I completed our Triple Crown of end-to-end bike rides and we decided to plan another trip, this time to Spain. Since we could catch a ferry from Plymouth to Santander we plumped for a tour of the Picos de Europa.

Ever since my days of editing *Climber* magazine this mountain range has been on my radar. Apparently, Spanish and Portuguese explorers named the range because they were the first mountains they glimpsed after sailing across the Atlantic, and fantastic mountains they are. From the outset, we knew any cycling route here would be hilly so we decided to take a soft option and disregard the temptation to put in big mileages. Our eventual circuit was in the region of 280 miles with around 25,000 feet of climbing, and we enjoyed a couple of walks too. The only downside of the trip was that out of nine nights we only camped on three of them – most of the campsites were closed for the season.

This was a bit of a nuisance because we had to carry the camping gear around with us, but we found some great, and very reasonably priced hotels, so it didn't hit us in the pockets too hard. The Plymouth to Santander ferry wasn't cheap but it was fairly luxurious and we had a smooth crossing to Santander. A number of folk had warned us that getting out of Santander and on to the coast road wasn't that easy so we did the smart thing by jumping aboard a terrific little single-track railway train to travel the forty-four miles to Unquera, close to the Picos de Europa National Park, for the grand total of five euros each. The loaded bikes travelled free.

From Unquera we headed for Potes, within sight of the big hills of the Picos. It was only twenty miles or so and we found a campsite that was open, although it was about a mile up a steep hill. However, it was a lovely campsite and we checked in for two nights. Our second day involved an out-and-back trip to the cable car at Fuente De, a fourteen-mile ride with an ascent of about 822 metres/2,700 feet. It took us a couple of hours to get there, but a mere forty minutes to get back down the hill to Potes. In between we took the cable car up to about 1,800 metres/6,000 feet and enjoyed a wander amongst the phenomenal limestone peaks. It was an extraordinary landscape, more of a moonscape, with some marvellous-looking ridges that we dared not attempt in cycling shoes.

The next day was potentially the biggy: about forty miles and about 1,800 metres/6,000 feet of climbing over the Puerto de San Glorio pass and then over another, smaller, pass to Posada de Valdeon. We used age as an excuse and decided, if we could, we'd break it into two days.

The San Glorio pass was long, but never terribly steep, and it was early afternoon by the time we crossed its summit. At the foot of the pass, in a tiny village called Llanaves de la Reina, we found a hotel.

One of the main problems with Spain, especially for hungry cyclists, is that the Spanish don't eat until late and in this hotel, which was otherwise great, the restaurant didn't open until 8.30p.m. We were famished by then and hastily devoured fish soup and a game stew. It was wonderful, and of course a nice bottle of local white wine washed it all nicely down. Our next day was short but the weather, which up until now had been about 26°C, finally broke. In pouring rain and almost freezing temperatures we trundled over a

1,520-metre/5,000-foot pass and raced down to Posada de Valdeon reaching speeds of 40mph. This time we didn't really want a camp-site, all we wanted was a hot shower where we could thaw out. We found one almost immediately, checked in and noticed through the window there was fresh snow on the mountain tops.

The weather improved substantially by lunchtime and we decided to take a walk along the Cares Gorge, a must-see in this part of Spain. The only problem was the start of the walk, in a village called Cain, lay about 600 metres/2,000 feet below us and while we could zoom down the six or seven miles, it would be a long haul back on the bikes at the end of our walk. After some soul searching we asked the *señorita* in the hotel if she could order us a taxi, and the driver agreed to come back for us after three hours once we had completed our wander through the narrow confines of the Cares Gorge.

That gave us enough time to see something of this fabulous place. The river crashes deep below formidable rock walls and we watched eagles and vultures high above us. I decided I had to return, and the following year brought Gina to walk the entire length of the gorge to Poncebos on the north side of the Picos range. It's a fabulous place.

Hamish and I had looked forward to the next day because we had been promised a twenty-eight-mile descent down to the town of Cangas de Onis. What we didn't know was that our day would start with a seven-mile climb over the Puerto de Panderruedas at 1,463 metres/4,800 feet. It was hot again on the climb and, by contrast, freezing in the shady descent. We had to continually stop in sunny spots to soak in some warmth, before crashing downhill again in the bitter cold of the shaded forest. We began to realise why Grand Tour riders stuff newspapers down the front of their jerseys on long descents. As soon we reached the lovely little village of Oseja de Sajambre we downed two large cups of hot coffee each.

The rest of the day was excellent, until we reached Cangas. It felt like a big town and neither of us like big towns so we cycled through it in search, yet again, of a campsite. It was closed, so we carried on to the very religious village of Covadonga, the houses dominated by a massive monastery and church, where we mixed with the pilgrims and those in search of a spiritual blessing. We even saw a priest, with holy water and incense, bless someone's motor bike. It all seemed rather surreal.

We had hoped to cycle uphill to the Covadonga Lakes the next morning but the weather was foul, so instead we decided to head for the coast for a change. We had assumed the seaside campsites would still be open but we were wrong so we headed back to the mountains and, you've guessed it, over another high pass. The downhill was wonderful though, through the little town of Poo (couldn't resist a photo for my wee grand-daughter Grace who falls about laughing whenever the word is mentioned), and on to a campsite – yippee – at Arenas de Cabrales. The only problem was that the campsite was about a mile outside town and the campsite bar was closed. We set up camp, had a shower, cooked a meal (we had a fortnight's worth of camp food to get through) and toddled into Arenas for a couple of beers and an unexpectedly fine end to the day.

Next day we would loop the loop so to speak, complete the circle, when a long and easy descent took us back to Panes and Unquera. Our final day involved a forty-mile bike ride along the coast back to Santander, a rolling undulating ride with a total ascent of about 914 metres/3,000 feet. It didn't matter, we knew we had a long and luxurious ferry crossing to recover.

The following year I returned with Gina in the campervan and spent a month there, enjoying some fabulous hillwalking and great days exploring ancient mountain villages. This mountain region of northern Spain is definitely one of Europe's best-kept secrets.

With the campervanning, cycling, packrafting and getting to the hills as often as I can there's life in the old dog yet, and it's all thanks to some expertly fitted orthotic insoles. Who'd have believed it?

Another semi-retirement ploy was rafting through Arizona's Grand Canyon with my sons Gordon and Gregor. Ever since they were teenagers I've promised them a boys-only trip somewhere special and, since Gina had little desire to go rafting, I thought it would be a great opportunity for the lads to have a trip with their old man.

My own fascination with the Grand Canyon began when I read

a wonderful book called *The Man Who Walked Through Time* by Colin Fletcher, a Welsh/American whose works have inspired legions of backpackers across the globe, including Chris Townsend and myself. On a personal level, the inspiration I've had from reading Colin Fletcher's books over the years has set a solid platform for my own understandings of the natural world and how I relate to it. His writings have delighted, motivated and amazed me for forty years and, although his writing style is no longer fashionable, I would argue that the quality of Fletcher's work is above such transitory notions.

I first became aware of Colin Fletcher through the enthusiasm of my old friend, the late Robin Adshead, author of *Backpacking in Britain*. Some time later I was given a copy of another of Fletcher's books, *The Complete Walker* by a publisher who asked if I could write something similar for a European market. In response, I produced a book called *The Backpackers' Handbook*, but it was a very, very pale shadow of Fletcher's worldwide best seller. Indeed, *The Complete Walker* is the book, along with its later editions, that made Colin Fletcher such a respected name in US backpacking circles. It's a how-to book that unashamedly concentrates on gear and how best to use it, but it's a how-to book that has become a literary classic. Fletcher's prose sucks you in and makes something as mundane as a cook-pot sound desperately exciting. It's when you become caught up in all this enthusiasm about outdoor gear that he tells you the gear is actually not that important after all.

Colin Fletcher was the first man to walk the length of the Grand Canyon. His book of the trip, *The Man Who Walked Through Time* is, in my opinion, the finest expedition book ever written. I make a habit of reading it at least once a year. Many years after his Grand Canyon expedition, when in his late sixties, Fletcher travelled the complete length of the Colorado River, backpacking from its source in the Rockies until he could float a raft. He then rafted downriver, through the white waters of the Grand Canyon, and eventually out to the Sea of Cortez. That expedition produced an outstanding book called *River* and, along with the previous book, made me determined, at some time in my life, to visit the Grand Canyon, one of nature's greatest creations.

This great cleavage in the earth's crust is 277 miles long, up to eighteen miles wide and attains a depth of over a mile (1,857 metres/6,093 feet). It is simply sensational, and I was well aware that I could never repeat Fletcher's walking route through it, for two reasons. Arguably I was now too old but, also, the creation of a couple of large reservoirs on the Colorado River meant that the river was now running higher than when Fletcher walked through. So, since neither of the lads, nor me, had any previous river-running experience of this kind we booked ourselves on what turned out to be a bit of a pleasure cruise. The 'rafts' that carried us along the Colorado River were massive, capable of taking twenty people plus tents and everything we needed to camp comfortably, if not luxuriously, along the way.

In about ten memorable days we rafted 277 miles and negotiated about two hundred sets of whitewater rapids between Lees Ferry in Arizona and Pearce Ferry on Lake Mead. We certainly negotiated the river very differently from the way Major John Wesley Powell and his small band of explorers did in 1869 when they became the very first men to successfully run the river but we had the opportunity to enjoy the exact same spectacle of river, cliffs, buttes and soaring rock buttresses.

Encompassing more than 1.2 million acres, the semi-arid canyon consists of raised plateaux, steep-walled canyons, desert basins at lower elevations and forests at higher elevations. The canyon walls provide an excellent record of three of the four eras of geological time, diverse fossil specimens, a vast array of geological features and rock types and numerous caves containing extensive and significant archaeological, biological, geological and paleontological resources. Even though the Grand Canyon is a desert, it abounds in plants and wildlife. Cactus and wildflowers dot the riverbanks, as well as cool glens with tumbling waterfalls and ferns. We caught glimpses of bighorn sheep, mule deer, coyotes and ringtail cats along the riverbanks and in tributary canyons. We also saw a wide range of birdlife including hawks, golden eagles, falcons, great blue herons and egrets, but without doubt the most thrilling event on a Grand Canyon rafting trip is riding the rapids.

The exhilaration we felt as our raft plunged through the waves is hard to describe. Only after passing through such rapids as Soap Creek, Hance, Sockdolager, Hermit, Crystal, and Lava Falls can you really appreciate the achievements of Major Powell and other early river pioneers. I think Gordon and Gregor would agree with me that our trip to Arizona fully lived up to its soubriquet of a once-in-a-lifetime expedition.

It's about this point in books like this that thoughts tend to turn to the future and authors like to dust down their crystal balls, and make predictions about what things will be like in ten, twenty or thirty years time. I'm not going to do that, and I'll tell you why. I could never have guessed the British public would vote to leave the EU and that Americans, who I always thought were fairly sensible people, would vote in a president like Donald Trump, so I'm not going to make any predictions about the future since anything could happen. I've never in my life known such uncertain times. However, I would like to examine several issues about the places that have so often been my redemption, the mountains and wild places of Scotland.

I recently had an interesting conversation with the film and television actor David Hayman. David was presenting a lovely television series for Scottish Television called *On Weir's Way* in which he visited some of the locations that Tom visited when filming his original *Weir's Way*. I assumed David wanted to talk to me about Tom and my relationship with him but he didn't. With the television camera rolling he took me completely by surprise and asked me what I thought the future held for planet earth. Wow, what a question!

I know, from my own interviewing techniques, that surprising an interviewee can often provide an answer that is completely honest because it has not been previously prepared or rehearsed or littered with deliberate ambiguity, so, right off the top of my head, or it may have been my heart, I confessed I was not optimistic. Not wanting to sound completely negative, I went on to explain that while I was not particularly optimistic about how mankind has treated the planet or the future of man's existence on it, I was convinced that the planet itself had the ability to simply slough us off and heal itself. In short, I wasn't optimistic about mankind's future, but I had little doubt the planet would survive.

In a later conversation with David, who helps run Spirit Aid, a humanitarian organisation here in Scotland and in Palestine, Afghanistan and Malawi, I learned that he is much more optimistic about mankind's future than I was, and I take heart from that. I hope he is right, but whatever happens, one thing is certain. We have to change our attitudes to how we treat the planet and that involves all of us. There is an old expression that suggests we 'think global, act local'. If you want to achieve change and improvement, you can't wait for global legislation or global action. The best course of action is to drive change yourself. I certainly won't have any great say in world economics or world health or whether global corporate greed will eventually be our downfall, but I can try and live sustainably at my own level. I can also try and influence politicans at a national level, something that I've been attempting to do for a long time, particularly in the areas of public access to the countryside and protecting our hills and wild places from developments that would spoil them.

When I was editor of *The Great Outdoors* I tried to make it a campaigning magazine. I tried to fight for the interests of walkers and mountain-goers but month after month I received letters from individuals threatening to cancel their subscriptions because the magazine was 'too political'. I admit *TGO* was inherently left-wing, because right-wingers have never been very keen on issues like access, freedom-to-roam or conservation in general, and I have no doubt we lost many readers over the years because of the political stance I took. Sadly, no outdoor magazine takes such a stance today. They are all obsessed with celebrity status, the best pubs in the Lake District or the endless liturgy of gear, gear, gear. It's no small wonder that outdoor types are not informed about the politics of the countryside, rarely inspired or encouraged to raise their own voice in protest.

I have no doubt that there will be those reading this who will say that after a week's work the last thing they want to do is get involved in lobbying politicians about wind farms, or bulldozed paths, or access issues. They just want to go to the hills and 'have a good time'. Well, that's fine, but please don't complain about your favourite Munro having a wind farm built on it, or that your favourite view is going to be spoiled by a line of pylons, or that the lovely natural footpath you once used is now a bulldozed track to carry shooting 'sportsmen' onto the hill.

We are losing the battle for our wild places. We badly need more hillwalkers and mountaineers to stand up to politicians and be counted. We urgently need thousands of voices raised in protest at developments on our wild lands. We badly need individuals of the calibre of John Muir to raise public awareness of the importance of wild land and why we should protect it. To remain silent is no longer an option and if we want to see any improvement then we all have to raise our voices, rally together, and support the conservation NGOs like the Ramblers, Mountaineering Scotland, the John Muir Trust and the National Trust for Scotland.

I've always had a fascination with the history of our wild places and an ongoing love affair with the tales and legends that have been handed down since time immemorial but, more recently, I've shifted my focus from the past to the future. Rather than consider those events and circumstances that have given us the landscapes we've inherited I've been wondering what the next throw of the dice will be for those areas we now regard as the wild places of Scotland.

'Throw of the dice' is, I think, a relevant term, for I doubt if much formal planning went into the creation of those areas we now consider to be wild, although it might be argued that the Clearances had an element of deliberation. Chance, happenstance, fate – call it what you will, but there's little doubt that our landscapes have evolved as they are because of the circumstances of the time: Culloden; the destruction of the clan system; the Clearances; the introduction of large-scale sheep farming; Victorian shooting estates; commercial afforestation; hydro power; wind power. Each element in the history of our wild lands has formed and shaped them into what we know today, areas that are often, and erroneously, described as wilderness.

In the half century that I've been climbing and exploring these areas of Scotland I suspect I may have enjoyed the best of it. While many of us complain from time to time about the monoculture aspect of deer management or grouse moor management (managing vast acres as a wet desert for the sake of sportsmen blasting some grouse from the sky) or erecting mile upon mile of ugly deer fences, relationships between shooting estates and hillwalkers have generally been based on mutual tolerance, and it's generally worked fairly well. While I, and many hillwalkers and mountaineers, can't understand the concept of shooting red deer stags or grouse as a form of pleasure, there is little doubt that in many areas of the Highlands shooting estates equate with local jobs and rural income. Take away the shooting lodges and the keepers' jobs and you risk losing the local shops and businesses that service them. However, as more and more shooting estates come up for sale, I wonder just what an alternative land use would be for these vast areas.

Very few of Scotland's private estates are run at a profit. They are, for the most part, the playthings of wealthy individuals or corporate businesses and huge swathes of Scotland sadly depend on such benefactors, questionable as they may be to many of us. I have always been a supporter of community ownership and have witnessed the successes of the likes of Assynt, Eigg and Knoydart and West and North Harris in the Hebrides. I'm confident we'll see more successful buy-outs in the future but what of those traditional estates that are still owned by corporations or absentee landlords? How can they be improved to help local people while maintaining the natural characteristics that have made them special?

We've seen the effect of the Highland Clearances and how a way of life that had existed for centuries was changed virtually overnight. The ruined shielings that I've often lingered by are a testament to that. We've seen the introduction of large-scale sheep farming in the Highlands and Islands and how that industry has had a chequered history in recent years. In many areas, conservation concerns have seen the removal of browsing sheep and a reduction in deer numbers in an attempt to protect young trees and encourage new growth. This has had a dramatic effect on the landscape and in the biodiversity of those areas. Glen Feshie, not far from where I live, is a prime example of new, forward thinking by landowners, in this case Danish clothing tycoon Anders Holch Povlsen.

Take visitors into most mountain areas of the Scottish Highlands and they will most probably gasp in wonder at the natural beauty that lies before them. The size and shape of the hills, the sheer expanse of sky and the humbling awareness of human insignificance is not unusual but in many cases those visitors will be gasping at a land that is degraded, shorn of its indigenous vegetation, bare of trees and lacking in biodiversity. Caledonia stern and wild, but, more often than not, treeless. It's well known that pine and birch woods once covered much of the Highlands but less than 1 per cent of this natural woodland remains and man is not entirely to blame. A wetter climate and peat formation have played their part as well as such activities as deliberate forest clearance by burning. Overgrazing by sheep and deer has had a dramatic effect on our landscapes.

In recent years serious attempts have been made to encourage the regeneration of the remnants of the Caledonian pine forest that once covered much of the Highlands. In Glen Affric, Rothiemurchus, Glen Tanar and Abernethy, to name a few, there is evidence of new growth as young pines, birches, rowans and aspen are given the opportunity to flourish. At the foot of Coire Ardair on Creag Meagaidh, near Laggan, a birch wood that was dying was brought back to life, life in all its biodiversity, by simply removing the browsing animals that fed off any young seedlings that dared to poke their heads through the earth.

Glenfeshie Estate, once described as the jewel in the crown of the Cairngorms, will always be associated with the nineteenth-century artist Sir Edwin Landseer and his Monarch of the Glen, the iconic red deer stag that has become a symbol to those who oppose the estate's plans to regenerate the woods by culling large numbers of deer. Anders Holch Povlsen wants to more than double the area of native woodland from the existing 1,900 hectares over the next few years and plans to achieve this by maintaining the number of deer at a lower density than previously.

Under Glenfeshie Estate's previous ownership, a large cull of red deer had taken place in partnership with the Red Deer Commission, a cull that led to ironic allegations of 'wildlife crime' by the Scottish Gamekeepers Association. After only a few years of this regeneration management the changes to the Feshie landscape are marked and positive. Young pines are growing on the roadside slopes, young birch trees are abundant and there is a freshness and vibrancy in the glen that suggests nothing less than complete renewal. Capercaillie have been seen again and blackcock numbers are rising. Red deer still roam the woodlands and the slopes around the glen, there are just fewer of them now.

Glen Feshie wears its 'jewel' description with some justification. The area has a long history of people living and working here, and during the eighteenth and nineteenth centuries, large quantities of pine timber were taken from the woods in the glen. This extraction continued before and during the first and second world wars. Today, by reducing the browsing effects of animals like deer and sheep the native trees have been given the opportunity to thrive again. Even after a few years the regeneration of the woodlands is impressive. Over the next few years, the estate hopes to more than double the area of native woodland from the existing 1,900 hectares to around 4,000 hectares. Some planting will be carried out in areas where the seed source is missing but most of the increase will come from natural regeneration. The changes in the glen have to be seen to be believed.

My great friend and neighbour in Newtonmore, the late Dick Balharry, who was one of the country's most respected naturalists, said to me not long before he died, 'On a recent visit to Feshie I was very impressed by the actions of estate staff that has led to the revival of this land. For fifty years I have witnessed the glen. Over that time I have had reason to be depressed regarding its future well being. Although as yet in its infancy, and still vulnerable to fire and grazing pressures, the promise for the future is optimistic. This has been a major undertaking and has at times been controversial. With adjacent estates showing similar shifts in land management, I wonder if, in the not too distant future, a red squirrel will be able to travel within native forest from Speyside to Deeside! The future of Glen Feshie is now on the right road to recovery but it needs all our support to ensure that it remains so.'

Glen Feshie is a success story, as is Creag Meagaidh where the native birch woods are prospering because of a reduction in deer numbers. I should point out that keepers are still employed on these estates. There has been no loss of jobs, one of the great fears of the anti-conservation lobby. Other estates are following suit, such as Corrour Estate in Lochaber and Coignafearn in Inverness-shire, but the big fear for many hill-goers is that more and more landowners, resident and absent, some under financial pressure, will be tempted into renting land to wind farm developers. Where a Scottish sporting estate could have been seen as a rich man's plaything with little income, many estates have become potential gold mines, earning their owners millions of pounds in land rental and government subsidy.

The current Scottish government has set ambitious targets for renewable energy and is determined to meet them, and that will mean more on-shore wind farms to fill the gap before off-shore renewables, including wave and tidal, become wholly viable. In many ways it's easy to understand the ambitions of the Scottish government. There are two issues at stake: future energy sources in a Scotland that the present government declares should be nuclear free, and the fight against climate change, formerly known as global warming.

Many people would agree that the future could be very bright for a Scotland that is rich in renewable sources, a Scotland that has lost its major industries over the past twenty-five years: coal mining, steel making and shipbuilding. Renewable energy could become the shining new industry of Scotland with wave power, tidal power, biomass, hydro and wind power in years to come providing all our energy needs with enough excess to sell some to our neighbours. At the moment, the only renewables making a significant contribution are hydro and on-shore wind. The other technologies have yet to come on-stream, and it may be some years before they do, but there could be a modicum of comfort here for those who don't like wind turbines. Most turbines have a life span of only twenty-five years and, it could be, that they will be made redundant by other technologies by the time they need to be replaced. Whatever happens to the blocks of concrete that hold them in place, or the miles of bulldozed tracks that currently service them, is another matter, but it's worth noting that it's unlikely that the present crop of wind turbines will be removed any time soon. As these huge turbines grow old they will be replaced by fewer, but taller turbines. That is already happening.

The current Scottish government, with its determination to promote renewables, has become a world leader in tackling climate change and as a promoter of climate justice, recognising and addressing the fact that those least responsible for climate change experience its greatest impacts. Climate change is a global issue and while it could be considered in years to come as an inconvenience and an occasional discomfort to those of us who live in Scotland, in other areas of the world its consequences will be catastrophic. In that sense, the Scottish government has recognised that a low-carbon economy is essential to allow us to play our part as a responsible member of the global community.

That's all very altruistic but does a low-carbon economy mean that the wild areas of Scotland, those areas that are recognised as a key component of Scotland's identity, bringing significant economic benefits, attracting visitors and tourists, will be sacrificed? Many people derive psychological and spiritual benefit from wild land, and such areas provide increasingly important havens for Scotland's wildlife. Are large wind farms the sacrifice we have to make for global justice and to ensure future energy needs?

I read a lot these days, particularly on social media, that Scotland's Highlands and Islands have been 'trashed' by development, particularly wind farms, but I personally disagree with that view. I can't say I'm in love with wind turbines but the sight of them in the far distance doesn't spoil a day for me. I know there are some places in Scotland where there are simply far too many turbines, but in the Highlands and Islands, where I tend to walk the most, on most days I don't see a single turbine, either in the distance or close at hand.

On one of our television walks, the *Pilgrims' Trail*, I wanted to note all the signs I found of past or present industrial activity in our wild places. We found all sorts of evidence of industry from the past but all the way from Iona, across the breadth of Scotland, we didn't see any wind turbines at all until we encountered the spinning blades of the Loch Luichart wind farm from Ben Wyvis, one of our most easterly Munros.

I'm not an apologist for the wind industry but I don't think exaggerating the problems is helpful in the long term. Far better to work with the government and ensure it keeps its promise of protecting the best of our wild lands from development. I'm proud that I managed to help coax Alex Salmond into agreeing that designated national scenic areas and national parks should be development free, and that it should be extremely difficult to get planning permission on those areas that have been recognised as Wild Land by Scottish Natural Heritage. I'm currently meeting with the government to encourage ministers to legislate to also make Wild Land map areas completely turbine-free. These are comparatively small steps but they all help.

Certainly some areas, notably the Scottish Borders, the Monadh Liath, Aberdeenshire and Easter Ross appear to have more than their fair share of turbines, but vast tracts of the Highlands and Islands are still turbine-free. The rhetoric of the Scottish government has also changed in the last few years. The emphasis in press statements is now about off-shore wind and marine renewables and I reckon we will see a greater emphasis on new hydro-electric projects.

While hydro isn't everyone's cup of tea at least we know it works – we now reap the benefits of the hydro schemes of the forties and fifties. The public acceptance of future schemes will largely depend on the geographical position of the new developments but hydro, for all the problems created during its construction phase, is surely preferable to covering the hills with highly visible, spinning windmills? With the amount of rainfall we have in this country it's surely criminal not to capitalise on it.

The need for reliable energy sources, the fight against climate change and the desire of Scottish political parties to re-industrialise Scotland means change and in some areas that change will be drastic. Things will never be the same again but my hope is that in years to come we could live in a country where energy is plentiful and secure, where we will be seen as a world leader in the fight for climate justice and where the best of our wild lands is safeguarded for future generations. I firmly believe that we have a great opportunity, here in this little country of ours, to get the best of all worlds.

The outdoor world has changed considerably since I took my first tentative steps on a mountain and I'm not just referring to the wind farms, the miles upon miles of bulldozed tracks across the hills, the new tracks to hydro schemes and all the other issues that have changed the landscapes of old. The creation of a Scottish Parliament in 1999 immediately gave us some of the best access legislation in the world and two national parks, legislation that would never have seen the light of day under a Westminster government. Both issues would have been thrown out by the landowning factions within the House of Lords.

There are also many more people enjoying the wild land of Scotland and I'm thinking not only of walkers and climbers but mountain bikers, paddlers, backcountry skiers and runners. Fell running was once a very specialised form of athletics and almost unknown outside the Lake District, where it's always been popular, but today I often meet more runners on the hills than walkers and it's great to see so many people keeping fit in such a way. There was a time not so long ago that you would have been severely criticised for going up a hill in a vest and shorts with a lightweight cagoule tied around your waist, but that seems almost normal nowadays.

I'm also delighted to see so many women on the hills, many in small groups but also individuals who have realised they are probably safer walking alone in the hills than they are in our towns and cities. I think we owe a great deal to Muriel Gray for that. Her book, *The First Fifty: Munro-bagging Without a Beard*, took a hefty swipe at those of us who probably took it all too seriously: the gear-freaks, the self-appointed guardians of the wilderness, the traditionalists and, of course, the old greybeards. I don't believe it's any coincidence that the number of females seen on the hills after the publication of this book, and the accompanying television series, *The Munro Show*, grew considerably. Muriel deserves a lot of credit for that.

I've no doubt our hills and wild places will continue to inspire and rejuvenate people for a long, long time to come and I look forward to taking my two granddaughters to the hills. Hopefully, they will have the opportunities I have had. When both my sons were born I became immediately aware of a new sense of responsibility and love and it's been much the same with the birth of my grandchildren. Someone once said that grandchildren were God's reward for being parents and I believe there is a lot of truth in that. You can have so much fun with them, smother them with love and affection, spoil them rotten, all without the immediate day-to-day concerns of raising youngsters in a world that can appear to be uncertain and circumspect.

Charlotte and Grace have changed the lives of Gina and me and we love being the doting grandparents. There's also a great satisfaction in being settled in a lovely part of the world with my two sisters living nearby and my own youngsters established in their own homes, making their own way in the world. I think, I hope, I still have a good number of years of work ahead, writing and making television programmes about the hills and mountains, and that Gina and I will continue to travel in our little campervan, exploring and taking every opportunity to peep over as many horizons as we can. Having said that, I've no doubt that from time to time difficulties will appear and I'll continue to rant and rage at various political decisions and continue to be surprised and depressed at some of the decisions of my fellow man but, whatever befalls, however black the future looks, I know exactly what to do. It may not cure the ills of the world, it may not entirely solve the immediate problems, but I know from experience that it will calm me down and give me the space to think things through logically and clearly.

I'll grab my boots, my pack and my trekking poles and head off to somewhere wild.

Thank goodness – there's always the hills.

SELECT BIBLIOGRAPHY

Hamish's Mountain Walk, Hamish Brown, Gollancz 1977. The much-loved narrative of the first non-stop round of Scotland's Munros. The original Munro-baggers guide.

Walking the Song, Hamish Brown, Sandstone Press 2016. A personal record of the author's many journeys and expeditions.

On the Crofter's Trail, David Craig, Birlinn, 2009 An excellent account of the Highland Clearances from the mouths of the relatives of those who were cleared. A masterly work.

Landmarks, David Craig, Jonathan Cape, 1995. David Craig is a man with a heart for the land. This book examines the significance of great rocks, cliffs and outcrops and the influence they have over those who climb them or live near them.

A High and Lonely Place, Jim Crumley, Jonathan Cape 1991. A radical look at the Cairngorms and how we have failed to protect this, the most important environmental site in the UK.

The Endless Knot: K2 Mountain of Dreams and Destiny, Kurt Diemberger, Vertebrate 2014. An account of the various attempts made by the author to climb K2. Lots of insights into why we climb mountains even in the midst of pain and tragedy.

Scottish Hill Names, Peter Drummond, Scottish Mountaineering Trust 2007. A must for anyone interested in the mountain names

of Scotland. A fascinating piece of research that also includes
phonetic pronunciations of all the Gaelic names.

Nature, Ralph Waldo Emerson, Beacon Press, first published 1836.
An illuminating essay on the natural world by one of America's
foremost philosophers.

The Complete Walker, Colin Fletcher, Knopf, 1984. The most
amusing, instructive and sensible how-to-do-it book on backpacking I've ever read.

The Man Who Walked Through Time, Colin Fletcher, Knopf 1968.
An account of the first foot traverse along the length of the
Grand Canyon. Packed full of wisdom and inspiration. The
finest outdoor book I have read.

The Thousand Mile Summer, Colin Fletcher, Knopf 1964.
Everything by Fletcher is good. This is an account of a summer
walking the length of California through desert heat and
mountain cold.

River, Colin Fletcher, Knopf 1997. Fletcher's latest offering takes to
the water of the Colorado River as he follows it from source to
mouth, first by backpacking to the source, then, when the water
became deep enough, by inflatable raft to the sea.

John Muir - The Eight Wilderness-Discovery Books, Introduced by
Terry Gifford, Baton Wicks, 1992. Everyone should read Muir.
It should be taught in our schools and our politicians should be
given regular tests on Muir's prophetic acclamations.

John Muir - His Life and Letters and Other Writings, Introduced by Terry
Gifford, Baton Wicks 1996. Fascinating insights into the character of
this Scot who became the father figure of modern ecology.

Highways and Byways in the West Highlands, Seton Gordon, 1995.

Reprint by Birlinn of the original 1935 edition of this classic work. Seton Gordon is one of the great outdoor writers of the 20th century. A walker, naturalist and piper he straddles the worlds of the recreational hill goer and the professional naturalist.

Highways and Byways in the Central Highlands, Seton Gordon, 1995. The accompanying volume to the above.

On the Other Side of Sorrow, James Hunter, Mainstream, 1995. An illuminating argument that suggests the romantic view of the Scottish Highlands may well be at odds with those who live and work there. An important book for anyone interested in the Scottish environment.

Beyond Backpacking, Ray Jardine, Adventure Lore Press, 1999. The seminal work on ultra-lightweight backpacking by a modern day guru of the art.

A Sand County Almanac, Aldo Leopold, Oxford University Press, 1949. The book in which Leopold sets out his ideals for a Land Ethic. Should be read by every student of landscape.

The Sunlit Summit: The Life of WH Murray, Robin Lloyd-Jones, Sandstone Press 2013. A wonderfully full and evocative biography of Bill Murray, a man who inspired a generation of climbers and hill goers.

Arctic Dreams, Barry Lopez, Picador 1987. A poetic and visionary account of several trips to the Arctic regions by one of America's finest outdoor essayists.

How to Shit in the Woods, Kathleen Meyer, Ten Speed Press, 1989. A must-have book for every backpacker and wild camper. Humorous and no-nonsense approach to walking softly in wild places.

The Munros: Scotland's Highest Mountains, Cameron McNeish,

Lomond Books, 1996. A guide to Scotland's Munros, the mountains of 3000ft and over.

The Wilderness World of Cameron McNeish, Cameron McNeish,The InPinn 2001. An eclectic mix of essays about hiking home and abroad with a good helping of home brewed hillwalking philosophies.

The Sutherland Trail, Cameron McNeish and Richard Else, Mountain Media 2009. A journey through North-West Scotland.

The Skye Trail, Cameron McNeish and Richard Else, Mountain Media 2010. A journey through the Isle of Skye.

Scotland End to End, Cameron McNeish and Richard Else, Mountain Media 2012. Walking the Scottish National Trail from Kirk Yetholm in the Scottish Borders to Cape Wrath.

Magic Mountains, Rennie McOwan, Mainstream 1996. A superbly researched collection of tales of odd happenings in the hills. Not a book to be read when solo backpacking on long, dark winter nights.

This Sunrise of Wonder, Michael Mayne, Harper Collins 1995. A deeply moving account of how the author came to unify his outer and inner worlds, the ordinariness and yet the extraordinariness of everything. Passionate and overflowing with wisdom.

Mountaineering in Scotland and Undiscovered Scotland, WH Murray, Diadem. The books which launched several thousand mountaineering careers. Classic accounts of pre-war mountaineering and hill walking expeditions in Scotland written by Scotland's most articulate mountain writer.

The Evidence of Things Not Seen: A Mountaineer's Tale, WH Murray, Baton Wicks 2002. The autobiography of Scotland's greatest mountain writer.

Spirits of Place, Jim Perrin, Gomer 1997. A powerful collection of essays, mostly on Wales, that describe the spirit of the people and the places held dear to the author, Britain's finest outdoor writer.

The Living Mountain, Nan Shepherd, Aberdeen University Press 1977. A celebration of the Cairngorms that contains some of the most insightful observations on these mountains I've ever read.

The Practice of the Wild, Gary Snyder, North Point Press 1990. A collection of essays which form a far-sighted articulation of what wildness and grace mean, using outdoor lessons to teach us how to live.

Walden, Henry David Thoreau, first published by Ticknor and Fields 1854. Thoreau's account of back-to-basics living. A wise, well-loved classic.

The Munros and Tops, Chris Townsend, Mainstream 1997. An account of the first continuous traverse of all Scotland's Munros and Tops.

Out There: A Voice From the Wild, Chris Townsend, Sandstone Press 2016. A series of well–argued essays that discuss the importance of wildness.

Scotland, Chris Townsend, Cicerone 2010. A comprehensive round-up of all Scotland's mountain ranges with good maps and excellent photographs. A must for any hillwalker in Scotland.

Walking Man: The Secret Life of Colin Fletcher, Robert Wehrman, Bookbaby 2016. A biography of the long distance backpacker and author Colin Fletcher.

The Scottish Lochs, Tom Weir, Constable 1970. A superbly researched description of Scotland's major lochs and many of the hills that rise beside them.

Weir's World, Tom Weir, Canongate 1994. An autobiography-of-sorts that illustrates the background and the motivations of this remarkable writer and broadcaster.

Biophilia, EO Wilson, Harvard University Press 1984. An eloquent statement of the conservation ethic. Wilson claims biophilia is the essence of our humanity, a state that binds us to all living species.

INDEX

Index